THEORY AND NEW APPLICATIONS OF SWARM INTELLIGENCE

Edited by **Rafael Parpinelli** and **Heitor S. Lopes**

Theory and New Applications of Swarm Intelligence
Edited by Rafael Parpinelli and Heitor S. Lopes

Published by InTech
Janeza Trdine 9, 51000 Rijeka, Croatia

Publishing Process Manager Romana Vukelic

Technical Editor Teodora Smiljanic

Cover Designer InTech Design Team

Additional hard copies can be obtained from orders@intechopen.com

Theory and New Applications of Swarm Intelligence, Edited by Rafael Parpinelli and Heitor S. Lopes
p. cm.
ISBN 978-953-51-0364-6

For EU product safety concerns:
IN TECH d.o.o., Prolaz Marije Krucifikse Kozulić 3, 51000 Rijeka, Croatia,
info@intechopen.com or visit our website at intechopen.com.

Meet the editors

Rafael S. Parpinelli is professor in the Computer Science Department at Santa Catarina State University (UDESC). He graduated in Computer Science (2000) from the Maringá State University (UEM), and got a M.Sc. degree in Computer Science (2001) from the Federal University of Technology - Paraná (UTFPR). He has been member of program committees for many international conferences and editorial boards of scientific journals. His research interests include data mining, bioinformatics, hybrid systems, and all kinds of bio-inspired algorithms.

Dr Heitor S. Lopes is Associate Professor at the Federal University of Technology Parana (UTFPR). He graduated in Electronic Engineering (1984), got a MSc degree in Biomedical Engineering (1990) and a PhD in Information Sciences (1996). Since 1992 he holds a research grant from the Brazilian National Research Council (CNPq) in the area of Computer Science. He has been member of program committees for many international conferences and editorial boards of scientific journals. His research interests include bioinformatics, evolutionary computation and high-performance computing.

Contents

Preface

Swarm Intelligence is a research field that studies the emergent collective intelligence of self-organized and decentralized simple agents. It is based on the social behavior that can be observed in nature, such as in flocks of birds, fish schools and bee hives, where a group of individuals with limited capabilities are able to emerge with intelligent solutions for complex problems. Since long ago, researchers in Computer Science have already realized the importance of emergent behaviors for complex problem solving. This book gathers together some recent advances on Swarm Intelligence, comprising new swarm-based optimization methods, hybrid algorithms and innovative applications. The contents of this book allows the reader to get acquainted with both theoretical and technical aspects and applications of Swarm Intelligence.

I would like to thank the authors that made this book possible and Dr. Heitor Silvério Lopes for all the help during the review process.

Dr. Rafael Stubs Parpinelli
Universidade do Estado de Santa Catarina (UDESC)
Brazil

1

Swarm-Based Metaheuristic Algorithms and No-Free-Lunch Theorems

Xin-She Yang
National Physical Laboratory
United Kingdom

1. Introduction

Metaheuristic algorithms, especially those based on swarm intelligence (SI), form an important part of contemporary global optimization algorithms (Kennedy and Ebarhart, 1995; Yang, 2008; Auger and Teytaud, 2010; Auger and Doerr, 2010; Blum and Roli, 2003; Neumann and Witt 2010; Parpinelli and Lopes, 2011). Good examples are particle swarm optimization (PSO) (Kennedy and Eberhart, 1995) and firefly algorithm (FA) (Yang, 2009). They work remarkably efficiently and have many advantages over traditional, deterministic methods and algorithms, and thus they have been applied in almost all area of science, engineering and industry (Floudas and Pardolos, 2009; Yang 2010a, Yang, 2010b; Yu et al., 2005).

The main characteristics of swarm intelligence is that multiple self-interested agents somehow work together without any central control. These agents as a population can exchange information, by chemical messenger (pheromone by ants), by dance (waggle dance by bees), or by broadcasting ability (such as the global best in PSO and FA). Therefore, all swarm-based algorithms are population-based. However, not all population-based algorithms are swarm-based. For example, genetic algorithms (Holland, 1975; Goldberg, 2002) are population-based, but they are not inspired by swarm intelligence (Bonabeau et al., 1999).

The mobile agents interact locally and under the right conditions they somehow form emergent, self-organized behaviour, leading to global convergence. The agents typically explore the search space locally, aided by randomization which increases the diversity of the solutions on a global scale, and thus there is a fine balance between local intensive exploitation and global exploration (Blue and Roli, 2003). Any swarm-based algorithms have to balance these two components; otherwise, efficiency may be limited. In addition, these swarming agents can work in parallel, and thus such algorithms are particularly suitable for parallel implementation, which leads to even better reduction in computing time.

Despite such a huge success in applications, mathematical analysis of algorithms remains limited and many open problems are still un-resolved. There are three challenging areas for algorithm analysis: complexity, convergence and no-free-lunch theory. Complexity analysis of traditional algorithms such as quick sort and matrix inverse are well-established, as these algorithms are deterministic. In contrast, complexity analysis of metaheuristics remains a challenging task, partly due to the stochastic nature of these algorithms. However, good results do exist, concerning randomization search techniques (Auger and Teytaud, 2010).

Convergence analysis is another challenging area. One of the main difficulties concerning the convergence analysis of metaheuristic algorithms is that no generic framework exists, though substantial studies have been carried out using dynamic systems and Markov processes. However, convergence analysis still remains one of the active research areas with many encouraging results (Clerc and Kennedy, 2002; Trelea, 2003; Ólafsson, 2006; Gutjahr, 2002).

In optimization, there is a so-called 'no-free-lunch (NFL) theorem' proposed by Wolpert and Mcready (1997), which states that any algorithm will *on average* perform equally well as a random search algorithm over *all* possible functions. In other words, two algorithms A and B will on average have equal performance;' that is, if algorithm A performs better than B for some problems, then algorithm B will outperform A for other problems. This means that there is no universally superior algorithm for all types of problems. However, this does not mean that some algorithms are not better than other algorithms for some *specific* types of problems. In fact, we do not need to measure performance on average for all functions. More often, we need to measure how an algorithm performs for a given class of problems. Furthermore, the assumptions of the NLF theorem are not valid for all cases. In fact, there are quite a few no-free-lunch (NFL) theorems (Wolpert and Mcready, 1997; Igel and Toussaint, 2003). While in well-posed cases of optimization where its functional space forms finite domains, NFL theorems do hold; however, free lunches are possible in continuous domains(Auger and Teytaud, 2010; Wolpert and Mcready 2005; Villalobos-Arias et al., 2005).

In this chapter, we intend to provide a state-of-the-art review of the recent studies of no-free-lunch theory and also free lunch scenarios. This enables us to view the NLF and free lunch in a unified framework, or at least, in a convenient way. We will also briefly highlights some of the convergence studies. Based on these studies, we will summarize and propose a series of recommendations for further research.

2. Swarm-based algorithms

There are more than a dozen of swarm-based algorithms using the so-called swarm intelligence. For a detailed introduction, please refer to Yang (2010b), and for a recent comprehensive review, please refer to Parpinelli and Lopes (2011). In this section, we will focus on the main chararcteristics and the ways that each algorithm generate new solutions, and we will not discuss each algorithm in details. Interested readers can follow the references listed at the end of this chapter and also refer to other chapters of this book.

2.1 Ant algorithms

Ant algorithms, especially the ant colony optimization (Dorigo and Stütle, 2004), mimic the foraging behaviour of social ants. Primarily, it uses pheromone as a chemical messenger and the pheromone concentration as the indicator of quality solutions to a problem of interest. As the solution is often linked with the pheromone concentration, the search algorithms often produce routes and paths marked by the higher pheromone concentrations, and therefore, ants-based algorithms are particular suitable for discrete optimization problems.

The movement of an ant is controlled by pheromone which will evaporate over time. Without such time-dependent evaporation, the algorithms will lead to premature convergence to the (often wrong) solutions. With proper pheromone evaporation, they usually behave very well.

There are two important issues here: the probability of choosing a route, and the evaporation rate of pheromone. There are a few ways of solving these problems, although it is still an area of active research. Here we introduce the current best method.

For a network routing problem, the probability of ants at a particular node i to choose the route from node i to node j is given by

$$p_{ij} = \frac{\phi_{ij}^{\alpha} d_{ij}^{\beta}}{\sum_{i,j=1}^{n} \phi_{ij}^{\alpha} d_{ij}^{\beta}}, \tag{1}$$

where $\alpha > 0$ and $\beta > 0$ are the influence parameters, and their typical values are $\alpha \approx \beta \approx 2$. ϕ_{ij} is the pheromone concentration on the route between i and j, and d_{ij} the desirability of the same route. Some *a priori* knowledge about the route such as the distance s_{ij} is often used so that $d_{ij} \propto 1/s_{ij}$, which implies that shorter routes will be selected due to their shorter traveling time, and thus the pheromone concentrations on these routes are higher. This is because the traveling time is shorter, and thus the less amount of the pheromone has been evaporated during this period.

This probability formula reflects the fact that ants would normally follow the paths with higher pheromone concentrations. In the simpler case when $\alpha = \beta = 1$, the probability of choosing a path by ants is proportional to the pheromone concentration on the path. The denominator normalizes the probability so that it is in the range between 0 and 1.

The pheromone concentration can change with time due to the evaporation of pheromone. Furthermore, the advantage of pheromone evaporation is that the system could avoid being trapped in local optima. If there is no evaporation, then the path randomly chosen by the first ants will become the preferred path as the attraction of other ants by their pheromone. For a constant rate γ of pheromone decay or evaporation, the pheromone concentration usually varies with time exponentially

$$\phi(t) = \phi_0 e^{-\gamma t}, \tag{2}$$

where ϕ_0 is the initial concentration of pheromone and t is time. If $\gamma t \ll 1$, then we have $\phi(t) \approx (1 - \gamma t)\phi_0$. For the unitary time increment $\Delta t = 1$, the evaporation can be approximated by $\phi^{t+1} \leftarrow (1 - \gamma)\phi^t$. Therefore, we have the simplified pheromone update formula:

$$\phi_{ij}^{t+1} = (1 - \gamma)\phi_{ij}^{t} + \delta\phi_{ij}^{t}, \tag{3}$$

where $\gamma \in [0, 1]$ is the rate of pheromone evaporation. The increment $\delta\phi_{ij}^t$ is the amount of pheromone deposited at time t along route i to j when an ant travels a distance L. Usually $\delta\phi_{ij}^t \propto 1/L$. If there are no ants on a route, then the pheromone deposit is zero.

There are other variations to this basic procedure. A possible acceleration scheme is to use some bounds of the pheromone concentration and only the ants with the current global best solution(s) are allowed to deposit pheromone. In addition, certain ranking of solution fitness can also be used.

2.2 Bee algorithms

Bees-inspired algorithms are more diverse, and some use pheromone and most do not. Almost all bee algorithms are inspired by the foraging behaviour of honey bees in nature. Interesting characteristics such as waggle dance, polarization and nectar maximization are often used to simulate the allocation of the foraging bee along flower patches and thus different search regions in the search space. For a more comprehensive review, please refer to Parpinelli and Lopes (2011).

Honeybees live in a colony and they forage and store honey in their constructed colony. Honeybees can communicate by pheromone and 'waggle dance'. For example, an alarming bee may release a chemical message (pheromone) to stimulate attack response in other bees. Furthermore, when bees find a good food source and bring some nectar back to the hive, they will communicate the location of the food source by performing the so-called waggle dances as a signal system. Such signaling dances vary from species to species, however, they will try to recruit more bees by using directional dancing with varying strength so as to communicate the direction and distance of the found food resource. For multiple food sources such as flower patches, studies show that a bee colony seems to be able to allocate forager bees among different flower patches so as to maximize their total nectar intake.

In the honeybee-based algorithm, forager bees are allocated to different food sources (or flower patches) so as to maximize the total nectar intake. The colony has to 'optimize' the overall efficiency of nectar collection, the allocation of the bees is thus depending on many factors such as the nectar richness and the proximity to the hive (Nakrani and Trovey, 2004; Yang, 2005; Karaboga, 2005; Pham et al., 2006)

Let $w_i(j)$ be the strength of the waggle dance of bee i at time step $t = j$, the probability of an observer bee following the dancing bee to forage can be determined in many ways depending on the actual variant of algorithms. A simple way is given by

$$p_i = \frac{w_i^j}{\sum_{i=1}^{n_f} w_i^j}, \tag{4}$$

where n_f is the number of bees in foraging process. t is the pseudo time or foraging expedition. The number of observer bees is $N - n_f$ when N is the total number of bees. Alternatively, we can define an exploration probability of a Gaussian type $p_e = 1 - p_i = \exp[-w_i^2/2\sigma^2]$, where σ is the volatility of the bee colony, and it controls the exploration and diversity of the foraging sites. If there is no dancing (no food found), then $w_i \to 0$, and $p_e = 1$. So all the bee explore randomly.

The virtual bee algorithm (VBA), developed by Xin-She Yang in 2005, is an optimization algorithm specially formulated for solving both discrete and continuous problems (Yang, 2005). On the other hand, the artificial bee colony (ABC) optimization algorithm was first developed by D. Karaboga in 2005. In the ABC algorithm, the bees in a colony are divided into three groups: employed bees (forager bees), onlooker bees (observer bees) and scouts. For each food source, there is only one employed bee. That is to say, the number of employed bees is equal to the number of food sources. The employed bee of an discarded food site is forced to become a scout for searching new food sources randomly. Employed bees share information with the onlooker bees in a hive so that onlooker bees can choose a food source to forage. Unlike the honey bee algorithm which has two groups of the bees (forager bees and observer bees), bees in ABC are more specialized (Karaboga, 2005; Afshar et al., 2007).

Similar to the ants-based algorithms, bee algorithms are also very flexible in dealing with discrete optimization problems. Combinatorial optimizations such as routing and optimal paths have been successfully solved by ant and bee algorithms. Though bee algorithms can be applied to continuous problems as well as discrete problems, however, they should not be the first choice for continuous problems.

2.3 Particle swarm optimization

Particle swarm optimization (PSO) was developed by Kennedy and Eberhart in 1995, based on the swarm behaviour such as fish and bird schooling in nature. Since then, PSO has generated much wider interests, and forms an exciting, ever-expanding research subject, called swarm intelligence. PSO has been applied to almost every area in optimization, computational intelligence, and design/scheduling applications.

The movement of a swarming particle consists of two major components: a social component and a cognitive component. Each particle is attracted toward the position of the current global best g^* and its own best location x_i^* in history, while at the same time it has a tendency to move randomly.

Let x_i and v_i be the position vector and velocity for particle i, respectively. The new velocity and location updating formulas are determined by

$$v_i^{t+1} = v_i^t + \alpha\epsilon_1[g^* - x_i^t] + \beta\epsilon_2[x_i^* - x_i^t]. \tag{5}$$

$$x_i^{t+1} = x_i^t + v_i^{t+1}, \tag{6}$$

where ϵ_1 and ϵ_2 are two random vectors, and each entry taking the values between 0 and 1. The parameters α and β are the learning parameters or acceleration constants, which can typically be taken as, say, $\alpha \approx \beta \approx 2$.

There are at least two dozen PSO variants which extend the standard PSO algorithm, and the most noticeable improvement is probably to use inertia function $\theta(t)$ so that v_i^t is replaced by $\theta(t)v_i^t$ where $\theta \in [0,1]$. This is equivalent to introducing a virtual mass to stabilize the motion of the particles, and thus the algorithm is expected to converge more quickly.

2.4 Firefly algorithm

Firefly Algorithm (FA) was developed by Xin-She Yang at Cambridge University (Yang,2008; Yang 2009), which was based on the flashing patterns and behaviour of fireflies. In essence, each firefly will be attracted to brighter ones, while at the same time, it explores and searches for prey randomly. In addition, the brightness of a firefly is determined by the landscape of the objective function.

The movement of a firefly i attracted to another more attractive (brighter) firefly j is determined by

$$x_i^{t+1} = x_i^t + \beta_0 e^{-\gamma r_{ij}^2}(x_j^t - x_i^t) + \alpha_t\, \epsilon_i^t, \tag{7}$$

where the second term is due to the attraction. The third term is randomization with α_t being the randomization parameter, and ϵ_i^t is a vector of random numbers drawn from a Gaussian distribution or uniform distribution. Here $\beta_0 \in [0,1]$ is the attractiveness at $r = 0$, and $r_{ij} = ||x_i^t - x_j^t||$ is the Cartesian distance. For other problems such as scheduling, any measure that can effectively characterize the quantities of interest in the optimization problem can be used as the 'distance' r. For most implementations, we can take $\beta_0 = 1$, $\alpha = O(1)$ and $\gamma = O(1)$.

Ideally, the randomization parameter α_t should be monotonically reduced gradually during iterations. A simple scheme is to use

$$\alpha_t = \alpha_0\delta^t, \quad \delta \in (0,1), \tag{8}$$

where α_0 is the initial randomness, while δ is a randomness reduction factor similar to that used in a cooling schedule in simulated annealing. It is worth pointing out that (7) is essentially a random walk biased towards the brighter fireflies. If $\beta_0 = 0$, it becomes a simple random walk. Furthermore, the randomization term can easily be extended to other distributions such as Lévy flights.

2.5 Bat algorithm

Bat algorithm is a relatively new metaheuristic, developed by Xin-She Yang in 2010 (Yang, 2010c). It was inspired by the echolocation behaviour of microbats. Microbats use a type of sonar, called, echolocation, to detect prey, avoid obstacles, and locate their roosting crevices in the dark. These bats emit a very loud sound pulse and listen for the echo that bounces back from the surrounding objects. Their pulses vary in properties and can be correlated with their hunting strategies, depending on the species. Most bats use short, frequency-modulated signals to sweep through about an octave, while others more often use constant-frequency signals for echolocation. Their signal bandwidth varies depends on the species, and often increased by using more harmonics.

Inside the bat algorithm, it uses three idealized rules:

1. All bats use echolocation to sense distance, and they also 'know' the difference between food/prey and background barriers in some magical way;
2. Bats fly randomly with velocity $\boldsymbol{v}_i$ at position $\boldsymbol{x}_i$ with a fixed frequency $f_{\min}$, varying wavelength λ and loudness A_0 to search for prey. They can automatically adjust the wavelength (or frequency) of their emitted pulses and adjust the rate of pulse emission $r \in [0,1]$, depending on the proximity of their target;
3. Although the loudness can vary in many ways, we assume that the loudness varies from a large (positive) A_0 to a minimum constant value $A_{\min}$.

BA has been extended to multiobjective bat algorithm (MOBA) by Yang (2011), and preliminary results suggested that it is very efficient.

2.6 Cuckoo search

Cuckoo search (CS) is one of the latest nature-inspired metaheuristic algorithms, developed in 2009 by Xin-She Yang and Suash Deb (Yang and Deb, 2009; Yang and Deb, 2010). CS is based on the brood parasitism of some cuckoo species. In addition, this algorithm is enhanced by the so-called Lévy flights, rather than by simple isotropic random walks. This algorithm was inspired by the aggressive reproduction strategy of some cuckoo species such as the *ani* and *Guira* cuckoos. These cuckoos lay their eggs in communal nests, though they may remove others' eggs to increase the hatching probability of their own eggs. Quite a number of species engage the obligate brood parasitism by laying their eggs in the nests of other host birds (often other species).

In the standard cuckoo search, the following three idealized rules are used:

- Each cuckoo lays one egg at a time, and dumps it in a randomly chosen nest;
- The best nests with high-quality eggs will be carried over to the next generations;
- The number of available host nests is fixed, and the egg laid by a cuckoo is discovered by the host bird with a probability $p_a \in [0,1]$. In this case, the host bird can either get rid of the egg, or simply abandon the nest and build a completely new nest.

As a further approximation, this last assumption can be approximated by a fraction p_a of the n host nests are replaced by new nests (with new random solutions). Recent studies suggest that cuckoo search can outperform particle swarm optimization and other algorithms (Yang and Deb, 2010). These are still topics of active research.

There are other metaheuristic algorithms which have not been introduced here, and interested readers can refer to more advanced literature (Yang, 2010b; Parpinelli and Lopes, 2011).

3. Intensification and diversification

Metaheuristics can be considered as an efficient way to produce acceptable solutions by trial and error to a complex problem in a reasonably practical time. The complexity of the problem of interest makes it impossible to search every possible solution or combination, the aim is to find good feasible solution in an acceptable timescale. There is no guarantee that the best solutions can be found, and we even do not know whether an algorithm will work and why if it does work. The idea is to have an efficient but practical algorithm that will work most the time and is able to produce good quality solutions. Among the found quality solutions, it is expected some of them are nearly optimal, though there is often no guarantee for such optimality.

The main components of any metaheuristic algorithms are: intensification and diversification, or exploitation and exploration (Blum and Roli, 2003; Yang, 2008; Yang, 2010b). Diversification means to generate diverse solutions so as to explore the search space on the global scale, while intensification means to focus on the search in a local region by exploiting the information that a current good solution is found in this region. This is in combination with the selection of the best solutions. Randomization techniques can be a very simple method using uniform distributions and/or Gaussian distributions, or more complex methods as those used in Monte Carlo simulations. They can also be more elaborate, from Brownian random walks to Lévy flights.

In general, intensification speeds up the convergence of an algorithm, however, it may lead to a local optimum, not necessarily the global optimality. On the other hand, diversification often slows down the convergence but increases the probability of finding the global optimum. Therefore, there is a fine balance beteween these seemingly competing components for any algorithm.

In ant and bee algorithms, intensification is usually achieved by pheromone and exchange of information so that all agents swarm together or follow similar routes. Diversification is achieved by randomization and probabilistic choices of routes. In PSO, intensification is controlled mainly by the use of the global best and individual best solutions, while diversification is plainly done using two random numbers or learning parameters.

For the standard FA, the global best is not used, though its use may increase the convergence rates for some problems such as unimodal problems or problems with some dominant modes. Intensification is subtly done by the attraction among fireflies and thus brightness is the information exchanged among adjacent fireflies. Diversification is carried out by the randomization term, either by random walks or by Lévy flights, in combination with a randomness-reduction technique similar to a cooling schedule in simulated annealing.

Intensification and diversification in the bat algorithm is controlled by a switch parameter. Intensification as well as diversification is also enhanced by the variations of loudness and pulse rates. In this sense, the mechanism is relatively simple, but very efficient in balancing the two key components.

In the cuckoo search, things become more subtle. Diversification is carried out in two ways: randomization via Lévy flights and feeding new solutions into randomly chosen nests. Intensification is achieved by a combination of elitism and the generation of solutions according to similarity (thus the usage of local information). In addition, a switch parameter (a fraction of abandoned nests) is used to control the balance of diversification and intensification.

As seen earlier, an important component in swarm intelligence and modern metaheuristics is randomization, which enables an algorithm to have the ability to jump out of any local optimum so as to search globally. Randomization can also be used for local search around the current best if steps are limited to a local region. When the steps are large, randomization can explore the search space on a global scale. Fine-tuning the randomness and balance of local search and global search is crucially important in controlling the performance of any metaheuristic algorithm.

4. No-free-lunch theorems

The seminal paper by Wolpert and Mcready in 1997 essentially proposed a framework for performance comparison of optimization algorithms, using a combination of Bayesian statistics and Markov random field theories. Let us sketch Wolpert and Macready's original idea. Assuming that the search space is finite (though quite large), thus the space of possible objective values is also finite. This means that objective function is simply a mapping $f : \mathcal{X} \mapsto \mathcal{Y}$, with $\mathcal{F} = \mathcal{Y}^{\mathcal{X}}$ as the space of all possible problems under permutation.

As an algorithm tends to produce a series of points or solutions in the search space, it is further assumed that these points are distinct. That is, for k iterations, k distinct visited points forms a time-ordered set

$$\Omega_k = \Big\{ \big(\Omega_k^x(1), \Omega_k^y(1)\big), ..., \big(\Omega_k^x(k), \Omega_k^y(k)\big) \Big\}. \tag{9}$$

There are many ways to define a performance measure, though a good measure still remains debatable (Shilane et al., 2008). Such a measure can depend on the number of iteration k, the algorithm a and the actual cost function f, which can be denoted by $P(\Omega_k^y \| f, k, a)$. Here we follow the notation style in seminal paper by Wolpert and Mcready (1997). For any pair of algorithms a and b, the NFL theorem states

$$\sum_f P(\Omega_k^y | f, k, a) = \sum_f P(\Omega_k^y | f, k, b). \tag{10}$$

In other words, any algorithm is as good (bad) as a random search, when the performance is averaged over all possible functions.

Along many relevant assumptions in proving the NFL theorems, two fundamental assumptions are: finite states of the search space (and thus the objective values), and the non-revisiting time-ordered sets.

The first assumption is a good approximation to many problems, especially in finite-digit approximations. However, there is mathematical difference in countable finite, and countable infinite. Therefore, the results for finite states/domains may not directly applicable to infinite domains. Furthermore, as continuous problem are uncountable, NFL results for finite domains will usually not hold for continuous domains (Auger and Teytaud, 2010).

The second assumption on non-revisiting iterative sequence is an over-simplification, as almost all metaheuristic algorithms are revisiting in practice, some points visited before will possibly be re-visited again in the future. The only possible exception is the Tabu algorithm with a very long Tabu list (Glover and Laguna, 1997). Therefore, results for non-revisiting time-ordered iterations may not be true for the cases of revisiting cases, because the revisiting iterations break an important assumption of 'closed under permutation' (c.u.p) required for proving the NFL theorems (Marshall and Hinton, 2010).

Furthermore, optimization problems do not necessarily concern the whole set of all possible functions/problems, and it is often sufficient to consider a subset of problems. It is worth pointing out active studies have carried out in constructing algorithms that can work best on specific subsets of optimization problems, in fact, NFL theorems do not hold in this case (Christensen and Oppacher, 2001).

These theorems are vigorous and thus have important theoretical values. However, their practical implications are a different issue. In fact, it may not be so important in practice anyway, we will discuss this in a later section.

5. Free lunch or no free lunch

The validity of NFL theorems largely depends on the validity of their fundamental assumptions. However, whether these assumptions are valid in practice is another question. Often, these assumptions are too stringent, and thus free lunches are possible.

5.1 Continuous free lunches

One of the assumptions is the non-revisiting nature of the k distinct points which form a time-ordered set. For revisiting points as they do occur in practice in real-world optimization algorithms, the 'closed under permutation' does not hold, which renders NFL theorems invalid (Schumacher et al., 2001; Marshall and Hinton, 2010). This means free lunches do exist in practical applications.

Another basic assumption is the finiteness of the domains. For continuous domains, Auger and Teytaud in 2010 have proven that the NFL theorem does not hold, and therefore they concluded that 'continuous free lunches exist'. Indeed, some algorithms are better than others. For example, for a 2D sphere function, they demonstrated that an efficient algorithm only needs 4 iterations/steps to reach the global minimum.

5.2 Coevolutionary and multiobjective free lunches

The basic NFL theorems concern a single agent, marching iteratively in the search space in distinct steps. However, Wolpert and Mcready proved in 2005 that NFL theorems do not hold under coevolution. For example, a set of players (or agents) in self-play problems can work together so as to produce a champion. This can be visualized as an evolutionary process of training a chess champion. In this case, free lunch does exist (Wolpert and Mcready, 2005). It is worth pointing out that for a single player, it tries to pursue the best next move, while for two players, the fitness function depend on the moves of both players. Therefore, the basic assumptions for NFL theorems are no longer valid.

For multiobjective optimization problems, things have become even more complicated. An important step in theoretical analysis is that some multiobjective optimizers are better than others as pointed out by Corne and Knowles (2003). One of the major reasons is that the archiver and generator in the multiobjective algorithms can lead to multiobjective free lunches.

Whether NFL holds or not, it has nothing to say about the complexity of the problems. In fact, no free lunch theorem has not been proved to be true for problems with NP-hard complexity (Whitley and Watson, 2005).

6. NFL theorems and meaning for algorithm developers

No-free-lunch theorems may be of theoretical importance, and they can also have important implications for algorithm development in practice, though not everyone agrees the real importance of these implications. In general, there are three kinds of opinions concerning the implications. The first group may simply ignore these theorems, as they argue that the assumptions are too stringent, and the performance measures based on average overall functions are irrelevant in practice (Whitley and Watson, 2005). Therefore, no practical importance can be inferred, and research just carries on.

The second kind is that NFL theorems can be true, and they can accept that the fact there is no universally efficient algorithm. But in practice some algorithms do performance better than others for a specific problem or a subset of problems. Research effort should focus on finding the right algorithms for the right type of problem. Problem-specific knowledge is always helpful to find the right algorithm(s).

The third kind of opinion is that NFL theorems are not true for other types of problems such as continuous problems and NP-hard problems. Theoretical work concerns more elaborate studies on extending NFL theorems to other cases or on finding free lunches (Auger and Teytaud, 2010). On the other hand, algorithm development continues to design better algorithms which can work for a wider range of problems, not necessarily all types of problems. As we have seen from the above analysis, free lunches do exist, and better algorithms can be designed for a specific subset of problems (Yang,2009; Yang and Deb, 2010).

Thus, free lunch or no free lunch is not just a simple question, it has important and yet practical importance. There is certain truth in all the above arguments, and their impacts on optimization community are somehow mixed. Obviously, in reality, the algorithms with problem-specific knowledge typically work better than random search, and we also realized that there is no universally generic tool that works best for all the problems. Therefore, we have to seek balance between speciality and generality, between algorithm simplicity and problem complexity, and between problem-specific knowledge and capability of handling black-box optimization problems.

7. Convergence analysis of metaheuristics

For convergence analysis, there is no mathematical framework in general to provide insights into the working mechanism, the complexity, stability and convergence of any given algorithm (He and Yu, 2001; Thikomirov, 2007). Despite the increasing popularity of metaheuristics, mathematical analysis remains fragmental, and many open problems concerning convergence analysis need urgent attention. In addition, many algorithms, though efficient, have not been proved their convergence, for example, harmony search usually converges well (Geem, 2009), but its convergence still needs mathematical analysis.

7.1 PSO

The first convergence analysis of PSO was carried out by Clerc and Kennedy in 2002 using the theory of dynamical systems. Mathematically, if we ignore the random factors, we can view the system formed by (5) and (6) as a dynamical system. If we focus on a single particle i and imagine that there is only one particle in this system, then the global best g^* is the same as its current best x_i^*. In this case, we have

$$v_i^{t+1} = v_i^t + \gamma(g^* - x_i^t), \quad \gamma = \alpha + \beta, \tag{11}$$

and

$$x_i^{t+1} = x_i^t + v_i^{t+1}. \tag{12}$$

Considering the 1D dynamical system for particle swarm optimization, we can replace g^* by a parameter constant p so that we can see if or not the particle of interest will converge towards p. By setting $u_t = p - x(t+1)$ and using the notations for dynamical systems, we have a simple dynamical system

$$v_{t+1} = v_t + \gamma u_t, \quad u_{t+1} = -v_t + (1-\gamma)u_t, \tag{13}$$

or

$$Y_{t+1} = AY_t, \quad A = \begin{pmatrix} 1 & \gamma \\ -1 & 1-\gamma \end{pmatrix}, \quad Y_t = \begin{pmatrix} v_t \\ u_t \end{pmatrix}. \tag{14}$$

The general solution of this dynamical system can be written as $Y_t = Y_0 \exp[At]$. The system behaviour can be characterized by the eigenvalues λ of A

$$\lambda_{1,2} = 1 - \frac{\gamma}{2} \pm \frac{\sqrt{\gamma^2 - 4\gamma}}{2}. \tag{15}$$

It can be seen clearly that $\gamma = 4$ leads to a bifurcation. Following a straightforward analysis of this dynamical system, we can have three cases. For $0 < \gamma < 4$, cyclic and/or quasi-cyclic trajectories exist. In this case, when randomness is gradually reduced, some convergence can be observed. For $\gamma > 4$, non-cyclic behaviour can be expected and the distance from Y_t to the center $(0,0)$ is monotonically increasing with t. In a special case $\gamma = 4$, some convergence behaviour can be observed. For detailed analysis, please refer to Clerc and Kennedy (2003). Since p is linked with the global best, as the iterations continue, it can be expected that all particles will aggregate towards the the global best.

7.2 Firefly algorithm

We now can carry out the convergence analysis for the firefly algorithm in a framework similar to Clerc and Kennedy's dynamical analysis. For simplicity, we start from the equation for firefly motion without the randomness term

$$x_i^{t+1} = x_i^t + \beta_0 e^{-\gamma r_{ij}^2}(x_j^t - x_i^t). \tag{16}$$

If we focus on a single agent, we can replace x_j^t by the global best g found so far, and we have

$$x_i^{t+1} = x_i^t + \beta_0 e^{-\gamma r_i^2}(g - x_i^t), \tag{17}$$

where the distance r_i can be given by the ℓ_2-norm $r_i^2 = ||g - x_i^t||_2^2$. In an even simpler 1-D case, we can set $y_t = g - x_i^t$, and we have

$$y_{t+1} = y_t - \beta_0 e^{-\gamma y_t^2} y_t. \tag{18}$$

We can see that γ is a scaling parameter which only affects the scales/size of the firefly movement. In fact, we can let $u_t = \sqrt{\gamma} y_t$ and we have

$$u_{t+1} = u_t[1 - \beta_0 e^{-u_t^2}]. \tag{19}$$

These equations can be analyzed easily using the same methodology for studying the well-known logistic map

$$u_t = \lambda u_t(1 - u_t). \tag{20}$$

Mathematical analysis and numerical simulations of (19) can reveal its regions of chaos. Briefly, the convergence can be achieved for $\beta_0 < 2$. There is a transition from periodic to chaos at $\beta_0 \approx 4$. This may be surprising, as the aim of designing a metaheuristic algorithm is to try to find the optimal solution efficiently and accurately. However, chaotic behaviour is not necessarily a nuisance, in fact, we can use it to the advantage of the firefly algorithm. Simple chaotic characteristics from (20) can often be used as an efficient mixing technique for generating diverse solutions. Statistically, the logistic mapping (20) for $\lambda = 4$ for the initial states in (0,1) corresponds a beta distribution

$$B(u, p, q) = \frac{\Gamma(p + q)}{\Gamma(p)\Gamma(q)} u^{p-1}(1 - u)^{q-1}, \tag{21}$$

when $p = q = 1/2$. Here $\Gamma(z)$ is the Gamma function

$$\Gamma(z) = \int_0^\infty t^{z-1} e^{-t} dt. \tag{22}$$

In the case when $z = n$ is an integer, we have $\Gamma(n) = (n - 1)!$. In addition, $\Gamma(1/2) = \sqrt{\pi}$. From the algorithm implementation point of view, we can use higher attractiveness β_0 during the early stage of iterations so that the fireflies can explore, even chaotically, the search space more effectively. As the search continues and convergence approaches, we can reduce the attractiveness β_0 gradually, which may increase the overall efficiency of the algorithm. Obviously, more studies are highly needed to confirm this.

7.3 Markov chains

Most theoretical studies use Markov chains/process as a framework for convergence analysis. A Markov chain is said be to regular if some positive power k of the transition matrix $\boldsymbol{P}$ has only positive elements. A chain is ergodic or irreducible if it is aperiodic and positive recurrent, which means that it is possible to reach every state from any state.

For a time-homogeneous chain as $k \to \infty$, we have the stationary probability distribution π, satisfying

$$\pi = \pi \mathbf{P}, \tag{23}$$

thus the first eigenvalue is always 1. This will lead to the asymptotic convergence to the global optimality θ_*:

$$\lim_{k \to \infty} \theta_k \to \theta_*, \tag{24}$$

with probability one (Gamerman, 1997; Gutjahr, 2002).

Now if look at the PSO and FA closely using the framework of Markov chain Monte Carlo, each particle in PSO or each firefly in FA essentially forms a Markov chain, though this Markov chain is biased towards to the current best, as the transition probability often leads to the acceptance of the move towards the current global best. Other population-based algorithms can also be viewed in this framework. In essence, all metaheuristic algorithms with piecewise, interacting paths can be analyzed in the general framework of Markov chain Monte Carlo. The main challenge is to realize this and to use the appropriate Markov chain theory to study metaheuristic algorithms. More fruitful studies will surely emerge in the future.

7.4 Other results

Limited results on convergence analysis exist, concerning finite domains, ant colony optimization (Gutjahr,2010; Sebastiani and Torrisi,2005), cross-entropy optimization, best-so-far convergence (Margolin, 2005), nested partition method, Tabu search, and largely combinatorial optimization. However, more challenging tasks for infinite states/domains and continuous problems. Many open problems need satisfactory answers.

On the other hand, it is worth pointing out that an algorithm can converge, but it may not be efficient, as its convergence rate could be typically low. One of the main tasks in research is to find efficient algorithms for a given type of problem.

8. Open problems

Active research on NFL theorems and algorithm convergence analysis has led to many important results. Despite this, many crucial problems remain unanswered. These open questions span a diverse range of areas. Here we highlight a few but relevant open problems.

Framework: Convergence analysis has been fruitful, however, it is still highly needed to develop a unified framework for algorithmic analysis and convergence.

Exploration and exploitation: Two important components of metaheuristics are exploration and exploitation or diversification and intensification. What is the optimal balance between these two components?

Performance measure: To compare two algorithms, we have to define a measure for gauging their performance (Spall et al., 2006). At present, there is no agreed performance measure, but what are the best performance measures ? Statistically?

Free lunches: No-free-lunch theorems have not been proved for continuous domains for multiobjective optimization. For single-objective optimization, free lunches are possible; is this true for multiobjective optimization? In addition, no free lunch theorem has not been proved to be true for problems with NP-hard complexity (Whitley and Watson, 2005). If free lunches exist, what are their implications in practice and how to find the best algorithm(s)?

Automatic parameter tuning: For almost all algorithms, algorithm-dependent parameters require fine-tuning so that the algorithm of interest can achieve maximum performance. At the moment, parameter-tuning is mainly done by inefficient, expensive parametric studies. In fact, automatic self-tuning of parameters is another optimization problem, and optimal tuning of these parameters is another important open problem.

Knowledge: Problem-specific knowledge always helps to find an appropriate solution? How to quantify such knowledge?

Intelligent algorithms: A major aim for algorithm development is to design better, intelligent algorithms for solving tough NP-hard optimization problems. What do mean by 'intelligent'? What are the practical ways to design truly intelligent, self-evolving algorithms?

9. Concluding remarks

SI-based algorithms are expanding and becoming increasingly popular in many disciplines and applications. One of the reasons is that these algorithms are flexible and efficient in solving a wide range of highly nonlinear, complex problems, yet their implementation is relatively straightforward without much problem-specific knowledge. In addition, swarming agents typically work in parallel, and thus parallel implementation is a natural advantage.

At present, swarm intelligence and relevant algorithms are inspired by some specific features of the successful biological systems such as social insects and birds. Though they are highly successful, however, these algorithms still have room for improvement. In addition to the above open problems, a truly 'intelligent' algorithm is yet to be developed. By learning more and more from nature and by carrying out ever-increasingly detailed, systematical studies, some truly 'smart' self-evolving algorithms will be developed in the future so that such smart algorithms can automatically fine-tune their behaviour to find the most efficient way of solving complex problems. As an even bolder prediction, maybe, some hyper-level algorithm-constructing metaheuristics can be developed to automatically construct algorithms in an intelligent manner in the not-too-far future.

10. References

[1] Afshar, A., Haddad, O. B., Marino, M. A., Adams, B. J., (2007). Honey-bee mating optimization (HBMO) algorithm for optimal reservoir operation, *J. Franklin Institute*, 344, 452-462.

[2] Auger, A. and Teytaud, O., Continuous lunches are free plus the design of optimal optimization algorithms, Algorithmica, 57, 121-146 (2010).

[3] Auger, A. and B. Doerr, B., *Theory of Randomized Search Heuristics: Foundations and Recent Developments*, World Scientific, (2010).

[4] Bonabeau, E., Dorigo, M., Theraulaz, G., (1999). *Swarm Intelligence: From Natural to Artificial Systems.* Oxford University Press.

[5] Blum, C. and Roli, A. (2003) Metaheuristics in combinatorial optimisation: Overview and conceptural comparision, *ACM Comput. Surv.*, Vol. 35, 268-308.

[6] Clerc, M. and J. Kennedy, J., The particle swarm - explosion, stability, and convergence in a multidimensional complex space, *IEEE Trans. Evolutionary Computation*, 6, 58-73 (2002).

[7] Corne D. and Knowles, J., Some multiobjective optimizers are better than others, *Evolutionary Computation*, CEC'03, 4, 2506-2512 (2003).

[8] Christensen, S. and Oppacher, F., (2001). Wath can we learn from No Free Lunch? in: *Proc. Genetic and Evolutionary Computation Conference* (GECCO-01), pp. 1219-1226 (2001).
[9] Dorigo, M. and Stütle, T., *Ant Colony Optimization*, MIT Press, (2004).
[10] Floudas, C. A. and Pardolos, P. M., *Encyclopedia of Optimization*, 2nd Edition, Springer (2009).
[11] Gamerman, D., *Markov Chain Monte Carlo*, Chapman & Hall/CRC, (1997).
[12] Glover, F. and Laguna, M. (1997) *Tabu Search*, Kluwer Academic Publishers, Boston.
[13] Goldberg, D. E., *The Design of Innovation: Lessons from and for Competent Genetic Algorithms*, Addison-Wesley, Reading, MA, (2002).
[14] Gutjahr, W. J., ACO algorithms with guaranteed convergence to the optimal solution, *Information Processing Letters*, 82, 145-153 (2002).
[15] Gutjahr, W. J., Convergence Analysis of Metaheuristics *Annals of Information Systems*, 10, 159-187 (2010).
[16] He, J. and Yu, X., Conditions for the convergence of evolutionary algorithms, *J. Systems Architecture*, 47, 601-612 (2001).
[17] Henderson, D., Jacobson, S. H., and Johnson, W., The theory and practice of simulated annealing, in: *Handbook of Metaheuristics* (Eds. F. Glover and G. A. Kochenberger), Kluwer Academic, pp. 287-319 (2003).
[18] Holland, J., *Adaptation in Natural and Artificial systems*, University of Michigan Press, Ann Anbor, (1975).
[19] Igel, C. and Toussaint, M., (2003). On classes of functions for which no free lunch results hold, *Inform. Process. Lett.*, 86, 317-321 (2003).
[20] Karaboga, D., (2005). An idea based on honey bee swarm for numerical optimization, Technical Report TR06, Erciyes University, Turkey.
[21] Kennedy, J. and Eberhart, R. (1995) 'Particle swarm optimisation', in: *Proc. of the IEEE Int. Conf. on Neural Networks*, Piscataway, NJ, pp. 1942-1948.
[22] Kirkpatrick, S., Gellat, C. D., and Vecchi, M. P. (1983) 'Optimisation by simulated annealing', *Science*, 220, 671-680.
[23] Nakrani, S. and Tovey, C., (2004). On Honey Bees and Dynamic Server Allocation in Internet Hosting Centers. *Adaptive Behaviour*, 12(3-4), 223-240.
[24] Neumann, F. and Witt, C., *Bioinspired Computation in Combinatorial Optimization: Algorithms and Their Computational Complexity*, Springer, (2010).
[25] Margolin, L., On the convergence of the cross-entropy method, *Annals of Operations Research*, 134, 201-214 (2005).
[26] Marshall, J. A. and Hinton, T. G., Beyond no free lunch: realistic algorithms for arbitrary problem classes, WCCI 2010 IEEE World Congress on Computational Intelligence, July 1823, Barcelona, Spain, pp. 1319-1324 (2010).
[27] Ólafsson, S., Metaheuristics, in: *Handbook on Simulation* (Eds. Nelson and Henderson), Handbooks in Operation Reserch and Management Science VII, Elsevier, pp. 633-654 (2006).
[28] Parpinelli, R. S., and Lopes, H. S., New inspirations in swarm intelligence: a survey, *Int. J. Bio-Inspired Computation*, 3, 1-16 (2011).
[29] Pham, D.T., Ghanbarzadeh, A., Koc, E., Otri, S., Rahim, S., and Zaidi, M., (2006). The Bees Algorithm Ű A Novel Tool for Complex Optimisation Problems, Proceedings of IPROMS 2006 Conference, pp.454-461
[30] Schumacher, C., Vose, M., and Whitley D., The no free lunch and problem description length, in: *Genetic and Evolutionary Computation Conference*, GECCO-2001, pp. 565-570 (2001).

[31] Sebastiani, G. and Torrisi, G. L., An extended ant colony algorithm and its convergence analysis, *Methodoloy and Computating in Applied Probability*, 7, 249-263 (2005).
[32] Shilane, D., Martikainen, J., Dudoit, S., Ovaska, S. J. (2008) 'A general framework for statistical performance comparison of evolutionary computation algorithms', *Information Sciences*, Vol. 178, 2870-2879.
[33] Spall, J. C., Hill, S. D., and Stark, D. R., Theoretical framework for comparing several stochastic optimization algorithms, in:*Probabilistic and Randomized Methods for Design Under Uncertainty*, Springer, London, pp. 99-117 (2006).
[34] Thikomirov, A. S., On the convergence rate of the Markov homogeneous monotone optimization method, *Computational Mathematics and Mathematical Physics*, 47, 817-828 (2007).
[35] Villalobos-Arias, M., Coello Coello, C. A., and Hernández-Lerma, O., Asymptotic convergence of metaheuristics for multiobjective optimization problems, *Soft Computing*, 10, 1001-1005 (2005).
[36] Whitley, D. and Watson, J. P., Complexity theory and the no free lunch theorem, in: *Search Methodolgies*, pp. 317-339 (2005).
[37] Wolpert, D. H. and Macready, W. G. (1997), No free lunch theorems for optimisation, *IEEE Transaction on Evolutionary Computation*, Vol. 1, 67-82.
[38] Wolpert, D. H. and Macready, W. G., Coevolutonary free lunches, *IEEE Trans. Evolutionary Computation*, 9, 721-735 (2005).
[39] Yang, X. S., (2005). Engineering optimization via nature-inspired virtual bee algorithms, IWINAC 2005, *Lecture Notes in Computer Science*, 3562, pp. 317-323.
[40] Yang, X. S. (2008), *Nature-Inspired Metaheuristic Algorithms*, Luniver Press.
[41] Yang, X. S. (2009), Firefly algorithms for multimodal optimisation, *Proc. 5th Symposium on Stochastic Algorithms, Foundations and Applications, SAGA 2009*, Eds. O. Watanabe and T. Zeugmann, Lecture Notes in Computer Science, Vol. 5792, 169-178.
[42] Yang, X. S. (2010a), Firefly algorithm, stochastic test functions and design optimisation, *Int. J. Bio-Inspired Computation*, 2, 78–84.
[43] Yang, X. S. (2010b), *Engineering Optimization: An Introduction with Metaheuristic Applications*, John Wiley and Sons, USA (2010).
[44] Yang, X. S., (2010c), A New Metaheuristic Bat-Inspired Algorithm, in: *Nature Inspired Cooperative Strategies for Optimization (NICSO 2010)* (Eds. J. R. Gonzalez et al.), Studies in Computational Intelligence, Springer Berlin, 284, Springer, 65-74 (2010).
[45] Yang X. S. and Deb S., (2009). Cuckoo search via Lévy flights, *Proceeings of World Congress on Nature & Biologically Inspired Computing* (NaBIC 2009, India), IEEE Publications, USA, pp. 210-214.
[46] Yang X. S. and Deb, S. (2010) Engineering optimisation by cuckoo search, *Int. J. Math. Modelling & Num. Optimisation*, Vol. 1, 330-343.
[47] Yang X. S., (2011), Bat algorithm for multi-objective optimisation, *Int. J. Bio-Inspired Computation*, 3 (5), 267-274 (2011).
[48] Yu L., Wang S. Y., Lai K.K. and Nakamori Y, Time Series Forecasting with Multiple Candidate Models: Selecting or Combining? *Journal of Systems Science and Complexity*, 18, No. 1, pp1-18 (2005).

2

Analysis of the Performance of the Fish School Search Algorithm Running in Graphic Processing Units

Anthony J. C. C. Lins, Carmelo J. A. Bastos-Filho, Débora N. O. Nascimento, Marcos A. C. Oliveira Junior and Fernando B. de Lima-Neto
Polytechnic School of Pernambuco, University of Pernambuco
Brazil

1. Introduction

Fish School Search (FSS) is a computational intelligence technique invented by Bastos-Filho and Lima-Neto in 2007 and first presented in Bastos-Filho et al. (2008). FSS was conceived to solve search problems and it is based on the social behavior of schools of fish. In the FSS algorithm, the search space is bounded and each possible position in the search space represents a possible solution for the problem. During the algorithm execution, each fish has its positions and weights adjusted according to four FSS operators, namely, feeding, individual movement, collective-instinctive movement and collective-volitive movement. FSS is inherently parallel since the fitness can be evaluated for each fish individually. Hence, it is quite suitable for parallel implementations.

In the recent years, the use of Graphic Processing Units (GPUs) have been proposed for various general purpose computing applications. Thus, GPU-based platforms afford great advantages on applications requiring intensive parallel computing. The GPU parallel floating point processing capacity allows one to obtain high speedups. These advantages together with FSS architecture suggest that GPU based FSS may produce marked reduction in execution time, which is very likely because the fitness evaluation and the update processes of the fish can be parallelized in different threads. Nevertheless, there are some aspects that should be considered to adapt an application to be executed in these platforms, such as memory allocation and communication between blocks.

Some computational intelligence algorithms already have been adapted to be executed in GPU-based platforms. Some variations of the Particle Swarm Optimization (PSO) algorithm suitable for GPU were proposed by Zhou & Tan (2009). In that article the authors compared the performance of such implementations to a PSO running in a CPU. Some tests regarding the scalability of the algorithms as a function of the number of dimensions were also presented. Bastos-Filho et al. (2010) presented an analysis of the performance of PSO algorithms when the random number are generated in the GPU and in the CPU. They showed that the XORshift Random Number Generator for GPUs, described by Marsaglia (2003), presents enough quality to be used in the PSO algorithm. They also compared different GPU-based versions of the PSO (synchronous and asynchronous) to the CPU-based algorithm.

Zhu & Curry (2009) adapted an Ant Colony Optimization algorithm to optimize benchmark functions in GPUs. A variation for local search, called SIMT-ACO-PS (*Single Instruction Multiple Threads - ACO - Pattern Search*), was also parallelized. They presented some interesting analysis on the parallelization process regarding the generation of ants in order to minimize the communication overhead between CPU-GPU. The proposals achieved remarkable speedups.

To the best of our knowledge, there is no FSS implementations for GPUs. So, in this paper we present the first parallel approach for the FSS algorithm suitable for GPUs. We discuss some important issues regarding the implementation in order to improve the time performance. We also consider some other relevant aspects, such as when and where it is necessary to set synchronization barriers. The analysis of these aspects is crucial to provide high performance FSS approaches for GPUs. In order to demonstrate this, we carried out simulations using a parallel processing platform developed by NVIDIA, called CUDA.

This paper is organized as follows: in the next Section we present an overview of the FSS algorithm. In Section 3, we introduce some basic aspects of the NVIDIA CUDA Architecture and GPU Computing. Our contribution and the results are presented in Sections 4 and 5, respectively. In the last Section, we present our conclusions, where we also suggest future works.

2. Fish School Search

Fish School Search (FSS) is a stochastic, bio-inspired, population-based global optimization technique. As mentioned by Bastos-Filho et al. (2008), FSS was inspired in the gregarious behavior presented by some fish species, specifically to generate mutual protection and synergy to perform collective tasks, both to improve the survivability of the entire group.

The search process in FSS is carried out by a population of limited-memory individuals - the fish. Each fish in the school represents a point in the fitness function domain, like the particles in the Particle Swarm Optimization (PSO) Kennedy & Eberhart (1995) or the individuals in the Genetic Algorithms (GA) Holland (1992). The search guidance in FSS is driven by the success of the members of the population.

The main feature of the FSS is that all fish contain an innate memory of their success - their weights. The original version of the FSS algorithm has four operators, which can be grouped in two classes: feeding and swimming. The Feeding operator is related to the quality of a solution and the three swimming operators drive the fish movements.

2.1 Individual movement operator

The individual movement operator is applied to each fish in the school in the beginning of each iteration. Each fish chooses a new position in its neighbourhood and then, this new position is evaluated using the fitness function. The candidate position $\vec{n}_i$ of fish i is determined by the Equation (1) proposed by Bastos-Filho et al. (2009).

$$\vec{n}_i(t) = \vec{x}_i(t) + rand[-1,1].step_{ind}, \quad (1)$$

where $\vec{x}_i$ is the current position of the fish in dimension i, rand[-1,1] is a random number generated by an uniform distribution in the interval [-1,1]. The $step_{ind}$ is a percentage of the search space amplitude and is bounded by two parameters ($step_{ind\_min}$ and $step_{ind\_max}$).

The $step_{ind}$ decreases linearly during the iterations in order to increase the exploitation ability along the iterations. After the calculation of the candidate position, the movement only occurs if the new position presents a better fitness than the previous one.

2.2 Feeding operator

Each fish can grow or diminish in weight, depending on its success or failure in the search for food. Fish weight is updated once in every FSS cycle by the feeding operator, according to equation (2).

$$W_i(t+1) = W_i(t) + \frac{\Delta f_i}{max(\Delta f)}, \tag{2}$$

where $W_i(t)$ is the weight of the fish i, $f[\vec{x}_i(t)]$ is the value for the fitness function (*i.e.* the amount of food) in $\vec{x}_i(t)$, Δf_i is the difference between the fitness value of the new position $f[\vec{x}_i(t+1)]$ and the fitness value of the current position for each fish $f[\vec{x}_i(t)]$, and the $max(\Delta f)$ is the maximum value of these differences in the iteration. A weight scale (W_{scale}) is defined in order to limit the weight of fish and it will be assigned the value for half the total number of iterations in the simulations. The initial weight for each fish is equal to $\frac{W_{scale}}{2}$.

2.3 Collective-instinctive movement operator

After all fish have moved individually, their positions are updated according to the influence of the fish that had successful individual movements. This movement is based on the fitness evaluation of the fish that achieved better results, as shown in equation (3).

$$\vec{x}_i(t+1) = \vec{x}_i(t) + \frac{\sum_{i=1}^{N} \Delta\vec{x}_{ind_i}\{f[\vec{x}_i(t+1)] - f[\vec{x}_i(t)]\}}{\sum_{i=1}^{N}\{f[\vec{x}_i(t+1)] - f[\vec{x}_i(t)]\}}, \tag{3}$$

where $\Delta\vec{x}_{ind_i}$ is the displacement of the fish i due to the individual movement in the FSS cycle. One must observe that $\Delta\vec{x}_{ind_i} = 0$ for fish that did not execute the individual movement.

2.4 Collective-volitive movement operator

The collective-volitive movement occurs after the other two movements. If the fish school search has been successful, the radius of the school should contract; if not, it should dilate. Thus, this operator increases the capacity to auto-regulate the exploration-exploitation granularity. The fish school dilation or contraction is applied to every fish position with regards to the fish school barycenter, which can be evaluated by using the equation (4):

$$\vec{B}(t) = \frac{\sum_{i=1}^{N} \vec{x}_i(t) W_i(t)}{\sum_{i=1}^{N} \vec{x}_i(t)}. \tag{4}$$

We use equation (5) to perform the fish school expansion (in this case we use sign $+$) or contraction (in this case we use sign $-$).

$$\vec{x}_i(t+1) = \vec{x}_i(t) \pm step_{vol} r_1 \frac{\vec{x}_i(t) - \vec{B}(t)}{d(\vec{x}_i(t), \vec{B}(t))}, \tag{5}$$

where r_1 is a number randomly generated in the interval $[0, 1]$ by an uniform probability density function. $d(\vec{x}_i(t), \vec{B}(t))$ evaluates the euclidean distance between the particle i and the barycenter. $step_{vol}$ is called volitive step and controls the step size of the fish. $step_{vol}$ is defined as a percentage of the search space range and is bounded by two parameters ($step_{vol\_min}$ and $step_{vol\_max}$). $step_{vol}$ decreases linearly from $step_{vol\_max}$ to $step_{vol\_min}$ along the iterations of the algorithm. It helps the algorithm to initialize with an exploration behavior and change dynamically to an exploitation behavior.

3. GPU computing and CUDA architecture

In recent years, Graphic Processing Units (GPU) have appeared as a possibility to drastically speed up general-purpose computing applications. Because of its parallel computing mechanism and fast float-point operation, GPUs were applied successfully in many applications. Some examples of GPU applications are physics simulations, financial engineering, and video and audio processing. Despite all successful applications, some algorithms can not be effectively implemented for GPU platforms. In general, numerical problems that present parallel behavior can obtain profits from this technology as can be seen in NVIDIA (2010a).

Even after some efforts to develop Applications Programming Interface (API) in order to facilitate the developer activities, GPU programming is still a hard task. To overcome this, NVIDIA introduced a general purpose parallel computing platform, named Computer Unified Device Architecture (CUDA). CUDA presents a new parallel programming model to automatically distribute and manage the threads in the GPUs.

CUDA allows a direct communication of programs, written in C programming language, with the GPU instructions by using minimal extensions. It has three main abstractions: a hierarchy of groups of threads, shared memories and barriers for synchronization NVIDIA (2010b). These abstractions allow one to divide the problem into coarse sub-problems, which can be solved independently in parallel. Each sub-problem can be further divided in minimal procedures that can be solved cooperatively in parallel by all threads within a block. Thus, each block of threads can be scheduled on any of the available processing cores, regardless of the execution order.

Some issues must be considered when modeling the Fish School Search algorithm for the CUDA platform. In general, the algorithm correctness must be guaranteed, once race conditions on a parallel implementation may imply in outdated results. Furthermore, since we want to execute the algorithm as fast as possible, it is worth to discuss where it is necessary to set synchronization barriers and in which memory we shall store the algorithm information.

The main bottleneck in the CUDA architecture lies in the data transferring between the host (CPU) and the device (GPU). Any transfer of this type may reduce the time execution performance. Thus, this operation should be avoided whenever possible. One alternative is to move some operations from the host to the device. Even when it seems to be unnecessary (not so parallel), the generation of data in the GPU is faster than the time needed to transfer huge volumes of data.

CUDA platforms present a well defined memory hierarchy, which includes distinct types of memory in the GPU platform. Furthermore, the time to access these distinct types of memory vary. Each thread has a private local memory and each block of threads has a shared memory accessible by all threads inside the block. Moreover, all threads can access the same global memory. All these memory spaces follow a memory hierarchy: the fastest one is the local memory and the slowest is the global memory; accordingly the smallest one is the local memory and the largest is the global memory. Then, if there is data that must be accessed by all threads, the shared memory might be the best choice. However, the shared memory can only be accessed by the threads inside its block and its size is not very large. On the FSS versions, most of the variables are global when used on kernel functions. Shared memory was also used to perform the barycenter calculations. Local memory were used to assign the thread, block and grid dimension indexes on the device and also to compute the specific benchmark function.

Another important aspect is the necessity to set synchronization barriers. A barrier forces a thread to wait until all other threads of the same block reach the barrier. It helps to guarantee the correctness of the algorithm running on the GPU, but it can reduce the time performance. Furthermore, threads within a block can cooperate among themselves by sharing data through some shared memory and must synchronize their execution to coordinate the memory accesses (see Fig. 1). Although the GPUs are famous because of their

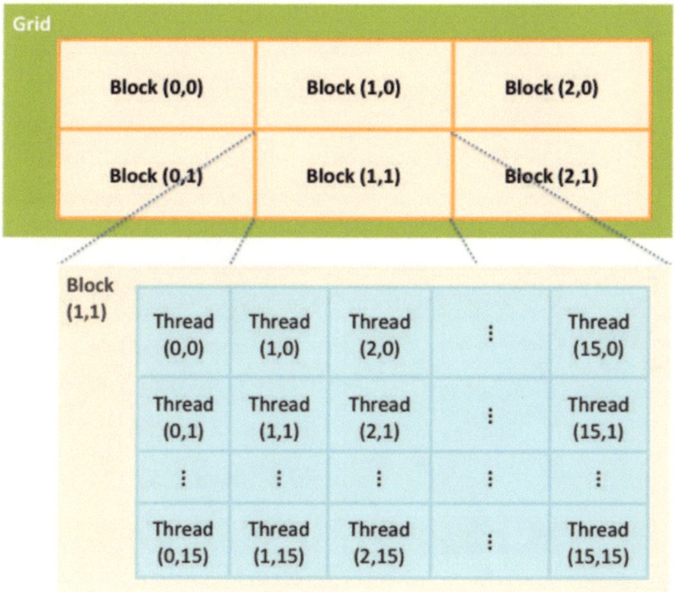

Fig. 1. Illustration of a Grid of Thread Blocks

parallel high precision operations, there are GPUs with only single precision capacity. Since many computational problems need double precision computation, this limitation may lead to bad results. Therefore, it turns out that these GPUs are inappropriate to solve some types of problems.

The CUDA capacity to execute a high number of threads in parallel is due to the hierarchical organization of these threads as a grid of blocks. A thread block is set of processes which cooperate in order to share data efficiently using a fast shared memory. Besides, a thread block must synchronize themselves to coordinate the accesses to the memory.

The maximum number of threads running in parallel in a block is defined by its number of processing units and its architecture. Therefore, each GPU has its own limitation. As a consequence, an application that needs to overpass this limitation have to be executed sequentially with more blocks, otherwise it might obtain wrong or, at least, outdated results.

The NVIDIA CUDA platform classify the NVIDIA GPUs using what they call Compute Capability as depicted in NVIDIA (2010b). The cards with double-precision floating-point numbers have Compute Capability 1.3 or 2.x. The cards with 2.x Capability can run up to 1,024 threads in a block and has 48 KB of shared memory space. The other ones only can execute 512 threads and have 16 KB of shared memory space.

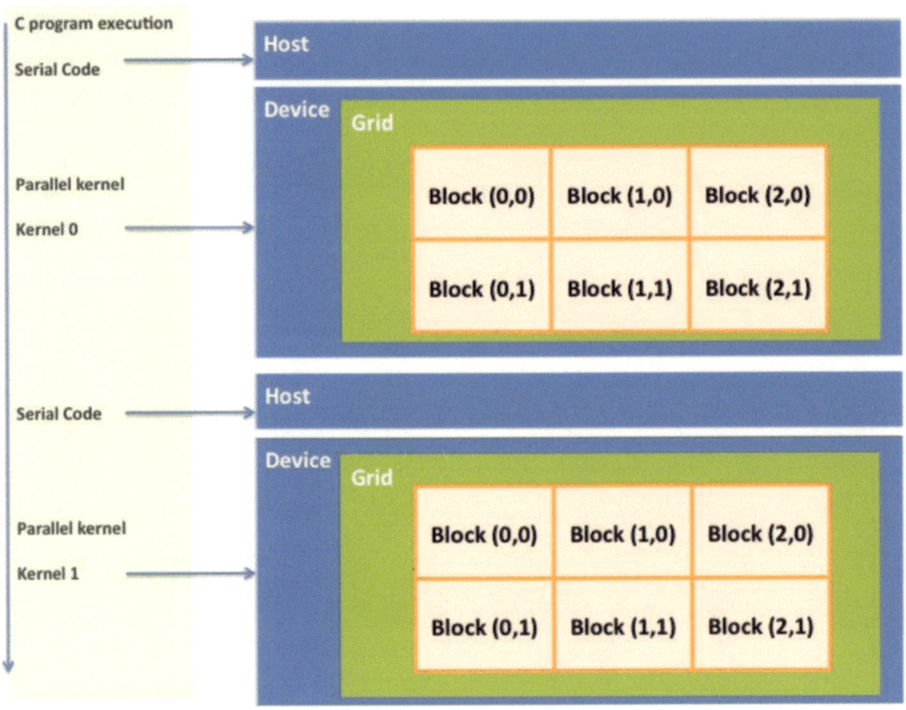

Fig. 2. CUDA C program structure

3.1 Data structures, kernel functions and GPU-operations

In order to process the algorithm in parallel, one must inform the CUDA platform the number of parallel copies of the Kernel functions to be performed. These copies are also known as parallel blocks and are divided into a number of execution threads.

The structures defined by grids can be split into blocks in two dimensions. The blocks are divided in threads that can be structured from 1 to 3 dimensions. As a consequence, the kernel functions can be easily instantiated (see Fig. 2). In case of a kernel function be invoked by the CPU, it will run in separated threads within the corresponding block. For each thread that executes a kernel function there is a thread identifier that allows one to access the threads within the kernel through two built-in variables *threadIdx* and *blockIdx*. The size of data to be processed or the number processors available in the system are used to define the number of thread blocks in a grid. The GPU architecture and its number of processors will define the maximum number of threads in a block. On the current GPUs, a thread block may contain up to 1024 threads. For this chapter, the simulations were made with GPUs that supports up to 512 threads. Table 1 presents the used configuration for grids, blocks and thread for each kernel function. Another important concept in CUDA architecture is related to Warp, which refers to 32 threads grouped to get executed in lockstep, *i.e.* each thread in a warp executes the same instruction on different data Sanders & Kandrot (2010). In this chapter, as already mentioned, the data processing is performed directly in the memories.

Type of Kernel Functions	Configurations		
	Blocks	Threads	Grids
Setting positions, movement operators	2	512	(512, 2)
Fitness and weights evaluations, feeding operator	1	36	(36, 1)

Table 1. Grids, Blocks and Threads per blocks structures and dimension sizes

CUDA defines different types of functions. A *Host function* can only be called and executed by the CPU. kernel functions are called only by the CPU and executed by the device (GPU). For these functions, the qualifier *__global__* must be used to allow one to access the functions outside the device. The qualifier *__device__* declares which kernel function can be executed in the device and which ones can only be invoked from the device NVIDIA (2010b).

The FSS pseudocode shown in algorithm 1 depicts which functions can be parallelized in GPUs.

4. Synchronous and asynchronous GPU-based Fish School Search

4.1 The synchronous FSS

The synchronous FSS must be implemented carefully with barriers to prevent any race condition that could generate wrong results. These barriers, indicated by *__syncthreads()* function in CUDA, guarantee the correctness but it comes with a caveat. Since the fish need to wait for all others, all these barriers harm the performance.

In the Synchronous version the synchronization barriers were inserted after the following functions (see algorithm 1): fitness evaluations, update new position, calculate fish weights, calculate barycenter and update steps values.

4.2 The asynchronous FSS

In general, an iteration of the asynchronous approach is faster than the synchronous one due to the absence of some synchronization barriers. However, the results will be probably worse, since the information acquired is not necessarily the current best.

Here, we propose two different approaches for Asynchronous FSS. The first one, called *Asynchronous - Version A*, presents some points in the code with synchronization barriers. In

Algorithm 0.1: Pseudocode of the Synchronous FSS

```
begin
    Declaration and allocation of memory variables for the Kernel operations;
    w ⟵ number_of_simulations;
    for i ⟵ 1 to Numberofiterations do
        Start timer event;
        /* calling Kernel functions                                    */
        Initialization_Positions;
        Initialization_Fish_Weights;
        Fitness_evaluation;
        Synchronization_Barrier;
        while number_of_iterations_not_achieved do
            /* Individual operator                                     */
            Calculate_New_Individual_Movement;
            Calculate_Fitness_for_New_Position;
            Update_New_Position;
            Synchronization_Barrier;
            Calculate_Fitness_Diference;
            /* Feeding operator                                        */
            Calculate_Fish_Weights;
            Synchronization_Barrier;
            Calculate_Weights_Difference;
            /* Collective Instinctive operator                         */
            Calculate_Instinctive_Movement;
            Update_New_Position;
            Synchronization_Barrier;
            /* Collective Volitive operator                            */
            Calculate_Barycentre;
            Synchronization_Barrier;
            Calculate_Volitive_Movement;
            Fitness_Evaluation;
            Synchronization_Barrier;
            /* Updating steps                                          */
            Update_Individual_Step;
            Update_Volitive_Step;
            Synchronization_Barrier;
        end
        /* Copy Kernel values to Host                                  */
        Copy_Kernel_Fitness_Value_To_Host;
        Stop timer event;
        Compute_Running_Time;
    end
    Free_memory_variables;
end
```

this case, were have maintained the synchronization barriers only in the functions used to update the positions and evaluate the barycenter. The pseudocode of the *Asynchronous FSS - Version A* is shown in algorithm 2. In the second approach, called *Asynchronous - Version B*, all the synchronization barriers were removed from the code in order to have a full asynchronous version. The pseudocode of the *Asynchronous FSS - Version B* is shown in algorithm 3.

Algorithm 0.2: Pseudocode of the Asynchronous FSS - Version A

```
begin
    Declaration and allocation of memory variables for the Kernel operations;
    w ⟵ number_of_simulations;
    for i ⟵ 1 to Numberofiterations do
        Start timer event;
        /* calling Kernel functions                                   */
        Initialization_Positions;
        Initialization_Fish_Weights;
        Fitness_evaluation;
        while number_of_iterations_not_achieved do
            /* Individual operator                                    */
            Calculate_New_Individual_Movement;
            Calculate_Fitness_for_New_Position;
            Update_New_Position;
            Synchronization_Barrier;
            Calculate_Fitness_Diference;
            /* Feeding operator                                       */
            Calculate_Fish_Weights;
            Calculate_Weights_Difference;
            /* Collective Instinctive operator                        */
            Calculate_Instinctive_Movement;
            Update_New_Position;
            Synchronization_Barrier;
            /* Collective Volitive operator                           */
            Calculate_Barycentre;
            Synchronization_Barrier;
            Calculate_Volitive_Movement;
            Fitness_Evaluation;
            /* Updating steps                                         */
            Update_Individual_Step;
            Update_Volitive_Step;
        end
        /* Copy Kernel values to Host                                 */
        Copy_Kernel_Fitness_Value_To_Host;
        Stop timer event;
        Compute_Running_Time;
    end
    Free_memory_variables;
end
```

Algorithm 0.3: Pseudocode of the Asynchronous FSS - Version B

```
begin
    Declaration and allocation of memory variables for the Kernel operations;
    w ←— number_of_simulations;
    for i ←— 1 to Numberofiterations do
        Start timer event;
        /* calling Kernel functions                                  */
        Initialization_Positions;
        Initialization_Fish_Weights;
        Fitness_evaluation;
        while number_of_iterations_not_achieved do
            /* Individual operator                                   */
            Calculate_New_Individual_Movement;
            Calculate_Fitness_for_New_Position;
            Update_New_Position;
            Calculate_Fitness_Diference;
            /* Feeding operator                                      */
            Calculate_Fish_Weights;
            Calculate_Weights_Difference;
            /* Collective Instinctive operator                       */
            Calculate_Instinctive_Movement;
            Update_New_Position;
            /* Collective Volitive operator                          */
            Calculate_Barycentre;
            Calculate_Volitive_Movement;
            Fitness_Evaluation;
            /* Updating steps                                        */
            Update_Individual_Step;
            Update_Volitive_Step;
        end
        /* Copy Kernel values to Host                                */
        Copy_Kernel_Fitness_Value_To_Host;
        Stop timer event;
        Compute_Running_Time;
    end
    Free_memory_variables;
end
```

5. Simulation setup and results

The FSS versions detailed in the previous section were implemented on the CUDA Platform. In this section we present the simulations executed in order to evaluate the fitness performance of these different approaches. We also focused on the analysis of the execution time.

In order to calculate the execution time for each simulation we have used the CUDA event API, which handles the time of creation and destruction events and also records the time of the events with the timestamp format NVIDIA (2010b).

We used a 1296 MHz GeForce GTX 280 with 240 Processing Cores to run the GPU-based FSS algorithms. All simulations were performed using 30 fish and we run 50 trial to evaluate the average fitness. All schools were randomly initialized in an area far from the optimal solution in every dimension. This allows a fair convergence analysis between the algorithms. All the random numbers needed by the FSS algorithm running on GPU were generated by a normal distribution using the proposal depicted in Bastos-Filho et al. (2010).

In all these experiments we have used a combination of individual and volitive steps at both initial and final limits with a percentage of the function search space Bastos-Filho et al. (2009). Table 2 presents the used parameters for the steps (individual and volitive). Three

Operator	Step value	
	Initial	Final
Individual	$10\%(2 * \max(searchspace))$	$1\%(2 * max(searchspace))$
Volitive	$10\%(Step_{ind,initial})$	$10\%(Step_{ind,final})$

Table 2. Initial and Final values for Individual and Volitive steps.

benchmark functions were used to employ the simulations and are described in equations (6) to (8). All the functions are used for minimization problems. The Rosenbrock function is a simple uni-modal problems. The Rastrigin and the Griewank functions are highly complex multimodal functions that contains many local optima.

The first one is Rosenbrock function. It has a global minimum located in a banana-shaped valley. The region where the minimum point is located is very easy to reach, but the convergence to the global minimum is hard to achieve. The function is defined as follows:

$$F_{Rosenbrock}(\vec{x}) = \sum_{i=1}^{n} x^2 \left[100(x_{i+1} - x_i^2)^2 + (1 - x_i)^2 \right]. \tag{6}$$

The second function is the generalized Rastrigin, a multi-modal function that induces the search to a deep local minima arranged as sinusoidal bumps:

$$F_{Rastrigin}(\vec{x}) = 10n + \sum_{i=1}^{n} \left[x_i^2 - 10cos(2\pi x_i) \right]. \tag{7}$$

Equation (8) shows the Griewank function, which is a multimodal function:

$$F_{Griewank}(\vec{x}) = 1 + \sum_{i=1}^{n} \frac{x_i^2}{4000} - \prod_{i=1}^{n} cos\left(\frac{x_i}{\sqrt{i}}\right). \tag{8}$$

All simulations were carried out in 30 dimensions. Table 3 presents the search space boundaries, the initialization range in the search space and the optima values. Figures 3, 4 and 5 present the fitness convergence along 10,000 iterations for the Rosenbrock, Rastrigin and

Function	Parameters		
	Search Space	Initialization	Optima
Rosenbrock	$-30 \leq \vec{x}_i \leq 30$	$15 \leq \vec{x}_i \leq 30$	1.0^D
Rastrigin	$-5.12 \leq \vec{x}_i \leq 5.12$	$2.56 \leq \vec{x}_i \leq 5.12$	0.0^D
Griewank	$-600 \leq \vec{x}_i \leq 600$	$300 \leq \vec{x}_i \leq 600$	0.0^D

Table 3. Function used: search space, initialization range and optima.

Griewank, respectively. Tables 4, 5 and 6 present the average value of the fitness and standard deviation at the 10,000 iteration for the Rosenbrock, Rastrigin and Griewank, respectively.

Analyzing the convergence of the fitness values, the results for the parallel FSS versions on the GPU demonstrate that there are no reduction on the quality performance over the original version running on the CPU. Furthermore, there is a slight improvement in the quality of the values found for the Rastrigin function (see Fig. 4), specially for the asynchronous FSS version B. It might occurs because the outdated data generated by the race condition can avoid premature convergence to local minima in multimodal problems.

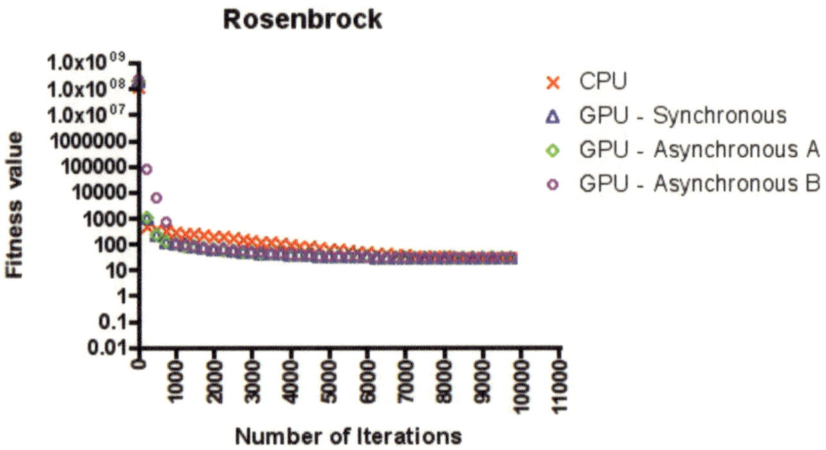

Fig. 3. Rosenbrock's fitness convergence as a function of the number of iterations.

Algorithm Version	Fitness	
	Average	Std Dev
CPU	28.91	0.02
GPU Synchronous	28.91	0.01
GPU Asynchronous A	28.91	0.01
GPU Asynchronous B	28.90	0.02

Table 4. The Average Value and Standard Deviation of the Fitness value at the 10,000 iteration for Rosenbrock function.

Tables 7, 8 and 9 present the average value and the standard deviation of the execution time and the speedup for the Rosenbrock, Rastrigin and Griewank functions, respectively.

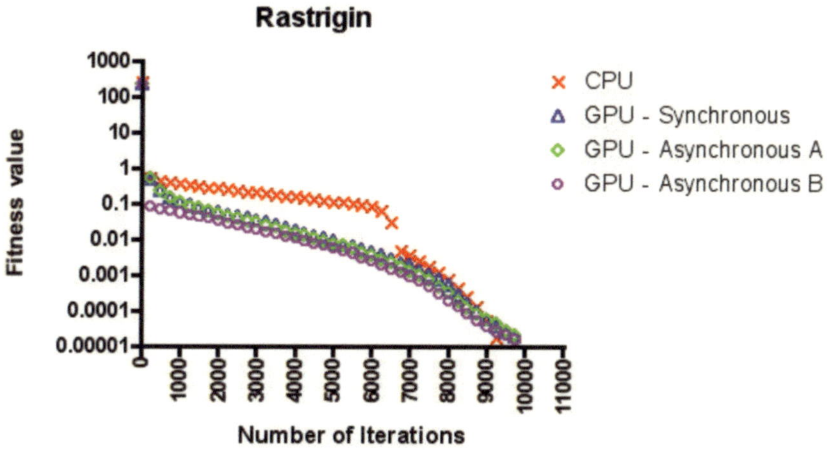

Fig. 4. Rastrigin's fitness convergence as a function of the number of iterations.

Algorithm Version	Fitness	
	Average	Std Dev
CPU	2.88e-07	5.30e-08
GPU Synchronous	1.81e-07	4.66e-08
GPU Asynchronous A	2.00e-07	2.16e-08
GPU Asynchronous B	1.57e-07	1.63e-08

Table 5. The Average Value and Standard Deviation of the Fitness value at the 10,000 iteration for Rastrigin function.

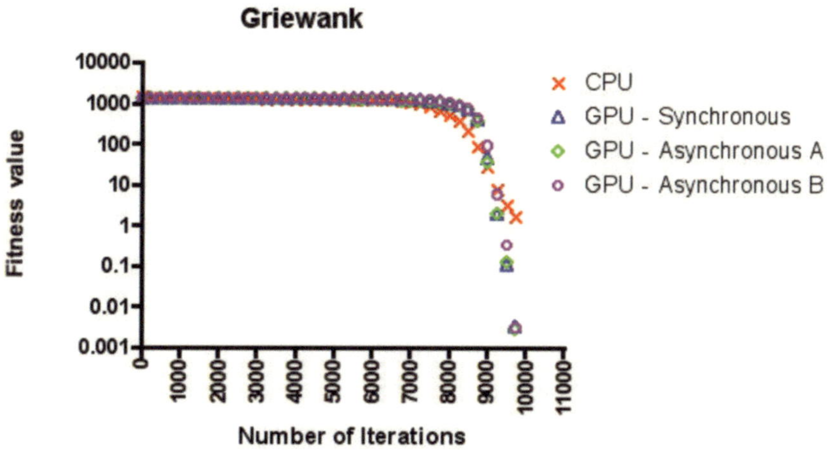

Fig. 5. Griewank's fitness convergence as a function of the number of iterations.

According to these results, all FSS implementations based on the GPU achieved a time performance around 6 times better than the CPU version.

Algorithm Version	Fitness	
	Average	Std Dev
CPU	1.67	0.74
GPU Synchronous	3.27e-05	3.05e-05
GPU Asynchronous A	2.91e-05	1.87e-05
GPU Asynchronous B	3.08e-05	1.54e-05

Table 6. The Average Value and Standard Deviation of the Fitness value at the 10,000 iteration for Griewank function.

Algorithm Version	Time (ms)		
	Average	Std Dev	Speedup
CPU	6691.08	1020.97	–
GPU Synchronous	2046.14	61.53	3.27
GPU Asynchronous A	1569.36	9.29	4.26
GPU Asynchronous B	1566.81	7.13	4.27

Table 7. The Average Value and Standard Deviation of the Execution Time and Speedup Analysis for Rosenbrock function.

Algorithm Version	Time (ms)		
	Average	Std Dev	Speedup
CPU	9603.55	656.48	–
GPU Synchronous	2003.58	2.75	4.79
GPU Asynchronous A	1567.08	2.11	6.13
GPU Asynchronous B	1568.53	4.40	6.13

Table 8. The Average Value and Standard Deviation of the Execution Time and Speedup Analysis for Rastrigin function.

Algorithm Version	Time (ms)		
	Average	Std Dev	Speedup
CPU	10528.43	301.97	–
GPU Synchronous	1796.07	2.77	5.86
GPU Asynchronous A	1792.43	2.88	5.87
GPU Asynchronous B	1569.36	9.30	6.71

Table 9. The Average Value and Standard Deviation of the Execution Time and Speedup Analysis for Griewank function.

6. Conclusion

In this chapter, we presented a parallelized version of the Fish School Search (FSS) algorithm for graphics hardware acceleration platforms. We observed a significant reduction of the computing execution time when compared to the original FSS version running on CPU. This swarm intelligence technique proved to be very well adapted to solving some optimization problems in a parallel manner. The computation time was significantly reduced and better optimization results were obtained more quickly with GPU parallel computing. Since FSS can be easily parallelized, we demonstrated that by implementing FSS in GPU one can benefit from the distributed float point processing capacity. We obtained a speedup around 6 for a cheap GPU-card. We expect to have a higher performance in more sophisticated GPU-based architectures. Since the Asynchronous version achieved the same fitness performance with a lower processing time, we recommend this option. As future work, one can investigate the performance in more complex problems and assess the scalability in more advanced platforms.

7. Acknowledgments

The authors would like to thank FACEPE, CNPq, UPE and POLI (Escola Politécnica de Pernambuco).

8. References

Bastos-Filho, C. J. A., Lima Neto, F. B., Lins, A. J. C. C., Nascimento, A. I. S. & Lima, M. P. (2008). A novel search algorithm based on fish school behavior, *Systems, Man and Cybernetics, 2008. SMC 2008. IEEE International Conference on*, pp. 2646 –2651.

Bastos-Filho, C. J. A., Lima-Neto, F. B., Sousa, M. F. C., Pontes, M. R. & Madeiro, S. S. (2009). On the influence of the swimming operators in the fish school search algorithm, *Systems, Man and Cybernetics, 2009. SMC 2009. IEEE International Conference on*, pp. 5012 –5017.

Bastos-Filho, C. J. A., Oliveira Junior, M. A. C., Nascimento, D. N. O. & Ramos, A. D. (2010). Impact of the random number generator quality on particle swarm optimization algorithm running on graphic processor units, *Hybrid Intelligent Systems, 2010. HIS '10. Tenth International Conference on* pp. 85–90.

Holland, J. H. (1992). *Adaptation in natural and artificial systems*, MIT Press, Cambridge, MA, USA.

Kennedy, J. & Eberhart, R. (1995). Particle swarm optimization, Vol. 4, pp. 1942–1948 vol.4. URL: *http://dx.doi.org/10.1109/ICNN.1995.488968*

Marsaglia, G. (2003). Xorshift rngs, *Journal of Statistical Software* 8(14): 1–6. URL: *http://www.jstatsoft.org/v08/i14*

NVIDIA (2010a). *CUDA C Best Practices Guide 3.2.*

NVIDIA (2010b). *NVIDIA CUDA Programming Guide 3.1.*

Sanders, J. & Kandrot, E. (2010). *CUDA By Example: an introduction to general-purpose GPU programming.*

Zhou, Y. & Tan, Y. (2009). Gpu-based parallel particle swarm optimization, *Evolutionary Computation, 2009. CEC '09. IEEE Congress on*, pp. 1493 –1500.

Zhu, W. & Curry, J. (2009). Parallel ant colony for nonlinear function optimization with graphics hardware acceleration, *Systems, Man and Cybernetics, 2009. SMC 2009. IEEE International Conference on*, pp. 1803 –1808.

3

Social Emotional Optimization Algorithm with Random Emotional Selection Strategy

Zhihua Cui[1,2], Yuechun Xu[1] and Jianchao Zeng[1]
[1]*Complex System and Computational Intelligence Laboratory, Taiyuan University of Science and Technology,*
[2]*State Key Laboratory of Novel Software Techchnology, Nanjing University, China*

1. Introduction

With the industrial and scientific developments, many new optimization problems are needed to be solved. Several of them are complex, multi-modal, high dimensional, non-differential problems. Therefore, some new optimization techniques have been designed, such as genetic algorithm, simulated annealing algorithm, Tabu search, etc. However, due to the large linkage and correlation among different variables, these algorithms are easily trapped to a local optimum and failed to obtain the reasonable solution.

Swarm intelligence (SI) is a recent research topic which mimics the animal social behaviors. Up to now, many new swarm intelligent algorithms have been proposed, such as group search optimizer[1], artificial physics optimization[2], firefly algorithm[3] and ant colony optimizer (ACO)[4]. All of them are inspired by different animal group systems. Generally, they are decentralized, self-organized systems, and a population of individuals are used to interacting locally. Each individual maintains several simple rules, and emergence of "intelligent" global behaviour are used to mimic the optimization tasks. The most famous one is particle swarm optimization.

Particle swarm optimization (PSO) [5-8] is a population-based, self-adaptive search optimization method motivated by the observation of simplified animal social behaviors such as fish schooling, bird flocking, etc. It is becoming very popular due to its simplicity of implementation and ability to quickly converge to a reasonably good solution. In a PSO system, multiple candidate solutions coexist and collaborate simultaneously. Each solution called a "particle", flies in the problem search space looking for the optimal position to land. A particle, as time passes through its quest, adjusts its position according to its own "experience" as well as the experience of neighboring particles. Tracking and memorizing the best position encountered build particle's experience. For that reason, PSO possesses a memory (i.e. every particle remembers the best position it reached during the past). PSO system combines local search method (through self experience) with global search methods (through neighboring experience), attempting to balance exploration and exploitation.

Human society is a complex group which is more effective than other animal groups. Therefore, if one algorithm mimics the human society, the effectiveness maybe more robust than other swarm intelligent algorithms which are inspired by other animal groups. With this manner, social emotional optimization algorithm (SEOA) was proposed by Zhihua Cui et al. in 2010[9-13]

In SEOA methodology, each individual represents one person, while all points in the problem space constructs the status society. In this virtual world, all individuals aim to seek the higher social status. Therefore, they will communicate through cooperation and competition to increase personal status, while the one with highest score will win and output as the final solution. In the experiments, social emotional optimization algorithm (SEOA) has a remarkable superior performance in terms of accuracy and convergence speed [9-13].

In this chapter, we proposed a novel improved social emotional optimization algorithm with random emotional selection strategy to evaluate the performance of this algorithm on 5 benchmark functions in comparison with standard SEOA and other swarm intelligent algorithms.

The rest of this paper is organized as follows: The standard version of social emotional optimization algorithm is presented in section 2, while the modification is listed in section 3. Simulation resutls are listed in section 4.

2. Standard social emotional optimization algorithm

In this paper, we only consider the following unconstrained problem:

$$min\, f(\vec{x}) \quad x \in [L,U]^D \subseteq R^D$$

In human society, all people do their work hardly to increase their social status. To obtain this object, people will try their bests to find the path so that more social wealthes can be rewarded. Inspired by this phenomenon, Cui et al. proposed a new population-based swarm methodology, social emotional optimization algorithm, in which each individual simulates a virtual person whose decision is guided by his emotion. In social emotional optimization algorithm methodology, each individual represents a virtual person, in each generation, he will select his behavior according to the corresponding emotion index. After the behavior is done, a status value is feedback from the society to confirm whether this behavior is right or not. If this choice is right, the emotion index of himself will increase, and vice versa.

In the first step, all individuals's emotion indexes are set to 1, with this value, they will choice the following behaviour:

$$\vec{x}_j(1) = \vec{x}_j(0) \oplus \text{Manner}_1 \tag{1}$$

where $\vec{x}_j(1)$ represents the social position of j's individual in the initialization period, the corresponding fitness value is denoted as the society status. Symbo $\oplus$ means the operation, in this paper, we only take it as addition operation +. Since the emotion index of j is 1, the movement phase $Manner_1$ is defined by:

$$Manner_1 = -k_1 \cdot rand_1 \cdot \sum_{w=1}^{L} (\vec{x}_w(0) - \vec{x}_j(0)) \tag{2}$$

where k_1 is a parameter used to control the emotion changing size, $rand_1$ is one random number sampled with uniform distribution from interval (0,1). The worst L individuals are selected to provide a reminder for individual j to avoid the wrong behaviour. In the initialization period, there is a little emotion affection, therefore, in this period, there is a little good experiences can be referred, so, $Manner_1$ simulates the affection by the wrong experiences.

In t generation, if individual j does not obtain one better society status value than previous value, the j's emotion index is decreased as follows:

$$BI_j(t+1) = BI_j(t) - \Delta \tag{3}$$

whereΔ is a predefined value, and set to 0.05, this value is coming from experimental tests. If individual j is rewarded a new status value which is the best one among all previous iterations, the emotion index is reset to 1.0:

$$BI_j(t+1) = 1.0 \tag{4}$$

Remark: According to Eq.(3), $BI_j(t+1)$ is no less than 0.0, in other words, if $BI_j(t+1) < 1.0$, then $BI_j(t+1) = 0.0$.

In order to simulate the behavior of human, three kinds of manners are designed, and the next behavior is changed according to the following three cases:

If $BI_j(t+1) < TH_1$

$$\vec{x}_j(t+1) = \vec{x}_j(t) \oplus Manner_2 \tag{5}$$

If $TH_1 \le BI_j(t+1) < TH_2$

$$\vec{x}_j(t+1) = \vec{x}_j(t) \oplus Manner_3 \tag{6}$$

Otherwise

$$\vec{x}_j(t+1) = \vec{x}_j(t) \oplus Manner_4 \tag{7}$$

Parameters TH_1 and TH_2 are two thresholds aiming to restrict the different behavior manner. For Case1, because the emotion index is too small, individual j prefers to simulate others successful experiences. Therefore, the symbol $Manner_2$ is updated with:

$$\begin{aligned}\text{Manner}_2 &= k_3 \cdot \text{rand}_3 \cdot (\vec{X}_{j,best}(t) - \vec{x}_j(t)) \\ &+ k_2 \cdot \text{rand}_2 \cdot (\vec{\text{Status}}_{best}(t) - \vec{x}_j(t))\end{aligned} \tag{8}$$

where $\vec{\text{Status}}_{best}(t)$ represents the best society status position obtained from all people previously. In other words, it is:

$$\vec{\text{Status}}_{best}(t) = \arg\ \min\{f(\vec{x}_w(h)) \mid 1 \le h \le t)\} \tag{9}$$

With the similar method, Manner_2 is defined:

$$\begin{aligned}\text{Manner}_3 &= k_3 \cdot \text{rand}_3 \cdot (\vec{X}_{j,best}(t) - \vec{x}_j(t)) \\ &+ k_2 \cdot \text{rand}_2 \cdot (\vec{\text{Status}}_{best}(t) - \vec{x}_j(t)) \\ &- k_1 \cdot \text{rand}_1 \cdot \sum_{w=1}^{L} (\vec{x}_w(0) - \vec{x}_j(0))\end{aligned} \tag{10}$$

where $\vec{X}_{j,best}(t)$ denotes the best status value obtained by individual j previously, and is defined by

$$\vec{X}_{j,best}(t) = \arg\ \min\{f(\vec{x}_j(h)) \mid 1 \le h \le t)\} \tag{11}$$

For Manner_4, we have

$$\begin{aligned}\text{Manner}_4 &= k_3 \cdot \text{rand}_3 \cdot (\vec{X}_{j,best}(t) - \vec{x}_j(t)) \\ &- k_1 \cdot \text{rand}_1 \cdot \sum_{w=1}^{L} (\vec{x}_w(0) - \vec{x}_j(0))\end{aligned} \tag{12}$$

Manner_2, Manner_3 and Manner_4 refer to three different emotional cases. In the first case, one individual's movement is protective, aiming to preserve his achievements (good experiences) in Manner_2 due to the still mind. With the increased emotion, more rewards are expected, so in Manner_3, a temporized manner in which the dangerous avoidance is considered by individual to increase the society status. Furthermore, when the emotional is larger than one threshold, it simulates the individual is in surged mind, in this manner, he lost the some good capabilities, and will not listen to the views of others, Manner_4 is designed to simulate this phenomenon.

To enhance the global capability, a mutation strategy, similarly with evolutionary computation, is introduced to enhance the ability escaping from the local optima, more details of this mutation operator is the same as Cai XJ[14], please refer to corresponding reference. The detail of social emotion optimization are listed as follows:

Step 1. Initializing all individuals respectively, the initial position of individuals randomly in problem space.
Step 2. Computing the fitness value of each individual according to the objective function.
Step 3. For individual j, determining the value $\vec{X}_{j,best}(0)$.
Step 4. For all population, determining the value $\vec{Status}_{best}(0)$.
Step 5. Determining the emotional index according to Eq.(5)-(7) in which three emotion cases are determined for each individual.
Step 6. Determining the decision with Eq. (8)-(12), respectively.
Step 7. Making mutation operation.
Step 8. If the criteria is satisfied, output the best solution; otherwise, goto step 3.

3. Random emotional selection strategy

To mimic the individual decision mechanism, emotion index $BI_j(t)$ is employed to simulate the personal decision mechanism. However, because of the determined emotional selection strategy, some stochastic aspects are omitted. To provide a more precisely simulation, we replace the determined emotional selection strategy in the standard SEOA with three different random manners to mimic the human emotional changes.

3.1 Gauss distribution

Gauss distribution is a general distribution, and in WIKIPEDIA is defined as "normalis a continuous probability distribution that is often used as a first approximation to describe real-valued random variables that tend to cluster around a single mean value. The graph of the associated probability density function is "bell"-shaped, and is known as the Gaussian function or bell curve" [15] (see Fig.1):

$$f(x)=\frac{1}{\sigma\sqrt{2\pi}}e^{-\frac{(x-\mu)^2}{2\sigma^2}}$$

where parameter μ is called the mean, σ^2 is the variance. The standard normal Gauss distribution is one special case with $\mu=0$ and $\sigma^2=1$.

3.2 Cauchy distribution

Cauchy distribution is also called Lorentz distribution, Lorentz(ian) function, or Breit-Wigner distribution. The probability density function of Cauchy distribution is

$$f(x,x_0,\gamma)=\frac{1}{\pi}\cdot\frac{\gamma}{(x-x_0)^2+\gamma^2}$$

where x_0 is the location parameter, specifying the location of the peak of the distribution, and γ is the scale parameter which specifies the half-width at half-maximum. The special case when $x_0 = 0$ and $\gamma = 1$ is called the standard Cauchy distribution with the probability density function

$$f(x) = \frac{1}{\pi(1+x^2)}$$

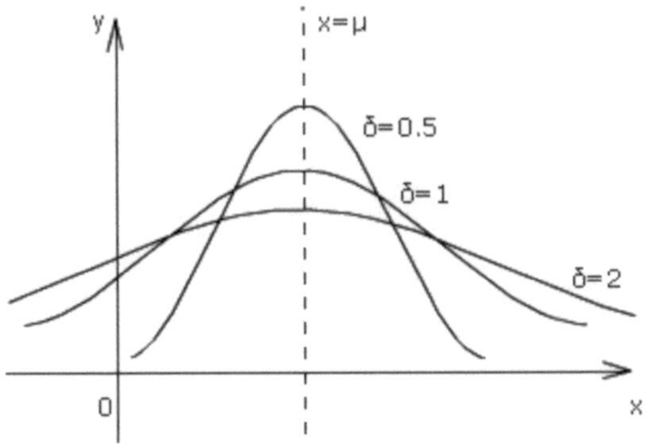

Fig. 1. Illustration of Probability Density Function for Gauss Distribution

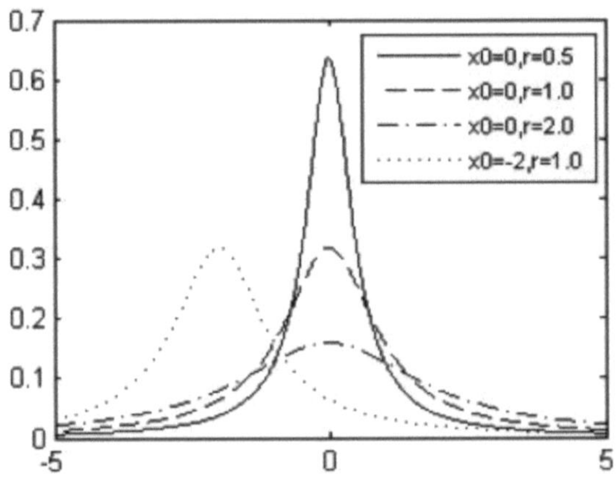

Fig. 2. Illustration of Probability Density Function for Cauchy Distribution

3.3 Levy distribution

In the past few years, there are more and more evidence from a variety of experimental, theoretical and field studies that many animals employ a movement strategy approximated by Levy flight when they are searching for resources. For example, wandering Albatross were observed to adopt Levy flight to adapted stochastically to their prey field[16]. Levy flight patterns have also been found in a laboratory-scale study of starved fruit flies. In a recent study by Sims[17], marine predators adopted Levy flights to pursuit Levy-like fractal distributions of prey density. In [18], the authors concluded that ``Levy flights may be a universal strategy applicable across spatial scales ranging from less than a meter, ..., to several kilometers, and adopted by swimming, walking, and airborne organisms". Shaped by natural selection, the Levy flights searching strategies of all living animals should be regarded as optimal strategies to some degree[19]. Therefore, it would be interesting to incorporate Levy flight into the SEOA algorithm to improve the performance.

Indeed, several studies have already incorporated Levy flight into heuristic search algorithms. In [20], the authors proposed a novel evolutionary programming with mutations based on the Levy probability distribution. In order to improve a swarm intelligence algorithm, Particle Swarm Optimizer, in [21], a novel velocity threshold automation strategy was proposed by incorporated with Levy probability distribution. In a different study of PSO algorithm[22], the particle movement characterized by a Gaussian probability distribution was replaced by particle motion with a Levy flight. A mutation operator based on the Levy probability distribution was also introduced to the Extremal Optimization (EO) algorithm[23].

Levy flights comprise sequences of straight-line movements with random orientations. Levy flights are considered to be 'scale-free' since the straight-line movements have no characteristic scale. The distribution of the straight-line movement lengths, L has a power-law tail:

$$P(L) \propto L^{-\mu}$$

where $1 < \mu < 3$.

The sum of the a set $\{L_i\}$ converge to the Levy distribution, which has the following probability density:

$$D_{\alpha,\gamma}(L) = \frac{1}{\pi}\int_0^{+\infty} e^{-\gamma q^{\alpha}} \cos(qL)dq$$

where α and γ are two parameters that control the sharpness of the graph and the scale unit of the distribution, respectively. The two satisfy $1 < \alpha < 2$ and $\gamma > 0$. For $\alpha \to 1$, the distribution becomes Cauchy distribution and for $\alpha \to 2$, the distribution becomes Gaussian distribution. Without losing generality, we set the scaling factor $\gamma = 1$.

Since, the analytic form of the Levy distribution is unknown for general α, in order to generate Levy random number, we adopted a fast algorithm presented in [24]. Firstly, Two independent random variables x and y from Gaussian distribution are used to perform a nonlinear transformation

$$v = \frac{x}{|y|^{\frac{1}{\alpha}}}$$

Then the random variable z:

$$z = \gamma^{\frac{1}{\alpha}} w$$

now in the Levy distribution is generated using the following nonlinear transformation

$$w = \{|K(\alpha) - 1| e^{\frac{-v}{C(\alpha)}} + 1\} \cdot v$$

where the values of parameters $K(\alpha)$ and $C(\alpha)$ are given in[24].

In each iteration, different random number $BI_j(t)$ is generated for different individual with Gauss distribution, Cauchy distribution and Levy fligh, then choices the different rules for different conditions according to Eq.(5)-(7).

4. Simulation

To testify the performance of proposed variant SEOA with random emotional selection strategy, five typical unconstraint numerical benchmark functions are chosen, and compared with standard particle swarm optimization (SPSO), modified particle swarm optimization with time-varying accelerator coefficients (TVAC)[25] and the standard version of SEOA (more details about the test suits can be found in [26]). To provide a more clearly insight, SEOA combined with Gauss distribution, Cauchy distribution and Levy distribution are denoted with SEOA-GD, SEOA-CD and SEOA-LD, respectively.

Sphere Model:

$$f_1(x) = \sum_{j=1}^{n} x_j^2$$

where $|x_j| \le 100.0$, and

$$f_1(x^*) = f_1(0,0,...,0) = 0.0$$

Rosenbrock Function:

$$f_2(x) = \sum_{j=1}^{n-1} [100(x_{j+1} - x_j^2)^2 + (x_j - 1)^2]$$

where $| \, |x_j| \le 30.0$, and

$$f_2(x^*) = f_1(0,0,...,0) = 0.0$$

Schwefel 2.26:

$$f_3(x) = -\sum_{i=1}^{n} \left(x_i \sin(\sqrt{|x_i|})\right),$$

where $|x_j| \le 500.0$, and

$$f_3(x^*) = f_3(420.9687,...,420.9687) = -418.98n$$

Rastrigin:

$$f_4(x) = \sum_{i=1}^{n} [x_i^2 - 10\cos(2\pi x_i) + 10]$$

where $|x_j| \le 5.12$, and

$$f_4(x^*) = f_4(0.0, ..., 0.0) = 0.0$$

Penalized Function2:

$$f_5(x) = 0.1\{\sin^2(3\pi x_1) + \sum_{j=1}^{n-1} (x_j - 1)^2 \cdot [1 + \sin^2(3\pi x_{j+1})] + (x_n - 1)^2$$

$$\cdot [1 + \sin^2(3\pi x_n)]\} + \sum_{j=1}^{n} u(x_j, 5, 100, 4)$$

where $|x_j| \le 50.0$, and

$$u(x_i, a, k, m) = \begin{cases} k(x_i - a)^m, x_i > a, \\ 0, -a \le x_i \le a, \\ k(-x_i - a)^m, x_i < -a. \end{cases}$$

$$y_i = 1 + \frac{1}{4}(x_i + 1)$$

$$f_5(x^*) = f_5(1, ..., 1) = 0.0$$

The inertia weight w is decreased linearly from 0.9 to 0.4 for SPSO and TVAC, accelerator coefficients c_1 and c_2 are both set to 2.0 for SPSO, as well as in TVAC, c_1 decreases from 2.5 to 0.5, while c_2 increases from 0.5 to 2.5. Total individuals are 100, and the velocity threshold v_{max} is set to the upper bound of the domain. The dimensionality is 30, 50, 100, 150, 200, 250 and 300. In each experiment, the simulation run 30 times, while each time the largest iteration is 50 times dimension, e.g. the largest iteration is 1500 for dimension 30. For SEOA, all parameters are used the same as Cui et al[9].

1. Comparison with SEOA-GD, SEOA-CD and SEOC-LD

From the Tab.1, we can find the SEOA-GD is the best algorithm for all 5 benchmarks especially for high-dimension cases. This phenomenon implies that SEOA-GD is the best choice between three different random variants.

2. Comparison with SPSO, TVAC and SEOA

In Tab.2, SEOA-GD is superior to other three algorithm in all benchmarks especially for multi-modal functions.

Based on the above analysis, we can draw the following conclusion:

SEOA-GD is the most stable and effective among three random variants, and is superior to other optimization algorithms significantly, e.g. SPSO, TVAC and SEOA. It is especially suit for high-dimensional cases.

Dimension	Algorithm	Mean Value	Standard Deviation
30	SEOA-GD	6.4355e-034	2.6069e-033
	SEOA-LD	2.4887e-019	1.3127e-018
	SEOA-CD	3.8304e-034	8.9763e-034
50	SEOA-GD	7.1686e-031	3.8036e-030
	SEOA-LD	2.5210e-016	7.5977e-016
	SEOA-CD	3.1894e-032	1.2666e-031
100	SEOA-GD	1.0111e-032	2.3768e-032
	SEOA-LD	3.8490e-013	1.1092e-012
	SEOA-CD	2.4269e-030	1.3091e-029
150	SEOA-GD	6.8757e-032	2.8083e-031
	SEOA-LD	5.7554e-012	3.1401e-011
	SEOA-CD	1.9043e-032	5.0848e-032
200	SEOA-GD	3.1075e-032	5.3236e-032
	SEOA-LD	1.1350e-009	4.4368e-009
	SEOA-CD	2.7272e-031	8.6026e-031
250	SEOA-GD	7.1304e-031	2.7851e-030
	SEOA-LD	9.0872e-010	1.9692e-009
	SEOA-CD	1.0602e-029	5.4445e-029
300	SEOA-GD	1.2563e-029	6.7502e-029
	SEOA-LD	3.3374e-009	6.4169e-009
	SEOA-CD	1.2338e-027	6.7241e-027

(a) Sphere Model

Dimension	Algorithm	Mean Value	Standard Deviation
30	SEOA-GD	1.9254e+001	3.1878e+001
	SEOA-LD	5.7495e+001	5.5242e+001
	SEOA-CD	1.7432e+001	3.6001e+001
50	SEOA-GD	1.2247e+001	2.4146e+001
	SEOA-LD	1.0847e+002	7.3577e+001
	SEOA-CD	3.1019e+001	4.6183e+001
100	SEOA-GD	3.3119e+001	5.7253e+001
	SEOA-LD	2.6886e+002	1.1566e+002
	SEOA-CD	3.4328e+001	5.7243e+001
150	SEOA-GD	3.2798e+001	5.0613e+001
	SEOA-LD	3.7234e+002	9.1565e+001
	SEOA-CD	5.6862e+001	8.7306e+001

200	SEOA-GD	7.4345e+001	6.7799e+001
	SEOA-LD	3.6658e+002	8.1035e+001
	SEOA-CD	9.5224e+001	1.2905e+002
250	SEOA-GD	7.9152e+001	1.7714e+002
	SEOA-LD	4.1573e+002	1.0684e+002
	SEOA-CD	7.0330e+001	9.5850e+001
300	SEOA-GD	7.8918e+001	1.0940e+002
	SEOA-LD	7.2125e+002	1.6142e+002
	SEOA-CD	9.2294e+001	1.7148e+002

(b) Rosenbrock

Dimension	Algorithm	Mean Value	Standard Deviation
30	SEOA-GD	-1.0935e+004	3.1474e+002
	SEOA-LD	-1.0485e+004	3.7499e+002
	SEOA-CD	-1.0846e+004	3.4926e+002
50	SEOA-GD	-1.8013e+004	4.3216e+002
	SEOA-LD	-1.7623e+004	5.6499e+002
	SEOA-CD	-1.7997e+004	4.5048e+002
100	SEOA-GD	-3.6064e+004	5.8230e+002
	SEOA-LD	-3.3434e+004	1.3006e+003
	SEOA-CD	-5.4032e+004	5.6218e+002
150	SEOA-GD	-5.3692e+004	6.5254e+002
	SEOA-LD	-4.5623e+004	2.5695e+003
	SEOA-CD	-5.4032e+004	5.6218e+002
200	SEOA-GD	-7.1830e+004	7.4485e+002
	SEOA-LD	-6.2516e+004	2.4362e+003
	SEOA-CD	-7.1926e+001	8.0021e+002
250	SEOA-GD	-9.0088e+004	1.0428e+003
	SEOA-LD	-7.3541e+004	4.0967e+003
	SEOA-CD	-8.9629e+004	8.8930e+002
300	SEOA-GD	-1.0853e+005	2.0551e+003
	SEOA-LD	-8.5244e+004	3.7267e+003
	SEOA-CD	-1.0788e+005	1.1546e+003

(c) Schwefel 2.26

Dimension	Algorithm	Mean Value	Standard Deviation
30	SEOA-GD	5.6381e-001	7.6996e-001
	SEOA-LD	1.1343e+001	5.1179e+000
	SEOA-CD	6.9647e-001	1.0170e+000
50	SEOA-GD	1.0945e+000	1.1787e+000
	SEOA-LD	3.5087e+001	1.3085e+001
	SEOA-CD	9.9496e-001	9.0513e-001

100	SEOA-GD	1.9927e+000	1.3044e+000
	SEOA-LD	6.7273e+001	1.9863e+001
	SEOA-CD	1.8904e+000	1.3156e+000
150	SEOA-GD	2.9849e+000	1.6317e+000
	SEOA-LD	1.6024e+002	3.0511e+001
	SEOA-CD	2.1557e+000	1.2823e+000
200	SEOA-GD	3.2502e+000	2.1216e+000
	SEOA-LD	2.1515e+002	4.3832e+001
	SEOA-CD	3.7145e+000	1.7709e+000
250	SEOA-GD	5.2733e+000	2.1884e+000
	SEOA-LD	2.4853e+002	4.8847e+001
	SEOA-CD	5.0743e+000	1.4861e+000
300	SEOA-GD	5.6049e+000	2.4578e+000
	SEOA-LD	4.4945e+002	8.3985e+001
	SEOA-CD	5.7376e+000	2.2881e+000

(d) Rastrigin

Dimension	Algorithm	Mean Value	Standard Deviation
30	SEOA-GD	6.7596e-020	3.7024e-019
	SEOA-LD	3.6502e-028	1.1039e-027
	SEOA-CD	3.5767e-032	5.3917e-032
50	SEOA-GD	2.8538e-022	1.5631e-021
	SEOA-LD	1.1715e-027	3.6895e-027
	SEOA-CD	4.3395e-026	2.3769e-025
100	SEOA-GD	3.7192e-030	1.7204e-029
	SEOA-LD	1.0191e-017	5.1895e-017
	SEOA-CD	6.6188e-021	3.6152e-020
150	SEOA-GD	2.0858e-030	5.0533e-030
	SEOA-LD	5.8928e-025	2.3415e-024
	SEOA-CD	3.0817e-019	1.6879e-018
200	SEOA-GD	2.9720e-026	1.5923e-025
	SEOA-LD	4.4726e-020	1.9939e-019
	SEOA-CD	1.4251e-030	2.9692e-030
250	SEOA-GD	6.7744e-024	3.7100e-023
	SEOA-LD	7.7143e-025	1.0616e-024
	SEOA-CD	3.0722e-023	1.6827e-022
300	SEOA-GD	2.7092e-030	4.7730e-030
	SEOA-LD	4.4726e-020	1.9939e-019
	SEOA-CD	1.6320e-026	7.5692e-026

(e) Penalized 2

Table 1. Comparison results between SEOA-GD, SEOA-CD and SEOA-LD

Dimension	Algorithm	Mean Value	Standard Deviation
30	SPSO	1.1470e-009	1.9467e-009
	TVAC	4.1626e-030	1.2140e-029
	SEOA	2.9026e-010	2.4315e-010
	SEOA-GD	6.4355e-034	2.6069e-033
50	SPSO	1.6997e-007	2.2555e-007
	TVAC	1.0330e-012	3.7216e-012
	SEOA	3.1551e-010	2.0241e-010
	SEOA-GD	7.1686e-031	3.8036e-030
100	SPSO	3.0806e-004	3.6143e-004
	TVAC	1.4014e-004	3.0563e-004
	SEOA	1.4301e-009	7.0576e-010
	SEOA-GD	1.0111e-032	2.3768e-032
150	SPSO	1.4216e-002	8.3837e-003
	TVAC	3.9445e-001	1.7831e+000
	SEOA	3.3950e-000	1.4518e-009
	SEOA-GD	6.8757e-032	2.8083e-031
200	SPSO	1.5234e-001	1.1698e-001
	TVAC	2.1585e-001	4.1999e-001
	SEOA	7.2473e-009	3.1493e-009
	SEOA-GD	3.1075e-032	5.3236e-032
250	SPSO	1.0056e+000	1.0318e+000
	TVAC	8.1591e-001	3.8409e+000
	SEOA	1.4723e-008	5.4435e-009
	SEOA-GD	7.1304e-031	2.7851e-030
300	SPSO	1.0370e+ 001	2.2117e+001
	TVAC	3.1681e+000	1.2412e+001
	SEOA	2.0420e-008	6.4868e-009
	SEOA-GD	1.2563e-029	6.7502e-029

(a) Sphere Model

Dimension	Algorithm	Mean Value	Standard Deviation
30	SPSO	5.6170e+001	4.3585e+001
	TVAC	3.3589e+001	4.1940e+001
	SEOA	4.7660e+001	2.8463e+001
	SEOA-GD	1.9254e+001	3.1878e+001
50	SPSO	1.1034e+002	3.7489e+001
	TVAC	7.8126e+001	3.2497e+001
	SEOA	8.7322e+001	7.4671e+001
	SEOA-GD	1.2247e+001	2.4146e+001
100	SPSO	4.1064e+002	1.0585e+002
	TVAC	2.8517e+002	9.8129e+001
	SEOA	1.3473e+002	5.4088e+001
	SEOA-GD	3.3119e+001	5.7253e+001

150	SPSO	8.9132e+002	1.6561e+002
	TVAC	1.6561e+002	6.4228e+001
	SEOA	2.2609e+002	9.6817e+001
	SEOA-GD	3.2798e+001	5.0613e+001
200	SPSO	2.9071e+003	5.4259e+002
	TVAC	8.0076e+002	2.0605e+002
	SEOA	2.9250e+002	9.2157e+001
	SEOA-GD	7.4345e+001	6.7799e+001
250	SPSO	7.4767e+003	3.2586e+003
	TVAC	1.3062e+003	3.7554e+002
	SEOA	3.4268e+002	9.0459e+001
	SEOA-GD	7.9152e+001	1.7714e+002
300	SPSO	2.3308e+004	1.9727e+004
	TVAC	1.4921e+003	3.4572e+002
	SEOA	3.8998e+002	5.1099e+001
	SEOA-GD	7.8918e+001	1.0940e+002

(b) Rosenbrock

Dimension	Algorithm	Mean Value	Standard Deviation
30	SPSO	-6.2762e+003	1.1354e+003
	TVAC	-6.7672e+003	5.7051e+002
	SEOA	-1.0716e+004	4.0081e+002
	SEOA-GD	-1.0935e+004	3.1474e+002
50	SPSO	-1.0091e+004	1.3208e+003
	TVAC	-9.7578e+003	9.6392e+002
	SEOA	-1.7065e+004	6.9162e+002
	SEOA-GD	-1.8013e+004	4.3216e+002
100	SPSO	-1.8148e+004	2.2012e+003
	TVAC	-1.7944e+004	1.5061e+003
	SEOA	-3.2066e+004	8.9215e+002
	SEOA-GD	-3.6064e+004	5.8230e+002
150	SPSO	-2.5037e+004	4.7553e+003
	TVAC	-2.7863e+004	1.6351e+003
	SEOA	-4.5814e+004	1.3892e+003
	SEOA-GD	-5.3692e+004	6.5254e+002
200	SPSO	-3.3757e+004	3.4616e+003
	TVAC	-4.0171e+004	4.3596e+003
	SEOA	-5.9469e+004	1.6065e+003
	SEOA-GD	-7.1830e+004	7.4485e+002
250	SPSO	-3.9984e+004	4.7100e+003
	TVAC	-4.7338e+004	3.7545e+003
	SEOA	-7.3460e+004	1.5177e+003
	SEOA-GD	-9.0088e+004	1.0428e+003

300	SPSO	-4.6205e+004	6.0073e+003
	TVAC	-5.6873e+004	3.5130e+003
	SEOA	-8.6998e+004	2.1240e+003
	SEOA-GD	-1.0853e+005	2.0551e+003

(c) Schwefel 2.26

Dimension	Algorithm	Mean Value	Standard Deviation
30	SPSO	1.7961e+001	4.2277e+000
	TVAC	1.5472e+001	4.2024e+000
	SEOA	1.8453e+001	5.6818e+000
	SEOA-GD	5.6381e-001	7.6996e-001
50	SPSO	3.9959e+001	7.9259e+000
	TVAC	3.8007e+001	7.0472e+000
	SEOA	3.8381e+001	9.6150e+000
	SEOA-GD	1.0945e+000	1.1787e+000
100	SPSO	9.3680e+001	9.9635e+000
	TVAC	8.4479e+001	9.4569e+000
	SEOA	8.0958e+001	1.1226e+001
	SEOA-GD	1.9927e+000	1.3044e+000
150	SPSO	1.5354e+002	1.2171e+001
	TVAC	1.3693e+002	2.0096e+001
	SEOA	1.3112e+002	1.5819e+001
	SEOA-GD	2.9849e+000	1.6317e+000 1.631749589612318e+000
200	SPSO	2.2828e+002	1.1196e+001
	TVAC	1.9920e+002	2.8291e+001
	SEOA	1.6894e+002	1.8414e+001
	SEOA-GD	3.2502e+000	2.1216e+000
250	SPSO	2.8965e+002	2.8708e+001
	TVAC	2.4617e+002	2.4220e+001
	SEOA	2.3165e+002	2.6751e+001
	SEOA-GD	5.2733e+000	2.1884e+000
300	SPSO	3.5450e+002	1.9825e+001
	TVAC	2.7094e+002	3.7640e+001
	SEOA	2.8284e+002	2.6353e+001
	SEOA-GD	5.6049e+000	2.4578e+000

(d) Rastrigin

Dimension	Algorithm	Mean Value	Standard Deviation
30	SPSO	5.4944e-004	2.4568e-003
	TVAC	9.3610e-027	4.1753e-026
	SEOA	9.7047e-012	5.7057e-012
	SEOA-GD	6.7596e-020	3.7024e-019

50	SPSO	6.4280e-003	1.0769e-002
	TVAC	4.9271e-002	2.0249e-001
	SEOA	2.5386e-011	4.0780e-011
	SEOA-GD	2.8538e-022	1.5631e-021
100	SPSO	3.8087e+001	1.8223e+001
	TVAC	3.7776e-001	6.1358e-001
	SEOA	2.6187e-010	5.3124e-010
	SEOA-GD	3.7192e-030	1.7204e-029
150	SPSO	1.6545e+002	5.5689e+001
	TVAC	1.2655e+000	1.4557e+000
	SEOA	1.8553e-009	2.9614e-009
	SEOA-GD	2.0858e-030	5.0533e-030
200	SPSO	1.8030e+003	2.8233e+003
	TVAC	3.7344e+000	2.6830e+000
	SEOA	2.9760e-006	1.2540e-005
	SEOA-GD	2.9720e-026	1.5923e-025
250	SPSO	6.7455e+003	9.5734e+003
	TVAC	2.8991e+000	1.3026e+000
	SEOA	1.8303e-007	1.5719e-007
	SEOA-GD	6.7744e-024	3.7100e-023
300	SPSO	3.2779e+004	4.4432e+004
	TVAC	3.7344e+000	2.6830e+000
	SEOA	2.9760e-006	1.2540e-005
	SEOA-GD	2.7092e-030	4.7730e-030

(e) Penalized 2

Table 2. Comparison results between SEOA-GD and SPSO, TVAC, SEOA

5. Conclusion

In standard version of social emotional optimization algorithm, all individuals' decision are influenced by one constant emotion selection strategy. However, this strategy may provide a wrong search selection due to some randomness omitted. Therefore, to further improve the performance, three different random emotional selection strategies are added. Simulation results show SEOA with Gauss distribution is more effective. Future research topics includes the application of SEOA to the other problems.

6. Acknowledgement

This paper were supported by the Key Project of Chinese Ministry of Education under Grant No.209021 and National Natural Science Foundation of China under Grant 61003053.

7. References

He S, Wu QH and Saunders JR. (2006) Group search optimizer an optimization algorithm inspired by animal searching behavior. *IEEE International Conference on Evolutionary Computation*, pp.973–990.

Xie LP, Tan Y, Zeng JC and Cui ZH. (2010) Artificial physics optimization: a brief survey. *International Journal of Bio-inspired Computation*, 2(5),291-302.

Yang XS. (2010) Firefly algorithm, stochastic test functions and design optimization. *International Journal of Bio-inspired Computation*, 2(2),78-84.

Laalaoui Y and Drias H. (2010) ACO approach with learning for preemptive scheduling of real-time tasks.*International Journal of Bio-inspired Computation*, 2(6),383-394.

Abraham S, Sanyal S and Sanglikar M. (2010) Particle swarm optimisation based Diophantine equation solver,*International Journal of Bio-inspired Computation*, 2(2),100-114.

Yuan DL and Chen Q. (2010) Particle swarm optimisation algorithm with forgetting character. *International Journal of Bio-inspired Computation*, 2(1),59-64.

Lu JG, Zhang L, Yang H and Du J. (2010) Improved strategy of particle swarm optimisation algorithm for reactive power optimization. *International Journal of Bio-inspired Computation*, 2(1),27-33.

Upendar J, Singh GK and Gupta CP. (2010) A particle swarm optimisation based technique of harmonic elimination and voltage control in pulse-width modulated inverters. *International Journal of Bio-inspired Computation*, 2(1),18-26.

Cui ZH and Cai XJ. (2010) Using social cognitive optimization algorithm to solve nonlinear equations. *Proceedings of 9th IEEE International Conference on Cognitive Informatics (ICCI 2010)*, pp.199-203.

Chen YJ, Cui ZH and Zeng JH. (2010) Structural optimization of lennard-jones clusters by hybrid social cognitive optimization algorithm. *Proceedings of 9th IEEE International Conference on Cognitive Informatics (ICCI 2010)*, pp.204-208

Cui ZH, Shi ZZ and Zeng JC. (2010) Using social emotional optimization algorithm to direct orbits of chaotic systems, *Proceedings of 2010 International Conference on Computational Aspects of Social Networks (CASoN2010)*, pp.389-395.

Wei ZH, Cui ZH and Zeng JC (2010) Social cognitive optimization algorithm with reactive power optimization of power system, *Proceedings of 2010 International Conference on Computational Aspects of Social Networks (CASoN2010)*, pp.11-14.

Xu YC, Cui ZH and Zeng JC (2010) Social emotional optimization algorithm for nonlinear constrained optimization problems, *Proceedings of 1st International Conference on Swarm, Evolutionary and Memetic Computing (SEMCCO2010)*, pp.583-590.

Cai XJ, Cui ZH, Zeng JC and Tan Y. (2008) Particle swarm optimization with self-adjusting cognitive selection strategy, *International Journal of Innovative Computing, Information and Control*. 4(4): 943-952.

http://en.wikipedia.org/wiki/Normal_distribution

G.M.Viswanathan, S.V.Buldyrev, S.Havlin, M.G.daLuz, E.Raposo and H.E.Stanley. (1999) Optimizing the success of random searches.*Nature*.401(911-914) .

D.W.Simsand. (2008) Scaling laws of marine predator search behavior. *Nature*.451:1098–1102.

A.M.Reynolds and C.J.Rhodes. (2009) The levy flight paradigm: random search patterns and mechanisms. *Ecology*.90(4):877 - 887.

G.A.Parkerand and J.MaynardSmith. (1990) Optimality theory in evolutionary biology. *Nature*.348(1):27 - 33.

C.Y.Lee and X.Yao. (2004) Evolutionary programming using mutations based on the levy probability distribution.*IEEE Transactions on Evolutionary Computation*.8(1):1 - 13.

X.Cai, J.Zeng, Z.H.Cui and Y.Tan. (2007) Particle swarm optimization using Levy probability distribution. *Proceedings of the 2nd International Symposium on Intelligence Computation and Application*, 353 - 361, Wuhan, China.

T.J.Richer and T.M.Blackwell. (2006) The levy particle swarm. *Proceedings of IEEE Congress on Evolutionary Computation*, 808 - 815.

M.R.Chen,Y.Z.Lu and G.Yang. (2006) Population-based extremal optimization with adaptive levy mutation for constrained optimization. *Proceedings of 2006 International Conference on Computational Intelligence and Security*, pp.258-261.November 3-6;Guangzhou,China.

R.N.Mantegna.(1994) Fast,accurate algorithm for numerical simulation of Levy stable stochastic processes. *Physical Review* E.49(5):4677 - 4683.

Ratnaweera A, Halgamuge SK and Watson HC. (2004) Self-organizing hierarchical particle swarm opitmizer with time-varying acceleration coefficients. *IEEE Transactions on Evolutionary Computation*, 8(3):240-255.

Yao X, Liu Y and Lin GM. (1999) Evolutionary programming made faster. *IEEE Transactions on Evolutionary Computation*, 3(2).82-102.

4

The Pursuit of Evolutionary Particle Swarm Optimization

Hong Zhang
Department of Brain Science and Engineering,
Kyushu Institute of Technology
Japan

1. Introduction

Particle swarm optimization inspired with the social behavior in flocks of birds and schools of fish is an adaptive, stochastic and population-based optimization technique which was created by Kennedy and Eberhart in 1995 (9; 12). As one of the representatives of swarm intelligence (20), it has the distinctive characteristics: information exchange, intrinsic memory, and directional search in contrast to genetic algorithms (GAs) (14) and genetic programming (GP) (16). Due to ease of understanding and implementation, good expression and expandability, higher searching ability and solution accuracy, the technique has been successfully applied to different fields of science, technology, engineering, and applications for dealing with various large-scale, high-grade nonlinear, and multimodal optimization problems (22; 23).

Although the mechanism of a plain particle swarm optimizer (the PSO) (13) is simple to implement with only a few parameters, in general, it can provide better computational results in contrast to other methods such as machine learning, neural network learning, genetic algorithms, tabu search, and simulated annealing (1). Nevertheless, like other optimization methods, an essential issue is how to make the PSO efficiently in dealing with different kinds of optimization problems. And it is well-known that the systematic selection of the parameter values in the PSO is one of fundamental manners to the end, and the most important especially for establishing a policy which determines the PSO with high search performance.

However, in fact how to properly determine the values of parameters in the PSO is a quite attractive but hard subject especially for a detailed analysis of higher order (7). The cause is because the search behavior of the PSO has very high indeterminacy. Usually, these parameter values related to internal stochastic factors need to be adjusted for keeping search efficiency (5).

As new development and expansion of the technique of meta-optimization[1], the above issue already can be settled by the method of evolutionary particle swarm optimization (EPSO) (27), which provides a good framework to systematically estimate appropriate values of

[1] Meta-optimization, in general, is defined as the process of using an optimization algorithm to automatically search the best optimizer from all computable optimizers.

parameters in a particle swarm optimizer corresponding to a given optimization problem without any prior knowledge. Based on the use of meta-optimization, it could be expected to not only efficiently obtain an optimal PSO, but also to quantitatively analyze the know-how on designing it. According to the utility and reality of the method of the EPSO, further deepening meta-optimization research, i.e. dynamic estimation approach, is an indispensable and necessary step for efficiently dealing with any complex optimization problems.

To investigate the potential characteristics and effect of the EPSO, here we propose and study to use two different criteria: a temporally cumulative fitness function of the best particle and a temporally cumulative fitness function of the entire particle swarm respectively to evaluate the search performance of the PSO in an estimation process. The goal of the attempt is to supply the demand for diversification satisfying some different specification to the optimizer.

Needless to say, the search behavior and performance of the PSO closely relies on the determined values of parameters in the optimizer itself. For revealing the inherent characteristics of the obtained PSOs, we also propose an indicator to measure the difference in convergence of the PSOs estimated by respectively implementing each criterion. Due to verify the effectiveness of the proposed method and different characters of the obtained results, computer experiments on a suite of multidimensional benchmark problems are carried out.

The rest of the paper is organized as follows. Section 2 introduces the related work on this study. Section 3 describes basic mechanisms of the PSO and EPSO, two different criteria, and an indicator in detail. Section 4 shows the obtained results of computer experiments applied to a suite of multidimensional benchmark problems, and analyzes the respective character of the estimated PSOs with using each criterion. Finally Section 5 gives the conclusion and discussion.

2. Related work

Until now, many researchers have paid much attention to the issue, i.e. effectually obtaining the PSO with high search performance, and proposed a number of advanced algorithms to deal with it. These endeavors can be basically divided into two approaches: manual estimation and mechanical estimation shown in Figure 1.

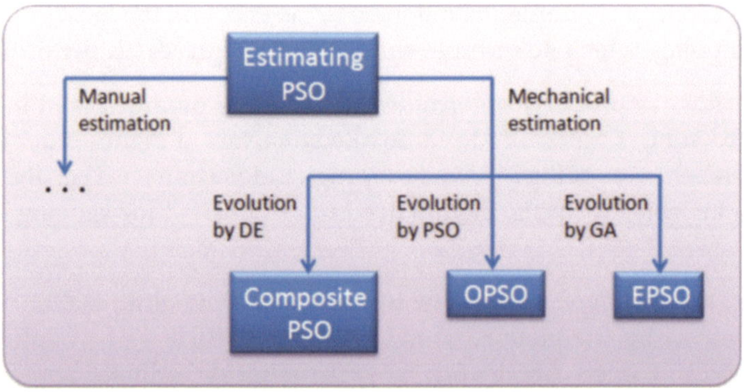

Fig. 1. Family of estimating PSO methods

Manual estimation is to try many values of parameters to find a proper set of parameter values in the PSO for dealing with various optimization problems reasonably well (2; 4; 10). Since its procedure belongs to a trial-and-error search, the computational cost is enormous, and the estimating accuracy is not enough.

In contrast to the above situation, mechanical estimation is to directly utilize evolutionary computation for achieving the task. A composite PSO (cPSO) (21) was proposed to estimate the parameter values of the PSO during optimization. In the cPSO, the differential evolution (DE) algorithm (24) is used to generate a difference vector of two randomly picked boundary vectors for parameter selection. In spite of the effect to the estimation, the internal stochastic factors in the DE have an enormous impact on the estimating process. Therefore, the recreation to obtain some similar results is difficult. This is the major shortcoming of the cPSO for certification.

In order to overcome the above mentioned weakness of instability in an estimation process, Meissner et al. proposed a method of optimized particle swarm optimization (OPSO) as an extension of the cPSO, which uses the PSO to deal with meta-optimization of the PSO heuristics (18). Zhang et al. independently proposed a method of evolutionary particle swarm optimization (EPSO) which uses a real-coded genetic algorithm with elitism strategy (RGA/E) to accomplish the same task (27). These methods are positive attempts of evolutionary computation applied for the design of the PSO itself, and give a marked tendency to deal with meta-optimization of analogous stochastic optimizers heuristics.

By comparing the mechanisms of both the OPSO and EPSO, we see that there are two big differences in achievement of estimating the PSO. The first one is on the judgment (selection) way used in evaluating the search performance of the PSO. The former uses an instantaneous fitness function and the PSO to estimation, and the latter uses a temporally cumulative fitness function and the RGA/E to estimation. The second one is on the estimating manner used in dealing with meta-optimization of the PSO heuristics.

Owing to the temporally cumulative fitness being the sum of an instantaneous fitness, fundamentally, the variation of the obtained parameter values, which comes from the stochastic influence in a dynamic evaluation process, can be vastly alleviated. According to this occasion, the use of the adopted criterion could be expected to give rigorous determination of the parameter values in the PSO, which will guide a particle swarm to efficiently find good solutions.

To investigate the potential characteristics of the EPSO, a temporally cumulative fitness function of the best particle and a temporally cumulative fitness function of the entire particle swarm are used for evaluating the search performance of the PSO to parameter selection. The former was reported in our previous work (27; 29). The latter is a proposal representing active behavior of entire particles inspired by majority decision in social choice for the improvement of the convergence and search efficiency of the entire swarm search (28).

The aim of applying the different criteria in estimating the PSO is to pursue the intrinsic difference and the inherent characters on designing the PSO with high search performance. For quantitative analysis to the obtained results, we also propose an indicator for judging the situation of convergence of the PSO, i.e. the different characteristics between the fitness value of the best particle and the average of fitness values of the entire swarm over time-step in search.

3. Basic mechanisms

For the sake of the following description, let the search space be N-dimensional, $\mathbf{S} \in \Re^N$, the number of particles in a swarm be P, the position of the ith particle be $\vec{x}^i = (x_1^i, x_2^i, \cdots, x_N^i)^T$, and its velocity be $\vec{v}^i = (v_1^i, v_2^i, \cdots, v_N^i)^T$, repectively.

3.1 The PSO

In the beginning of the PSO search, the particle's position and velocity are generated randomly, then they are updated by

$$\begin{cases} \vec{x}^i_{k+1} = \vec{x}^i_k + \vec{v}^i_{k+1} \\ \vec{v}^i_{k+1} = c_0\vec{v}^i_k + c_1\vec{r}_1 \otimes (\vec{p}^i_k - \vec{x}^i_k) + c_2\vec{r}_2 \otimes (\vec{q}_k - \vec{x}^i_k) \end{cases}$$

where c_0 is an inertia coefficient, c_1 and c_2 are coefficients for individual confidence and swarm confidence, respectively. $\vec{r}_1$ and $\vec{r}_2 \in \Re^N$ are two random vectors in which each element is uniformly distributed over the interval $[0,1]$, and the symbol $\otimes$ is an element-wise operator for vector multiplication. $\vec{p}^i_k (= arg \max_{j=1,\cdots,k} \{g(\vec{x}^i_j)\}$, where $g(\cdot)$ is the fitness value of the ith particle at k time-step) is the local best position of the ith particle up to now, and $\vec{q}_k (= arg \max_{i=1,2,\cdots} \{g(\vec{p}^i_k)\})$ is the global best position among the whole particle swarm. In the original PSO, $c_0 = 1.0$ and $c_1 = c_2 = 2.0$ are used (12).

To prevent particles spread out to infinity in the PSO search, a boundary value, v_{max}, is introduced into the above update rule to limit the biggest velocity of each particle by

$$\begin{cases} v^{ij}_{k+1} = v_{max}, & if\ v^{ij}_{k+1} > v_{max} \\ v^{ij}_{k+1} = -v_{max}, & if\ v^{ij}_{k+1} < -v_{max} \end{cases}$$

where v^{ij}_{k+1} is the jth element of the ith particle's velocity $\vec{v}^i_{k+1}$.

For attaining global convergence of the PSO, the studies of theoretical analysis were minutely investigated (3; 5; 6). Clerc proposed a canonical particle swarm optimizer (CPSO) and analyzed its dynamical behavior. According to Clerc's constriction method, the parameter values in the equivalent PSO are set to be $c_0^\star = 0.7298$ and $c_1^\star = c_2^\star = 1.4960$. Since the value of the inertia coefficient $c_0^\star$ is less than 1.0, the CPSO has better convergence compared to the original PSO. Consequently, it is usually applied for solving many practice problems as the best parameter values to search (17).

Although the set of the parameter values, $(c_0^\star, c_1^\star, c_2^\star)$, is determined by a rigid analysis in a low-dimensional case, it is hard to declare that these parameter values are whether the surely best ones or not for efficiently dealing with different kinds of optimization problems, especially in a high-dimensional case. To distinguish the truth of this fact, correctly obtaining the information on the parameter values of the equivalent PSO by evolutionary computation is expected to make clear.

3.2 The EPSO

In order to certainly deal with meta-optimization of the PSO heuristics, the EPSO is composed of two loops: an outer loop and an inner loop. Figure 2 illustrates a flowchart of the EPSO run. The outer loop is a real-coded genetic algorithm with elitism strategy (RGA/E) (26). The inner loop is the PSO. This is an approach of dynamic estimation. They exchange the necessary information each other during the whole estimating process. Especially, as information transmission between the loops in each generation, the RGA/E provides each parameter set of parameter values, $\vec{c}^j = (c_0^j, c_1^j, c_2^j)$ (the j-th individual in a population, $j \in J$, where J is the number of individuals), to the PSO, and the PSO returns the values of the fitness function, $F(c_0^j, c_1^j, c_2^j)$, corresponding to the given parameter set to the RGA/E. By the evolutionary computation, the RGA/E simulates the survival of the fittest among individuals over generations for finding the best parameter values in the PSO.

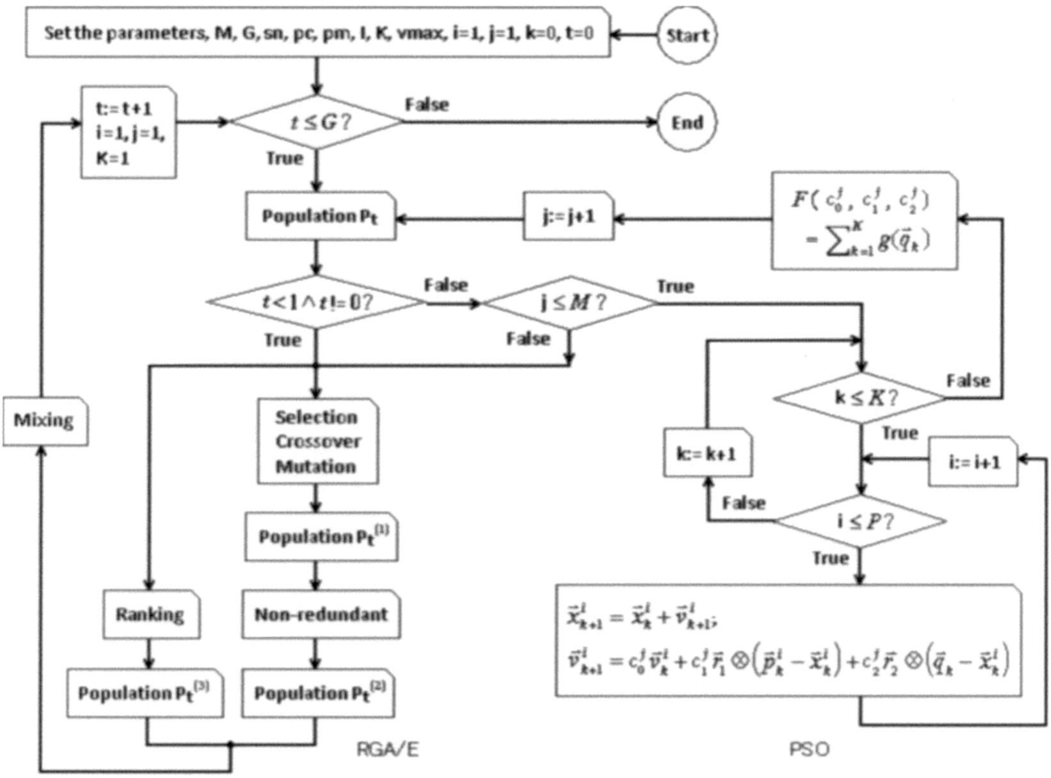

Fig. 2. A flowchart of the EPSO

As genetic operations in the RGA/E, roulette wheel selection, BLX-α crossover, random mutation, non-redundant strategy, and elitism strategy are used for efficiently finding an optimal individual (i.e. an optimal PSO) from the population of parameter values of the PSO. On being detailed, further refer to (33).

3.3 Two different criteria

To reveal the potential characteristics of the EPSO in estimation, two criteria are applied for evaluating the search performance of the PSO. The first criterion is a temporally cumulative fitness function of the best particle, which is defined as

$$F_1(c_0^j, c_1^j, c_2^j) = \sum_{k=1}^{K} g(\vec{q}_k)\big|_{c_0^j, c_1^j, c_2^j} \tag{1}$$

where K is the maximum number of iterations in the PSO run. The second criterion is a temporally cumulative fitness function of the entire particle swarm, which is defined as

$$F_2(c_0^j, c_1^j, c_2^j) = \sum_{k=1}^{K} \bar{g}_k\big|_{c_0^j, c_1^j, c_2^j} \tag{2}$$

where $\bar{g}_k = \sum_{i=1}^{P} g(\vec{x}_k^i)/P$ is the average of fitness values over the entire particle swarm at time-step k.

As an example, Figure 3 illustrates the relative evaluation between two pairs of the criteria, $\{g(\vec{q}_k), \bar{g}_k\}$ and $\{F_1, F_2\}$, during the evolutionary computation. It is clearly observed that the properties of the instantaneous fitness functions, $g(\vec{q}_k)$ and $\bar{g}_k$, are quite different. Namely, while the change of $g(\vec{q}_k)$ is monotonous increment, the change of $\bar{g}_k$ is non-monotonous increment with violent stochastic vibration. In contrast to this, the criteria, F_1 and F_2, are all monotonous increment with a minute vibration.

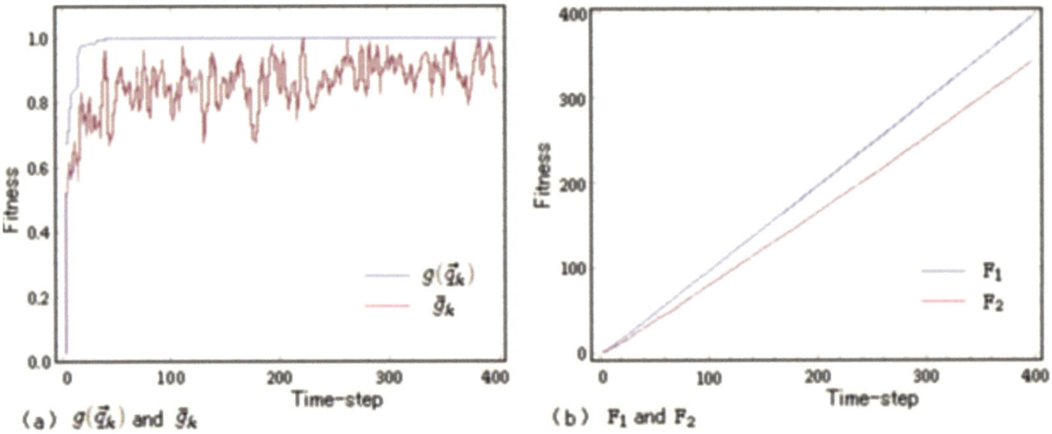

Fig. 3. Comparison of two pairs of the used fitness functions

Because both F_1 and F_2 are the sum of instantaneous fitness functions, $g(\vec{q}_k)$ and $\bar{g}_k$, over time-step, in theory, their variance is inversely proportional to the interval of summation. Thus, they could lead to vastly inhibit noise which comes from dynamic evaluation to the estimation. This property indicates that which of both F_1 and F_2 is well suitable for evaluating the search performance of the PSO, regardless of the difference in objects of evaluation themselves.

3.4 A convergence indicator

Looking from another viewpoint, the above difference in evaluational form can be considered as the disparty between the values of the temporally cumulative fitness function of the best particle and the average of fitness values over the entire particle swarm.

According to the concept of different characteristics, we propose to set the following convergence time-step, k_{max}, as a convergence indicator for measurement.

$$\forall k \geq k_{max}, \quad g(\vec{q}_k) - \bar{g}_k \leq \tau, \tag{3}$$

where τ is a positive tolerance coefficient.

It is clear that the shorter the convergence time-step is, the faster the convergence of particles is. Since most particles quickly converge on an optimal solution or a near-optimal solution, the convergence indicator, k_{max}, shows the conversion of difference of the different characteristics from increasing to decreasing, which representing a change of process, and indirectly records the index of diversity of the swarm over time-step in search.

4. Computer experiments

To facilitate comparison and analysis of the potential characteristics of the EPSO, the following suite of multidimensional benchmark problems (25) is used in the next experiments.

Sphere function:

$$f_{Sp}(\vec{x}) = \sum_{d=1}^{N} x_d^2$$

Griewank function:

$$f_{Gr}(\vec{x}) = \frac{1}{4000} \sum_{d=1}^{N} x_d^2 - \prod_{d=1}^{N} cos\Big(\frac{x_d}{\sqrt{d}}\Big) + 1$$

Rastrigin function:

$$f_{Ra}(\vec{x}) = \sum_{d=1}^{N} \Big(x_d^2 - 10\, cos(2\pi x_d) + 10\Big)$$

Rosenbrock function:

$$f_{Ro}(\vec{x}) = \sum_{d=1}^{N-1} 100\big(x_{d+1} - x_d^2\big)^2 + (1 - x_d)^2$$

The following fitness function in the search space, $\mathbf{S} \in (-5.12, 5.12)^N$, is defined by

$$g_\omega(\vec{x}) = \frac{1}{f_\omega(\vec{x}) + 1} \tag{4}$$

where the subscript, ω, stands for one of the followings: Sp (*Sphere*), Gr (*Griewank*), *Ra* (*Rastrigin*), and *Ro* (*Rosenbrock*). Since the value of each function, $f_\omega(\vec{x})$, at the optimal solution is zero, the largest fitness value, $g_\omega(\vec{x})$, is 1 for all given benchmark problems.

Figure 4 illustrates the distribution of each fitness function in two-dimensional space. It is clearly shown that the properties of each problem, i.e. the *Sphere* problem is an unimodal with axes-symmetry, the *Rosenbrock* problem is an unimodal with axes-asymmetry, and the *Griewank* and *Rastrigin* problems are multimodal with different distribution density and axes-symmetry.

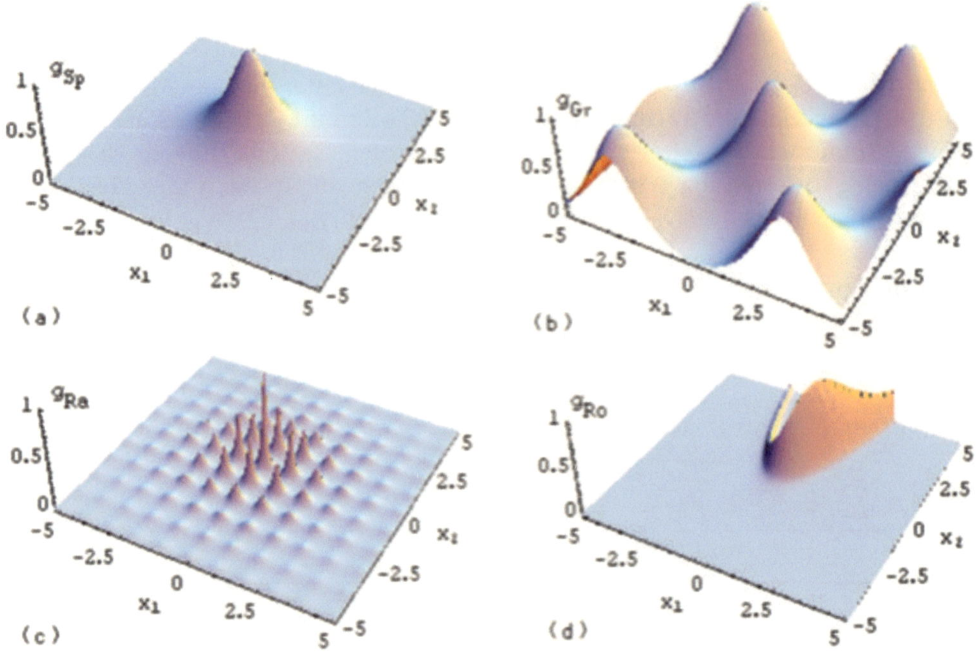

Fig. 4. Fitness functions corresponding to the given benchmark problems in two-dimensional space. (a) The *Sphere* problem, (b) The *Griewank* problem, (c) The *Rastrigin* problem, (d) The *Rosenbrock* problem.

4.1 Experimental condition

Table 1 gives the major parameters used in the EPSO run for parameter selection in the next experiments. As initial condition of the EPSO, positions of particles are set in random, and the corresponding velocities are set to zero.

Note that the constant, v_{max}, is used to arbitrarily limit the maximum velocity of each particle in search. Both non-redundant search and roulette wheel selection in genetic operations have not parameter to set. The smaller number of individuals, particles and iterations is chosen in order to acquire the balance between estimating accuracy and computing speed. As for the estimating accuracy, it can be guaranteed by repetitively taking average of the results.

On regarding the parameter setting for the genetic operations in the RGA/E, concretely, some experimental results reveal that bigger probability works better in generating superior

Parameters	Value
the number of individuals, J	10
the number of generations, G	20
the number of elite individuals, s_n	2
probability of BLX-2.0 crossover, p_c	0.5
probability of mutation, p_m	0.5
the number of particles, P	10
the number of iterations, K	400
the maximum velocity, v_{max}	5.12

Table 1. Major parameters in the EPSO run

individuals (33). This is the reason why the probability of crossover and mutation is set to 0.5 for efficient parameter selection.

4.2 Experimental results (1)

Computer experiments on estimating the PSO are carried out for each five-dimensional benchmark problem. It is to be noted that the appropriate values of parameters in the PSO are estimated under the condition, i.e. each parameter value is non-negative.

Based on the distribution of the resulting parameter values, $\hat{c}_0$, $\hat{c}_1$, and $\hat{c}_2$, within the top-twenty optimizers taken from the all obtained PSOs, they are divided into four groups, namely, *a*-type: $\hat{c}_0 = 0, \hat{c}_1 = 0, \hat{c}_2 > 0$; *b*-type: $\hat{c}_0 = 0, \hat{c}_1 > 0, \hat{c}_2 > 0$; *c*-type: $\hat{c}_0 > 0, \hat{c}_1 = 0, \hat{c}_2 > 0$; and *d*-type: $\hat{c}_0 > 0, \hat{c}_1 > 0, \hat{c}_2 > 0$. Doing this way is to adequately improve the accuracy of parameter selection, because each type of the obtained PSOs has stronger probability which solves the given benchmark problems regardless of the frequencies corresponding to them within the top-twenty optimizers.

Table 2 gives the resulting values of parameters in each type of the obtained PSOs, criterion values and frequencies. According to the statistical results, the following features and judgments are obtained.

1. The estimated PSOs are non-unique, and the parameter values in each optimizer are quite different from that in the original PSO or equivalent PSO.
2. The values of inertia coefficient, $\hat{c}_0$, and the coefficient for individual confidence, $\hat{c}_1$, could be zero, but the value of coefficient for swarm confidence, $\hat{c}_2$, is always non-zero, which plays an essential role in finding a solution to any given problem.
3. For the PSO in *d*-type cases, an overlapping phenomenon in each parameter value appears with the corresponding standard deviation (SD) in many cases. The variation of the respective SD indicates the adaptable range to each parameter value and the difficulty to obtain appropriate parameter value for handling the given problem.
4. For *Rastrigin* problem, both of $\hat{c}_1$ and $\hat{c}_2$ drastically exceed 1 in the criterion F_1 case. This suggests that the search behavior of the PSO is required to be more randomization extensively for enhancing the search performance to find an optimal solution or near-optimal solutions in search space. For the *Griewank* and *Rosenbrock* problems, $\hat{c}_1$

Problem	Dim.		Cumulative fitness	PSO	Parameter $\hat{c}_0$	$\hat{c}_1$	$\hat{c}_2$	Freq.
Sphere	5	F_1	395.3±0.7	*a*-type	0	0	2.4961±0.2468	20%
			–	*b*-type	–	–	–	–
			394.6±0.8	*c*-type	0.1975±0.0187	0	2.4665±0.3573	45%
			394.1±0.5	*d*-type	0.6770±0.2326	1.1293±0.0939	0.9375±0.6567	35%
		F_2	392.5±0.8	*a*-type	0	0	2.2990±0.1614	15%
			393.0±1.4	*b*-type	0	0.2397±0.1007	2.2867±0.1602	15%
			–	*c*-type	–	–	–	–
			392.2±0.5	*d*-type	0.4656±0.1514	0.9807±0.6100	1.3073±0.5850	70%
Griewank	5	F_1	–	*a*-type	–	–	–	–
			–	*b*-type	–	–	–	–
			396.8±0.0	*c*-type	0.1707±0.0000	0	0.6224±0.0000	5%
			396.6±0.6	*d*-type	0.5101±0.2669	2.0868±0.4260	1.0258±0.6117	95%
		F_2	–	*a*-type	–	–	–	–
			394.7±0.0	*b*-type	0	3.3247±0.0000	0.6994±0.0000	5%
			–	*c*-type	–	–	–	–
			394.8±0.8	*d*-type	0.4821±0.1911	1.2448±0.5229	1.6101±0.6596	95%
Rastrigin	5	F_1	–	*a*-type	–	–	–	–
			–	*b*-type	–	–	–	–
			396.0±0.0	*c*-type	1.0578±0.0000	0	82.171±0.0000	5%
			395.7±0.5	*d*-type	1.3459±0.5439	10.286±3.5227	24.929±21.857	95%
		F_2	230.0±20.9	*a*-type	0	0	3.8991±0.0681	100%
			–	*b*-type	–	–	–	–
			–	*c*-type	–	–	–	–
			–	*d*-type	–	–	–	–
Rosenbrock	5	F_1	–	*a*-type	–	–	–	–
			–	*b*-type	–	–	–	–
			298.4±3.7	*c*-type	0.6804±0.0000	0	2.1825±0.0000	10%
			317.1±18.8	*d*-type	0.9022±0.0689	1.3097±0.5619	0.7614±0.1689	90%
		F_2	–	*a*-type	–	–	–	–
			295.5±9.0	*b*-type	0	4.0370±0.5740	1.9494±0.1237	20%
			312.4±26.7	*c*-type	0.8033±0.0000	0	0.5165±0.0000	20%
			310.5±36.3	*d*-type	0.7042±0.0492	0.7120±0.3631	1.5028±0.6779	60%

Table 2. Estimated appropriate values of parameters in the PSO, cumulative fitness values, and frequencies in the top-twenty optimizers. The PSO in *a*-type: $\hat{c}_0 = 0, \hat{c}_1 = 0, \hat{c}_2 > 0$; The PSO in *b*-type: $\hat{c}_0 = 0, \hat{c}_1 > 0, \hat{c}_2 > 0$; The PSO in *c*-type: $\hat{c}_0 > 0, \hat{c}_1 = 0, \hat{c}_2 > 0$; in *d*-type: $\hat{c}_0 > 0, \hat{c}_1 > 0, \hat{c}_2 > 0$. The symbol "-" signifies no result corresponding to contain type of the PSO.

drastically exceeds 1 under the condition of $\hat{c}_0 = 0$. This suggests that there is a choice to adapt the spacial condition in using the criterion F_2 case for improving search performance of the PSO.

5. The average of the fitness values, F_1, is larger than that of F_2 except for the *Rosenbrock* problem. And the frequencies corresponding to the PSO in d-type are higher than other types for a majority given problems.

It is understood that the estimated PSOs related to each given benchmark problem are obtained by implementing the EPSO without any prior knowledge. The signification of the existence of the four types of the obtained PSOs reflects the possibility of problem-solving.

4.3 Performance analysis

For inspecting the results of the EPSO using two different criteria, we measure the search ability of each estimated PSO by the average of parameter values in Table 2, and show the obtained fitness values with 20 trials in Figure 5.

It is observed from Figure 5 that the search ability of the PSO estimated by using the criterion F_1 is superior to that by using the criterion F_2 except for the *Sphere* and *Griewank* problems. Therefore, the obtained results declare that the criterion F_1 is suitable for generating the PSO with higher adaptability in search compared with the criterion F_2. The cause is obvious, i.e. all of particles rapidly move in close to the global best position, $\vec{q}_k$, found by themselves up to now. About the fact, it can be confirmed by the following experiments. However, such improvement of the search performance of the entire particle swarm, in general, restricts active behavior of each particle, and will lose more chances for finding an optimal solution or near-optimal solutions.

For investigating the different characteristics, we measure the convergence time-step for each estimated PSO in d-type with the highest search ability in Figure 6. According to the different characteristics, for instance, the disparity between two criteria, i.e. $g(\vec{q}_k) - \bar{g}_k$, maximum tolerance, τ_{max}, and the convergence time-step, k_{max}, is shown in Figure 6.

In comparison with the difference between two criteria in the optimization, Table 3 gives the convergence time-step, k_{max}, of the original PSO, and the estimated PSO under the condition of the maximum tolerance, $\tau_{max}(=\max_{k=1\cdots K}(g(\vec{q}_k) - \bar{g}_k))$, corresponding to each given problem.

Problem	Convergence time-step, k_{max}		
	Original PSO	EPSO (F_1)	EPSO (F_2)
Sphere	236.1±95.63	8.100±2.268	7.200±2.375
Griewank	249.4±108.0	4.350±2.814	4.150±2.224
Rastrigin	363.4±92.40	224.2±152.3	99.15±52.83
Rosenbrock	397.4±2.370	34.15±7.862	25.72±8.672

Table 3. The convergence time-step for the original PSO and the estimated PSO.

Based on the results on the search performance (SP) and the convergence time-step (CT) in Table 3, the dominant relationship on their different characteristics is indicated as follows.

SP: $\text{EPSO}(F_1) \succ \text{EPSO}(F_2) \succ \text{Original PSO}$

CT: $\text{EPSO}(F_2) \succ \text{EPSO}(F_1) \succ \text{Original PSO}$

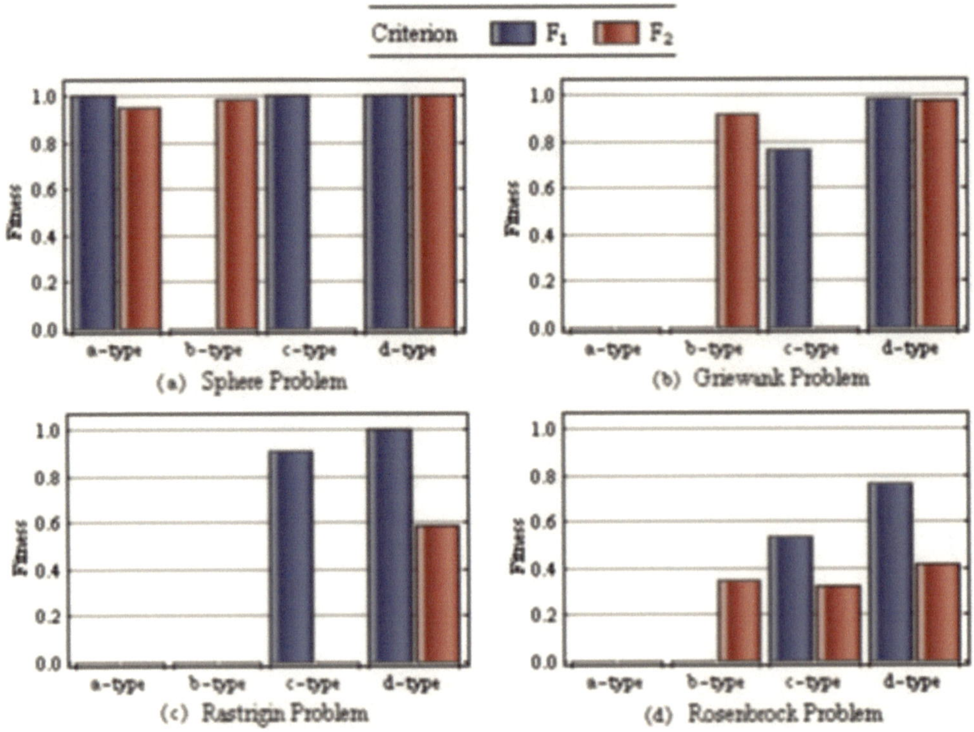

Fig. 5. The search ability of each estimated PSO

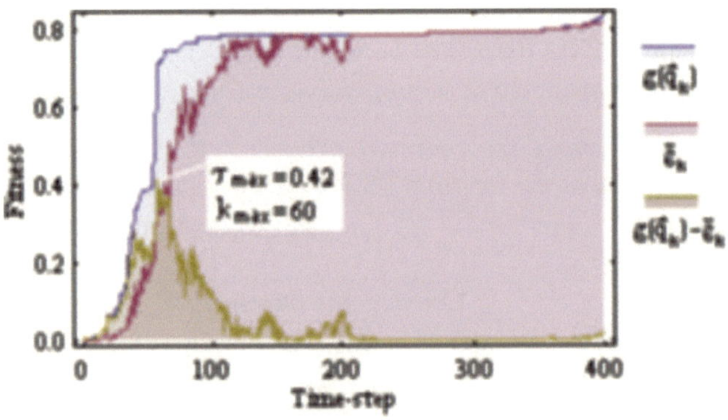

Fig. 6. The disparity in criterion, $g(\vec{q}_k) - \bar{g}_k$.

In comparison with both SP and CT, it is considered that the criterion F_1 well manages the trade-off between exploitation and exploration than that the criterion F_2 does. And the search performance of the original PSO is the lowest. These results indicate that these parameters, $c_0 = 1.0$ and $c_1 = c_2 = 2.0$, cannot manage the trade-off between exploration and exploitation in its heuristics well, so the original PSO is unreasonable for efficiently solving different optimization problems to conclude.

Table 4 gives the results of implementing the EPSO, the original PSO, the original CPSO, OPSO, and RGA/E. We can see that the search performance of the PSOs optimized by the

EPSO using the criterion F_1 is superior to that by the original PSO, the original CPSO, OPSO, and RGA/E for the given benchmark problems except the *Sphere* problem.

Problem	Dim.	Original PSO	Original CPSO	EPSO(F_1)	EPSO(F_2)	OPSO	RGA/E
Sphere	5	0.9997±0.0004	**1.0000**±0.0000	**1.0000**±0.0000	0.9830±0.0399	**1.0000**±0.000	0.9990±0.0005
Griewank	5	0.9522±0.0507	0.8688±0.0916	**0.9829**±0.0129	0.9826±0.0311	0.9448±0.0439	0.9452±0.0784
Rastrigin	5	0.1828±0.1154	0.6092±0.2701	**1.0000**±0.0000	0.6231±0.3588	0.2652±0.1185	0.9616±0.0239
Rosenbrock	5	0.4231±0.2208	0.6206±0.2583	**0.7764**±0.2723	0.5809±0.2240	0.3926±0.1976	0.3898±0.2273

Table 4. The obtained results of the EPSO, the original PSO, the original CPSO, OPSO, and RGA/E (the mean and the standard deviation of fitness values in each optimizer). The values in bold signify the best results for each problem.

Specially, the fact of what the search performance by the estimated PSO is superior to that by the original CPSO demonstrates the effectiveness of the proposed criteria, which emphasizes the importance of executing the EPSO to parameter selection.

4.4 Experimental results (2)

For further identifying the effectiveness of the EPSO, the following experiments are carried out for each benchmark problem in ten- and twenty-dimensional cases.

According to the better search performance corresponding to each type of the PSO in Section 4.3, Table 5 shows the obtained results of the PSO in d-type, their criterion values and frequencies. To demonstrate the search performance of these PSO in Table 5, Table 6 gives the obtained results for the EPSO using two different criteria, the original PSO, the original CPSO, OPSO, and RGA/E. Similar to the results of five-dimensional case in Table 4, it is confirmed that the search performance of the PSO optimized by the EPSO using the criterion F_1 is superior to that by the criterion F_2, and is also superior to that by the original PSO, the original CPSO, OPSO, and RGA/E for the given benchmark problems except for the *Rastrigin* problem.

Comparison with the values of parameters of the estimated PSO in different dimensional cases for the *Rastrigin* problem, we observe that the values of the estimated PSO, $\hat{c}_0$, are less than 1.0 in ten- and twenty-dimensional cases. Just as which the inertia coefficient is less than 1.0, so that the PSO cannot explore over a wide search space due to the origins of premature convergence and stagnation.

However, why the ideal results in five-dimensional case cannot be reappeared for dealing with same problem in ten- and twenty-dimensional cases, the causes may be associated with the experimental condition such as the number of generations $G = 20$, and iterations $K = 400$ of the EPSO run. Since they are too little, appropriate values of parameters in the PSO cannot be found without enough possibility in a bigger search space.

To testify the truth of the supposition, we tried to use the PSO in d-type by the criterion F_1 in Table 2 as a proxy for solving the ten- and twenty-dimensional *Rastrigin* problems. Under such circumstances, the resulting search performance of the EPSO with the criterion F_1 are

Problem	Dim.	Cumulative fitness		PSO	Parameter			Freq.
					$\hat{c}_0$	$\hat{c}_1$	$\hat{c}_2$	
Sphere	10	F_1	380.8±1.9	*d*-type	0.8022±0.0224	1.6485±0.4327	0.7468±0.1453	100%
		F_2	375.9±2.6	*d*-type	0.7654±0.0468	1.3853±0.5210	0.8777±0.0439	95%
Griewank	10	F_1	389.9±1.4	*d*-type	0.7620±0.0016	1.5490±0.7157	0.7587±0.2100	95%
		F_2	386.4±1.4	*d*-type	0.7318±0.1111	1.3844±0.3688	1.2278±0.3945	100%
Rastrigin	10	F_1	59.79±14.8	*d*-type	0.5534±0.1462	2.1410±0.5915	2.0062±1.0027	25%
		F_2	32.61±5.8	*d*-type	0.3596±0.1740	3.3035±1.6040	1.2856±1.4118	55%
Rosenbrock	10	F_1	155.1±45.2	*d*-type	0.7050±0.2830	1.6254±0.8717	1.9030±0.5038	90%
		F_2	122.0±59.9	*d*-type	1.0159±0.0279	1.6045±0.4152	0.4983±0.1048	100%
Sphere	20	F_1	326.4±7.1	*d*-type	0.9091±0.0425	2.2427±0.1360	0.4249±0.0675	100%
		F_2	320.1±9.6	*d*-type	0.8860±0.0000	1.9482±0.1912	0.6693±0.1157	100%
Griewank	20	F_1	374.8±2.1	*d*-type	0.9717±0.0093	1.7877±0.2686	0.6989±0.1442	100%
		F_2	370.3±3.0	*d*-type	0.9738±0.0000	1.6542±0.3106	0.7064±0.0330	70%
Rastrigin	20	F_1	10.33±1.0	*d*-type	0.9776±0.0198	1.3934±0.2050	0.2179±0.0561	70%
		F_2	8.48±1.4	*d*-type	0.8920±0.0000	1.7465±0.4156	0.4155±0.2469	100%
Rosenbrock	20	F_1	10.49±1.7	*d*-type	0.9237±0.0000	1.9173±0.2636	0.8158±0.1274	100%
		F_2	10.93±2.3	*d*-type	0.8680±0.1128	0.9377±0.6782	1.0402±0.2969	100%

Table 5. Estimated appropriate values of parameters in the PSO, criterion values and frequencies in the top-twenty optimizers. The PSO in *d*-type: $\hat{c}_0 > 0, \hat{c}_1 > 0, \hat{c}_2 > 0$.

below.

$$\begin{cases} 0.7048 \pm 0.4536 \ in \ \ ten - dimensional \ \ case \\ 0.1160 \pm 0.3024 \ in \ \ twenty - dimensional \ \ case \end{cases}$$

We can see that the average of fitness values in each case is not only better than the old one in Table 6, but also is better than that of the RGA/E. Therefore, it is demonstrated that the above supposition is correct and the generality of the estimated result of the EPSO.

Problem	Dim.	Original PSO	Original CPSO	EPSO (F_1)	EPSO (F_2)	OPSO	RGA/E
Sphere	10	0.8481±0.0995	0.9518±0.2153	**0.9985**±0.0048	0.9599±0.1465	0.9980±0.0077	0.9957±0.0028
	20	0.0912±0.0662	0.2529±0.3654	**0.9791**±0.0512	0.9328±0.2132	0.6939±0.3131	0.9207±0.0290
Griewank	10	0.7290±0.1506	0.7025±0.1475	**0.9547**±0.0621	0.9282±0.1138	0.8236±0.1835	0.9136±0.1415
	20	0.6752±0.1333	0.6593±0.1653	**0.9174**±0.1657	0.9028±0.1565	0.8073±0.1742	0.8816±0.1471
Rastrigin	10	0.0600±0.0346	0.0336±0.0156	0.6319±0.0370	0.0936±0.0783	0.0321±0.0255	**0.6693**±0.2061
	20	0.0084±0.0019	0.0065±0.0010	0.0162±0.0075	0.0148±0.0046	0.0147±0.0033	**0.0844**±0.0292
Rosenbrock	10	0.0928±0.0423	0.0899±0.0763	**0.1467**±0.1694	0.1388±0.0811	0.0825±0.0719	0.1243±0.0650
	20	0.0012±0.0019	0.0070±0.0103	**0.0293**±0.0217	0.0193±0.0186	0.0084±0.0108	0.0108±0.0082

Table 6. The obtained results of the EPSO, the original PSO, the original CPSO, and RGA/E (the mean and the standard deviation of fitness values in each method). The values in bold signify the best results for each problem.

5. Conclusion and discussion

We presented the method of evolutionary particle swarm optimization which provides a good framework to effectually estimate appropriate values of parameters in the PSO corresponding to a given optimization problem. Two different criteria, i.e. a temporally cumulative fitness function of the best particle and a temporally cumulative fitness function of the whole particle swarm, are adopted to use for evaluating the search performance of the PSO without any prior knowledge.

According to the synthetic results of both the search performance and convergence time-step, it is confirmed that the criterion F_1 has higher adaptability in search than that by the criterion F_2. On the other hand, these experimental results also clearly indicated that the PSO with higher adaptability is available when we have a passionate concern for the behavior of the best particle in evaluation, and the PSO with faster convergence is available when we have a passionate concern for the behavior of the entire swarm in evaluation.

As well as we observed, specially the results of the PSO estimated by the criterion F_2 having higher convergence easily tend to be trapped in local minima. This phenomenon suggests that estimating the PSO alone is not enough, and that a valid effective method for alleviating premature convergence and stagnation is of necessity. We also tested how to obtain the PSO with high search performance in a high-dimensional case by using the knowledge obtained in low-dimensional case, and showed the effectiveness of the use of this way.

It is left for further study to investigate the relation between search ability and faster convergence. By obtaining the *Pareto* front of 2-objective optimization (8; 23), the know-how on designing the PSO can be generally interpreted not only at model selection level but also at multi-objective level.

Nevertheless, it is necessary to argue a method reduced name EPSO (19) as a supplementary explanation. The method was created by Miranda et al. in 2002 for improving the search performance of th PSO. Although the concepts of evolutionary computation such as selection and mutation are used to the PSO search process and the effect of adaptation could be obtained, its mechanism is similar to the cPSO (21) and is completely different from the EPSO described in Section 3.2.

Generally, the following three manners can be used for improving the search performance of the PSO. (1) Optimizing the PSO, i.e. rationally managing the trade-off between exploitation and exploration by adopting appropriate values of parameters in the PSO; (2) Enforcing the intelligence of the PSO search, i.e. practicing intellectual action in optimization; (3) Unifying the mentioned (1) and (2) manners for acquiring more efficiency to search. Needless to say, the third manner in particular is successful among them. This is because the search capability of the PSO can be easily improved by the combination of capacity and intellectuality. In recent years, a number of studies and investigations regarding the third manner are focused, and being accepted flourishingly (11; 15; 30–32).

Accordingly, it is also left for further study to still handle the above hard problems with powerful hybrid techniques such as blending a local search and the PSO search for further increasing search ability, and introducing the mechanism of diversive curiosity into the PSO for raising the search performance of a single particle swarm or even multiple particle swarms with hybrid and intelligent search (34) to exploration.

6. Acknowledgment

This research was partially supported by Grant-in-Aid Scientific Research(C)(22500132) from the Ministry of Education, Culture, Sports, Science and Technology, Japan.

7. References

[1] A. Abraham, H. Guo and H. Liu, "Swarm Intelligence: Fondations, Perspectives and Applications, Swarm Intelligence Systems," in N. Nedjah and L. Mourelle (Eds.), *Studies in Computational Intelligence* (SCI), Springer-Verlag, Germany, pp.3-25, 2006.

[2] T. Beielstein, K. E. Parsopoulos and M. N. Vrahatis, "Tuning PSO Parameters Through Sensitivity Analysis," Technical Report of the Collaborative Research Center 531, *Computational Intelligence* CI–124/02, University of Dortmund, 2002.

[3] E. F. Campana, G. Fasano, D. Peri, and A. Pinto, "Particle Swarm Optimization: Efficient Globally Convergent Modifications," in C. A. Motasoares et al. (Eds.), *III European Conference on Computational Mechanics Solids, Structures and Coupled Problems in Engineering*, Springer Netherlands, pp.412-429, 2006.

[4] A. Carlisle and G. Dozier, "An Off-The-Shelf PSO," in *Proceedings of the Workshop on Particle Swarm Optimization*, Indianapolis, IN, USA, 2001, pp.1-6.

[5] M. Clerc and J. Kennedy, "The particle swarm-explosion, stability, and convergence in a multidimensional complex space," *IEEE Transactions on Evolutionary Computation*, vol.6, no.1, pp.58-73, 2002.

[6] M. Clerc, *Particle Swarm Optimization*, Iste Publishing Co., 2006.

[7] J. D. Cohen, S. M. McClure and A. J. Yu, "Should I stay or should I go? How the human brain manages the trade-off between exploitation and exploration," *Philosophical Transactions of the Royal Society*, Part B, no.362, pp.933-942. 2007.

[8] K. Deb, *Multi-Objective Optimization using Evolutionary Algorithms*, John Wiley & Sons, Ltd, 2001.

[9] R. C. Eberhart, and J. Kennedy, "A new optimizer using particle swarm theory," in *Proceedings of the sixth International Symposium on Micro Machine and Human Science*, Nagoya, Japan, 1995, pp.39-43.

[10] R. C. Eberhart and Y. Shi, "Comparing inertia weights and constriction factors in particleswarm optimization," in *Proceedings of the 2000 IEEE Congress on Evolutionary Computation*, La Jolla, CA, USA, 2000, vol.1, pp.84-88.

[11] M. El-Abd and M. S. Kamel, "A Taxonomy of Cooperative Particle Swarm Optimizers," *International Journal of Computational Intelligence Research*, vol.4, nol.2, pp.137-144, 2008.

[12] J. Kennedy and R. C. Eberhart, "Particle swarm optimization," in *Proceedings of the 1995 IEEE International Conference on Neural Networks*, Perth, Austrilia, 1995, pp.1942-1948.

[13] J. Kennedy, "In Search of the Essential Particle Swarm," in *Proceedings of the 2006 IEEE Congress on Evolutionary Computations*, Vancouver, BC, Canada, 2006, pp.6158-6165.

[14] J. Holland, *Adaptation in Natural and Artificial Systems*, University of Michigan Press, Ann Arbor, 1975.

[15] X. Hu and R. C. Eberhart, "Adaptive Particle Swarm Optimization: Detection and Response to Dynamic Systems", in *Proceedings of the 2002 IEEE Congress on Evolutionary Computations*, Honolulu, HI, USA, 2002, vol.2, pp.1666-1670.

[16] J. R. Koza, *Genetic Programming: A Paradigm for Genetically Breeding Populations of Computer Programs to Solve Problems*, Stanford University Computer Science Department technical report STAN-CS-90-1314, 1990.

[17] J. Lane, A. Engelbrecht and J. Gain, "Particle Swarm Optimization with Spatially Meaningful Neighbours," in *Proceedings of Swarm Intelligence Symposium* (SIS2008), St. Louis, MO, USA, 2008, pp.1-8.

[18] M. Meissner, M. Schmuker and G. Schneider, "Optimized Particle Swarm Optimization (OPSO) and its application to artificial neural network training," *BMC Bioinformatics*, vol.7, no.125, 2006.

[19] V. Miranda and N. Fonseca, "EPSO – Evolutionary Particle Swarm Optimization, a New Algorithm with Applications in Power Systems," *Transmission and Distribution Conference and Exhibition 2002: Asia Pacific, IEEE/PES*, 2002, vol.2, pp.745-750.

[20] R. S. Parpinelli and H. S. Lopes, "New inspirations in swarm intelligence: a survey," *International Journal of Bio-Inspired Computation*, vol.3, no.1, pp.1-16, 2011.

[21] K. E. Parsopoulos and M. N. Vrahatis, "Recent approaches to global optimization problems through Particle Swarm Optimization," *Natural Computing*, vol.1, pp.235-306, 2002.

[22] R. Poli, J. Kennedy and T. Blackwell, "Particle swarm optimization – An overview," *Swarm Intelligence*, vol.1, pp.33-57, 2007.

[23] M. Reyes-Sierra and C. A. Coello Coello, "Multi-Objective Particle Swarm Optimizers: A Survey of the State-of-the-Art," *International Journal of Computational Intelligence Research*, vol.2, no.3, pp.287-308, 2006.

[24] R. Storn and K. Price, "Differential evolution - a simple and efficient heuristic for global optimization over continuous space," *Journal of Global Optimization*, vol.11, pp.341-359, 1997.

[25] P. N. Suganthan, N. Hansen, J. J. Liang, K. Deb, Y.-P. Chen, A. Auger and S. Tiwari, (2005). Problem Definitions and Evaluation Criteria for the CEC 2005, Available: http://www.ntu.edu.sg/home/epnsugan/index_files/CEC-05/Tech-Report-May-30-05.pdf.

[26] H. Zhang and M. Ishikawa, "A Hybrid Real-Coded Genetic Algorithm with Local Search," in *Proceedings of the 12th International Conference on Neural Information Processing* (ICONIP2005), Taipei, Taiwan, ROC, 2005, pp.732-737.

[27] H. Zhang and M. Ishikawa, "Evolutionary Particle Swarm Optimization (EPSO) – Estimation of Optimal PSO Parameters by GA," in *Proceedings of The IAENG International MultiConference of Engineers and Computer Scientists 2007* (IMECS 2007), Hong Kong, China, 2007, vol.1, pp.13-18.

[28] H. Zhang and M. Ishikawa, "Performance Comparison of Fitness Functions in Evolutionary Particle Swarm Optimization," in *Proceedings of the 26th IASTED International Conference on Artificial Intelligence and Applications*, Innsbruck, Austria, 2008, pp.301-306.

[29] H. Zhang and M. Ishikawa, "Evolutionary Particle Swarm Optimization – Metaoptimization Method with GA for Estimating Optimal PSO Methods," in Castillo,

O. et al. (Eds.), *Trends in Intelligent Systems and Computer Engineering*, Lecture Notes in Electrical Engineering 6, Springer-Verlag, Germany, pp.75-90, 2008.
[30] H. Zhang and M. Ishikawa, "Particle Swarm Optimization with Diversive Curiosity – An Endeavor to Enhance Swarm Intelligence," *IAENG International Journal of Computer Science*, vol.35, Issue 3, pp.275-284, 2008.
[31] H. Zhang and M. Ishikawa, "Characterization of Particle Swarm Optimization with Diversive Curiosity," *Journal of Neural Computing and Applications*, vol.18, no.5, pp.409-415, 2009.
[32] H. Zhang and M. Ishikawa, "Particle Swarm Optimization with Diversive Curiosity and Its Applications," in Ao, S. et al. (Eds.), *Trends in Communication Technologies and Engineering Science*, Lecture Notes in Electrical Engineering 33, Springer Netherlands, pp.335-349, 2009.
[33] H. Zhang and M. Ishikawa, "The performance verification of an evolutionary canonical particle swarm optimizer," *Neural Networks*, vol.23, Issue 4, pp.510-516, 2010.
[34] H. Zhang, "A New Expansion of Cooperative Particle Swarm Optimization," in *Proceedings of the 17th International Conference on Neural Information Processing* (ICONIP2010), in Kevin K. W. Wong (Eds.), Neural Information Processing – Theory and Algorithms, LNCS 6443, Sydney, Australia, 2010, pp.593-600.

5

Volitive Clan PSO - An Approach for Dynamic Optimization Combining Particle Swarm Optimization and Fish School Search

George M. Cavalcanti-Júnior, Carmelo J. A. Bastos-Filho
and Fernando B. de Lima-Neto
Polytechnic School of Pernambuco, University of Pernambuco
Brazil

1. Introduction

The optima solutions for many real-world problems may vary over the time. Therefore, optimization algorithms to solve this type of problem should present the capability to deal with dynamic environments, in which the optima solutions can change during the algorithm execution. Many swarm intelligence algorithms have been proposed in the last years, and in general, they are inspired in groups of animals, such as flocks of birds, schools of fish, hives of bees, colonies of ants, etc. Although a lot of swarm-based algorithms were already proposed, just some of them were designed to tackle dynamic problems.

One of the most used swarm intelligence algorithms is the Particle Swarm Optimization (*PSO*). Despite the fast convergence capability, the standard version of the *PSO* can not tackle dynamic optimization problems. It occurs mainly because the entire swarm often increases the exploitation around a good region of the search space, consequently reducing the overall diversity of the population. Some variations of the *PSO*, such as *Charged PSO* proposed by Blackwell & Bentley (2002) and *Heterogeneous PSO* proposed by Leonard et al. (2011), have been proposed in order to increase the capacity to escape from regions within the search space where the global optimum is not located anymore.

The topology of the *PSO* defines the communication schema among the particles and it plays an important hole in the performance of the algorithm. The topology can influence in the trade-off between the convergence velocity and the quality of the solutions. In general, *PSO* topologies that benefit diversity, *e.g.* local and Von Neumann, are used to handle dynamic optimization problems. Carvalho and Bastos-Filho (Carvalho & Bastos-Filho, 2009a) presented a dynamic topology based on clan behaviors, which improves the *PSO* performance in various benchmark functions. This approach was named *Clan PSO*.

On the other hand, another swarm intelligence algorithm proposed in 2008, called the Fish School Search algorithm (*FSS*) (Bastos Filho, de Lima Neto, Lins, Nascimento & Lima, 2009), presents a very interesting feature that can be very useful for dynamic environments. *FSS* has an operator, called collective-volitive, which is capable to self-regulate automatically the exploration-exploitation trade-off during the algorithm execution.

Since the *PSO algorithm* converges faster than the *FSS*, but can not self-adapt the granularity of the search, Cavalcanti-Júnior *et al.* (Cavalcanti-Júnior et al., 2011) have incorporated the *FSS* volitive operator into the *PSO* in order to allow diversity generation after an stagnation process. The algorithm was named *Volitive PSO*. On dynamic optimization benchmark functions, this algorithm obtained better results than some *PSO* approaches created to tackle dynamic optimization problems, such as the *Charged PSO* (Blackwell & Bentley, 2002).

We believe that one can profit better results in multimodal search spaces if we deploy a collaborative multi-swarm approach in the *Volitive PSO*. Thus, we propose in this chapter to run independently the volitive operator in each one of the clans of the *Clan PSO* algorithm.

The chapter is organized as follows: Sections 2, 3, 4 and 5 present the background on *PSO*, *Clan PSO*, *FSS* and *Volitive PSO*, respectively. In Section 6 we put forward our contribution, the *Volitive Clan PSO*. In Section 7 we present the simulation setup. In Sections 8 we analyze the dynamics of our proposal and compare it to previous approaches. In Section 9.1 and 9.2 we present, respectively, some simulation results regarding the dependence on the parameters and compare our proposal to previous approaches in terms of performance. In Section 10 we give our conclusions.

2. *PSO* (Particle Swarm Optimization)

PSO is a population-based optimization algorithm inspired by the behavior of flocks of birds. The standard approach is composed by a swarm of particles, where each one has a position within the search space $\vec{x}_i$ and each position represents a possible solution for the problem. The particles fly through the search space of the problem searching for the best solution, according to the current velocity $\vec{v}_i$, the best position found by the particle itself ($\vec{P}_{best_i}$) and the best position found by the neighborhood of the particle i during the search so far ($\vec{N}_{best_i}$). One of the most used approach was proposed by Shi and Eberhart (Shi & Eberhart, 1998). This approach is also called *Inertia PSO*. According to their approach, the velocity of a particle i is evaluated at each iteration of the algorithm by using the following equation:

$$\vec{v}_i(t+1) = w\vec{v}_i(t) + r_1c_1[\vec{P}_{best_i}(t) - \vec{x}_i(t)] + r_2c_2[\vec{N}_{best_i}(t) - \vec{x}_i(t)], \tag{1}$$

where r_1 and r_2 are numbers randomly generated in the interval $[0,1]$ by an uniform probability density function. The inertia weight (w) controls the influence of the previous velocity and balances the exploration-exploitation behavior along the process. c_1 and c_2 are called cognitive and social acceleration constants, respectively, and weight the influence of the memory of the particle and the information acquired from the neighborhood.

The position of each particle is updated based on the updated velocity of the particle, according to the following equation:

$$\vec{x}_i(t+1) = \vec{x}_i(t) + \vec{v}_i(t+1). \tag{2}$$

The communication topology defines the neighborhood of the particles and, as a consequence, the flow of information through the particles. There are two basic topologies: global (Figure 1(a)) and local (Figure 1(b)). In the former, each particle shares and acquires information directly from all other particles, *i.e.* all particles use the same social memory, often referred as $\vec{G}_{best}$. In the local topology, each particle only share information with two neighbors and the social memory is not the same within the whole swarm. This approach, often called $\vec{L}_{best}$, helps to avoid a premature attraction of all particles to a single spot point in the search space, but presents a slower convergence.

Many other topologies were already proposed to overcome this trade-off. One promising topology, called *Clan PSO*, has a dynamic structure and outperforms the standard topologies in multimodal search spaces.

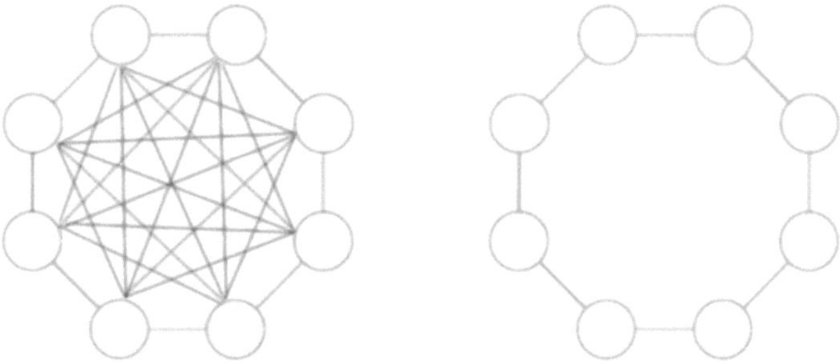

(a) Global best topology. (b) Local best topology.

Fig. 1. Two basic topologies used in PSO.

3. *Clan PSO*

Clans are groups of individuals united by a kinship and each clan has at least one guide. Inspired by these leadership characteristics, Carvalho and Bastos-Filho (Carvalho & Bastos-Filho, 2009a) proposed a topology called *Clan PSO*. As a part of the topology, each clan is composed by particles which are connected to the other particles of the same clan in order to share information quickly, as shown in the example depicted in Figure 2. The algorithm

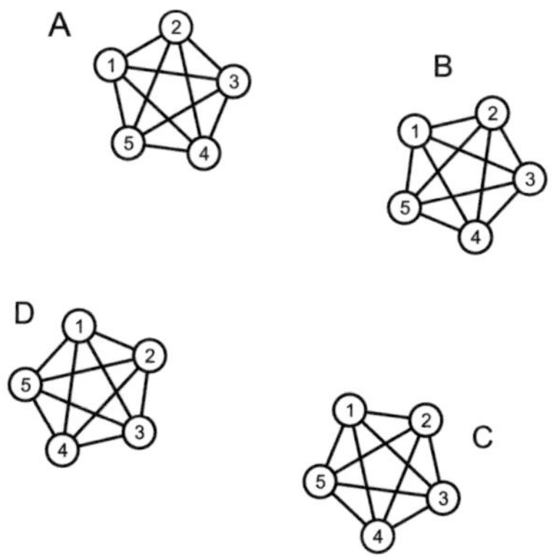

Fig. 2. Topology used within the clans for the *Clan PSO* with 4 clans with 5 particles.

has two phases executed in every iteration, the delegation of the leaders and the conference of the leaders. In previous works, Carvalho and Bastos-Filho (Carvalho & Bastos-Filho, 2009a) recommended to use just some few clans in order to avoid extra overhead within the iteration. More details about them are given in the following subsections.

3.1 Delegation of the leaders

At each iteration, each clan singly performs an independent *PSO* and the particle that obtained the best position within the clan is delegated as a leader of the clan in the iteration. Figure 3 illustrates an example with the leader delegated in each clan.

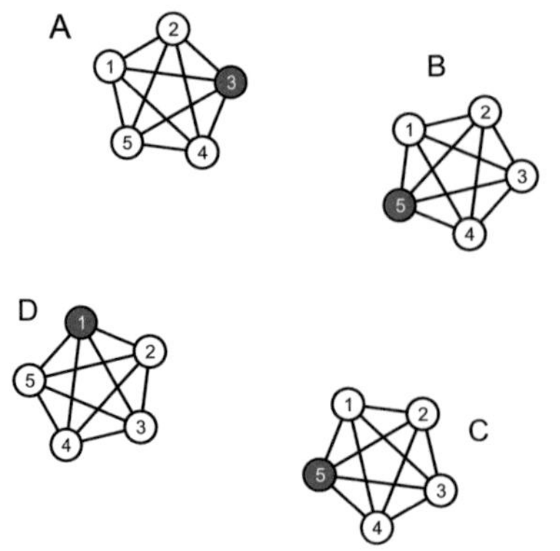

Fig. 3. Leaders delegated in the clans (A, B, C, D).

3.2 Conference of the leaders

After the Delegation, the leaders of each clan are selected and a new virtual swarm is composed by them. A *PSO* with the leaders can be ran using global (Figure 4(a)) or local (Figure 4(b)) topology. The former induces a faster convergence, while the latter allows more exploitation.

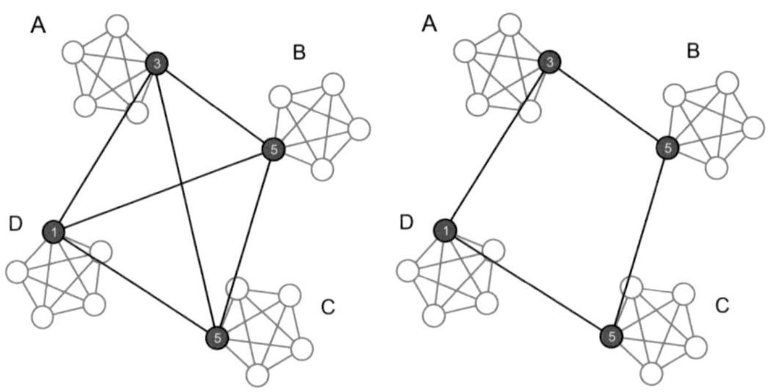

(a) Global conference. (b) Local conference.

Fig. 4. Leaders conference illustrations.

We will use the following nomenclature along the paper: <number of clans> x <particles per clan>. This means that if the swarm configuration is 4x5 particles, then the whole swarm contains 4 clans and each clan has 5 particles.

4. *FSS* (Fish School Search)

The Fish School Search (*FSS*) is an optimization algorithm based on the gregarious behavior of schools. It was firstly proposed by Bastos-Filho *et al.* (Bastos Filho, de Lima Neto, Lins,

Nascimento & Lima, 2009). In the *FSS*, each fish represents a solution for the problem and the success of a fish during the search process is indicated by its weight. The FSS has four operators, which are executed for each fish of the school at each iteration: (i) individual movement; (ii) feeding; (iii) collective-instinctive movement; and (iv) collective-volitive movement. Since we will use only the feeding and collective-volitive movement operators in our proposal, we detail them in the following subsections.

4.1 Feeding operator

The feeding operator determines the variation of the fish weight at each iteration. A fish can increase or decrease its weight depending, respectively, on the success or failure during the search process. The weight of the fish is evaluated according to the equation (3):

$$W_i(t+1) = W_i(t) + \frac{\Delta f_i}{max(|\Delta f|)}, \tag{3}$$

where $W_i(t)$ is the weight of the fish i, Δf_i is the variation of the fitness function between the new position and the current position of the fish, $max(|\Delta f|)$ is the absolute value of the highest fitness variation among all fish in the current iteration. There is a parameter w_{scale} that limits the maximum weight of the fish. The weight of each fish can vary between 1 and w_{scale} and has an initial value equal to $\frac{w_{scale}}{2}$.

4.2 Collective-volitive movement operator

This operator controls the granularity of the search executed by the fish school. When the whole school is achieving better results, the operator approximates the fish aiming to accelerate the convergence toward a good region. On the contrary, the operator spreads the fish away from the barycenter of the school and the school has more chances to escape from a local optimum. The fish school expansion or contraction is applied as a small drift to every fish position regarding the school barycenter, which can be evaluated by using the equation (4):

$$\vec{B}(t) = \frac{\sum_{i=1}^{N} \vec{x}_i(t) W_i(t)}{\sum_{i=1}^{N} \vec{x}_i(t)}. \tag{4}$$

We use equation (5) to perform the fish school expansion (in this case we use sign $+$) or contraction (in this case we use sign $-$).

$$\vec{x}_i(t+1) = \vec{x}_i(t) \pm step_{vol} r_1 \frac{\vec{x}_i(t) - \vec{B}(t)}{d(\vec{x}_i(t), \vec{B}(t))}, \tag{5}$$

where r_1 is a number randomly generated in the interval $[0, 1]$ by an uniform probability density function. $d(\vec{x}_i(t), \vec{B}(t))$ evaluates the euclidean distance between the particle i and the barycenter. $step_{vol}$ is called volitive step and controls the step size of the fish and is defined as a percentage of the search space range. The $step_{vol}$ is bounded by two parameters ($step_{vol\_min}$ and $step_{vol\_max}$) and decreases linearly from $step_{vol\_max}$ to $step_{vol\_min}$ along the iterations of the algorithm. It helps the algorithm to initialize with an exploration behavior and change dynamically to an exploitation behavior.

5. *Volitive PSO*

Volitive PSO is a hybridization of the *FSS* and the *PSO* algorithms and it was proposed by (Cavalcanti-Júnior et al., 2011). The algorithm uses two *FSS* operators in the *Inertia PSO*, the feeding and the collective-volitive movement. Each particle becomes a weighted particle, where the weights are used to define the collective-volitive movement, resulting in an expansion or contraction of the school. As a results, the *Volitive PSO* presents good features of the *PSO* and the *FSS* to tackle dynamic problems. These features are, respectively, fast convergence and the capacity to self-regulate the granularity of the search by using the volitive operator. Figure 5 illustrates the features aggregated in the *Volitive PSO*.

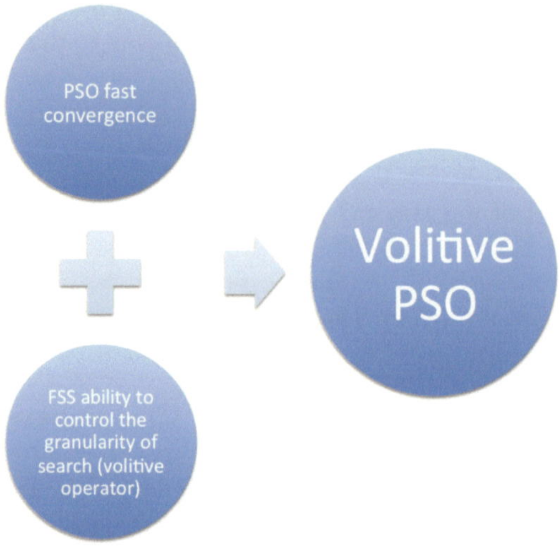

Fig. 5. Illustration of the features presented by the *Volitive PSO*.

In the *Volitive PSO*, the $step_{vol}$ decreases according to the equation (6).

$$step_{vol}(t+1) = step_{vol}(t)\frac{100 - decay_{vol}}{100}, \tag{6}$$

where $decay_{vol}$ is the volitive step decay percentage which must be in the interval $[0, 100]$.

The $step_{vol}$ is reinitialized to $step_{vol\_max}$ when a change in the environment is detected in order to allow the algorithm to increase the diversity within the population. The detection of a change is performed by using a sentry particle as presented in (Carlisle & Dozier, 2002). In this case, the fitness is evaluated in the end of each iteration and in the beginning of the next iteration. Thus, immediately after an environment change, the algorithm has more capacity to escape from an old optima due to the larger steps of the volitive movement. As $step_{vol}$ is decreased along the iterations, the algorithm gradually changes from exploration to exploitation mode.

6. Our proposal: *Volitive clan PSO*

We propose here to include the volitive operator into the *Clan PSO*. In our approach, each clan runs a Volitive PSO separately and the weights of the individuals of each clan are treated independently. As a consequence, each clan can perform independent volitive movements, shrinking or expanding its radius depending on its success or failure. The multi-swarm proposal with the volitive movement is the main difference to the approach proposed by Cavalcanti-Júnior et al. (2011). The pseudocode of our proposal is depicted in algorithm 1. We observed that the *Volitive Clan PSO* returned better results for dynamic environments when we run *PSOs* with local topology either within the clans and in the conference of the leaders.

Algorithm 1: Pseudocode of the *Volitive Clan PSO*.

Initialize parameters and particles;
while *the stop condition is not reached* **do**
  Update the sentry particle;
  if *the sentry particle detected a change* **then**
    reinitialize $step_{vol}$;
  foreach *clan of the swarm* **do**
    foreach *particle of the clan* **do**
      Update the velocity and the position of the particle using local topology using equations (1) and (2), respectively;
    Execute the feeding operator in the clan using equation (3);
    Execute the collective-volitive movement operator in the clan using equation (5);
    foreach *particle of the clan* **do**
      Evaluate the fitness of the particle;
      Evaluate $\vec{P}_{best}$ and $\vec{N}_{best}$;
    Delegate the leader of the clan;
  Perform the conference of the Leaders using local topology;
  Update the sentry particle;

7. Simulation setup

All experiments were developed in JAVA and executed in a computer with a 2.40GHz Core 2 Quad processor and 8GB RAM memory running Linux operational system.

7.1 Benchmark function

We used the DF1 benchmark function proposed by Morrison & De Jong (1999) in our simulations. DF1 is composed by a set of random peaks with different heights and slopes. The number of peaks, their heights, slopes, and positions within the search space are adjustable. As those three components can change during the execution, then they are called dynamic components. The function for a N-dimensional space is defined according to the equation (7).

$$f(\vec{x}) = max_{i=1,2,\ldots,P}[H_i - S_i\sqrt{\sum(\vec{x} - \vec{x}_i)^2}], \tag{7}$$

where P is the number of peaks (peak i is centered in the position $\vec{x}_i$), H_i is the peak height and S_i is the peak slope. The values for x_{id}, H_i and S_i are bounded.

The dynamic components of the environment are updated using discrete steps. The DF1 uses a logistics function to control the generation of different step sizes. The parameter used to calculate the steps is adjusted according to the equation (8).

$$e_i = re_{i-1}(1 - e_{i-1}), \quad (8)$$

where r is a constant in the interval [1,4]. As r increases, more simultaneous results for e are achieved. As r gets closer to 4, the behavior becomes chaotic.

In the simulations presented in the Sections 9.1 and 9.2, we use 10 dimensions, 10 or 50 peaks and search space bounds $[-50, 50]^d$ for all dimensions. All peaks have a constant slope along the execution that is determined in the beginning of each simulation randomly in the interval $[1, 7]$. All peaks move around the bounded search space independently and their height vary in the interval $[10, 50]$, both for each 100 iterations. For Section 8 we use a search space with 2 dimensions.

We simulate an environment with high severity changes. For all dynamic components the scale parameter was set to 0.5. This parameters is a value between 0 and 1, which multiplies the result of the logistics function for each environment change. Thus, the scale parameter control the severity of the change of each dynamic component. The coefficient r of the logistic function is equal to 2.1 for all dynamic components.

All environments are generated using the same seed for the random number. Thus, the initial environment conditions are the same for all simulations. However, the dynamics of the environment over the algorithm execution are different for each simulation. For the box plot graphs, we evaluate the performance of the algorithms over 30 independent simulations with 10,000 iterations each one.

7.2 Performance metric

To measure the performance of an optimization algorithm in a dynamic environment a good metric should reflect the performance of the algorithm across the entire range of environment dynamics. Accordingly, we use in all experiments the mean fitness, which was introduced by Morrison (Morrison, 2003). The mean fitness is the average over all previous fitness values, as defined below:

$$F_{mean}(T) = \frac{\sum_{t=1}^{T} F_{best}(t)}{T}, \quad (9)$$

where T is the total number of iterations and F_{best} is the fitness of the best particle after iteration t. The advantage of the mean fitness is that it represents the entire algorithm performance history.

7.3 Algorithms setup

The cognitive acceleration coefficient (c_1) of the *PSO* is set initially to 2.5 and decreases linearly to 0.5 along 100 iterations (that corresponds to the frequency of the environment change). On the other hand, the social acceleration coefficient (c_2) is initially equal to 0.5 and increases linearly to 2.5 over the same change interval. For every 100 iterations, c_1 and c_2 are reinitialized. Thus, the algorithms has more capacity to generate diversity after an environment change and consequently is more capable to explore the search space looking for new optima. Gradually, the algorithm increases the exploitation until another environment change occurs, then it return to the first step of this process. We used the inertia weight (w) equal to 0.729844 and a total number of 54 particles for all algorithms.

On the *Charged PSO*, c_1 and c_2 are constant and equal to 1.49618. 50% of the particles are charged with charge value 16, both according to the specification presented in (Blackwell & Bentley, 2002). The parameters p and p_{core} are set to 1 and 30, respectively, according to Blackwell Leonard et al. (2011).

For the parameters in *Clan PSO*, *Volitive PSO* and *Volitive Clan PSO*, we use the same configuration used in the *PSO*. For the algorithms which use the volitive operator, we use $w_{scale} = 5000$ and $step_{vol\_min} = 0.01\%$, according to Bastos-Filho, Lima-Neto, Sousa & Pontes (2009).

8. Analysis of the dynamics of the algorithms

The following requirements are necessary to reach good performance in dynamic optimization: i) generation of diversity to explore the search space after an environment change, and ii) quick convergence to a new optimum. These capabilities can lead the algorithm to track optima solutions. In this section we analyze the dynamic behavior of our proposal and compare it to some other previous PSO approaches.

Figures 6, 7 and 8 present the positions of the particles for the *PSO* using Local topology with 54 particles (*PSO-L*), *Clan PSO* with 3 clans and 18 particles per clan (*ClanPSO-L 3x18*) and *Volitive Clan PSO* with 3 clans and 18 particles per clan (*Volitive Clan PSO-L 3x18*), respectively, for the two dimensional dynamic DF1 function (Morrison & De Jong, 1999). In the clan-based approaches, we used Local topology in the conference of leaders. In this analysis, we used the Global topology within the clans for the *Clan PSO* and the Local topology within the clans for the *Volitive Clan PSO*. All algorithms are deployed to maximize the DF1 function, where each red region represents a peak which changes its height and position after 100 iterations. The value for the peak height can be inferred by the legend situated on the right side of each graph. All figures show the positions of the particles: (a) just before an environment change, (b) just after an environment change and (c) 10, (d) 30, (e) 50 and (f) 100 iterations after the environment change.

From Figure 6, it is possible to observe that the *PSO-L* swarm is located in an outdated optimum position in the first iterations after the change in the environment. Because *PSO-L* does not have any mechanism to generate diversity after the swarm convergence, the swarm slows down to find another optimum, and just can find it because of the inertia term and reinitialization of c_1 and c_2. Figure 6(d) shows that most of the particles is located at an optimum which is not the global one after 30 iterations. One can observe that some particles escaped to other optima after 50 and 100 iterations, as shown in Figure 6(e) and 6(f). Nevertheless, the swarm could not generate diversity enough to explore farther regions of the search space in order to find other optima which could be the global one.

The *ClanPSO-L* presents a slightly worse behavior when compared to the *PSO-L*. Figure 7(a) shows that the swarm converged to a single spot and, after the environment change (Figure 7(b)), the whole swarm tends to move towards the optimum which is closest to this spot (Figures 7(c), 7(d)). Even after more iterations after the environment change, the swarm was not capable to generate diversity and, as a consequence, was not able to find an optimum far from the initial spot, as shown in Figures 7(e) and 7(f). This behavior occurs because every clan uses global topology, which strong attracts the whole sub-swarm to a single spot.

Unlike the *PSO-L* and the *ClanPSO-L*, the *Volitive Clan PSO* has a mechanism to generate diversity after an environment change. Comparing Figures 8(a) and 8(b), we can observe that the swarm spreads away from the barycenter after the change. It occurs because immediately after the change, the particles assess their positions and check that they are in a worse position than the last iteration because of the change in the environment. Because of this, the swarm tends to decrease its weight according to the feeding operator and it consequently triggers the collective-volitive operator to expand the swarm radius by repelling particles from the barycenter (Figure 8(b)). In Figures 8(c) and 8(d) one can observe that the swarm is still performing exploration, but the particles also begin to approximate themselves in order to converge to another optimum. Finally, in Figure 8(f) the swarm splits in three sub-swarms and each one is located in a different optimum. We believe that each sub-swarm is a clan since we are using the 3x18 configuration. Summarizing, Figure 8 shows that the *Volitive Clan PSO* is capable to generate diversity in order to escape from outdated optima.

9. Simulation results

9.1 Parametric analysis

In this section we analyse the impact of some parameters on the performance of the *Volitive Clan PSO*. We tested the following values for $decay_{vol}$: 0%, 5% and 10%, combined with $step_{vol\_max}$ values equals to 30%, 40%, 50%, 60%, 70% and 80% of the search space range. We observed that the best results for the *Volitive Clan PSO* were achieved with Local topology within the clans and in the conference of the leaders. Therefore, we used these configurations in all experiments presented in this section.

Figure 9 provides the performance for different values of $decay_{vol}$ and $step_{vol\_max}$ for the configuration 3x18. The bests results were achieved for $decay_{vol} = 5\%$, as shown in Figure 9(b). One can observe that it is necessary to balance the $decay_{vol}$ value. If $decay_{vol} = 0\%$, then the algorithm is not allowed to exploit. On the other hand, if $decay_{vol}$ is higher, then $step_{vol}$ decays too fast and causes a premature convergence of the swarm.

According to results showed in Figure 9, we selected $decay_{vol} = 5\%$ and $step_{vol\_max} = 60\%$ to compare different configurations of clans. We assessed the following clans configurations: 1x54, 3x18, 6x9 and 9x6. Figure 10 shows the results. One can observe that the best performance was achieved for 3x18 particles. Therefore, we used this configuration to compare the performance to other algorithms (experiments presented in the Section 9.2).

9.2 Performance comparison

We compare all algorithms in two situations: without reinitializing particles and reinitializing 50% of particles for every environment change. The second situation is a common approach to generate diversity in algorithms when dealing with dynamic problems (Leonard et al., 2011). In both situations we performed simulations with 10 and 50 peaks for the DF1 benchmark function.

Figure 11 shows the box plots for the performance of the algorithms in terms of Mean Fitness for 10 dimensions and 10 peaks. Comparing the Figures 11(a) and 11(b) we can observe that the algorithms that uses the volitive operator achieved better results in both situations. Besides, the results observed for the *Volitive PSO* and the *Volitive Clan PSO* did not change significantly when the reinitialization procedure is used (see Tables 0(a) and 0(b)). In fact, the

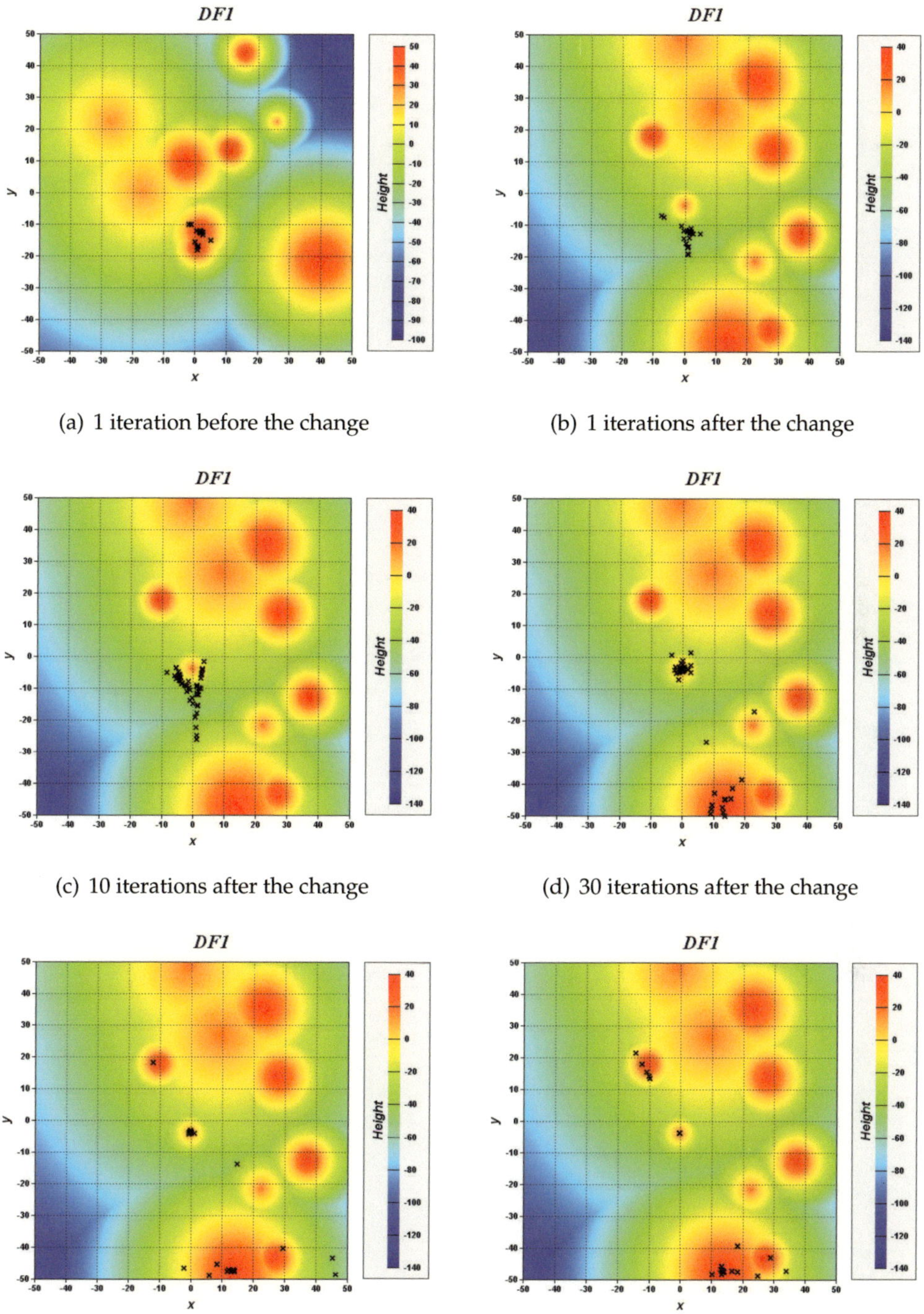

(a) 1 iteration before the change

(b) 1 iterations after the change

(c) 10 iterations after the change

(d) 30 iterations after the change

(e) 50 iterations after the change

(f) 100 iterations after the change

Fig. 6. Positions of the particles for the *PSO-L* in a dynamic environment.

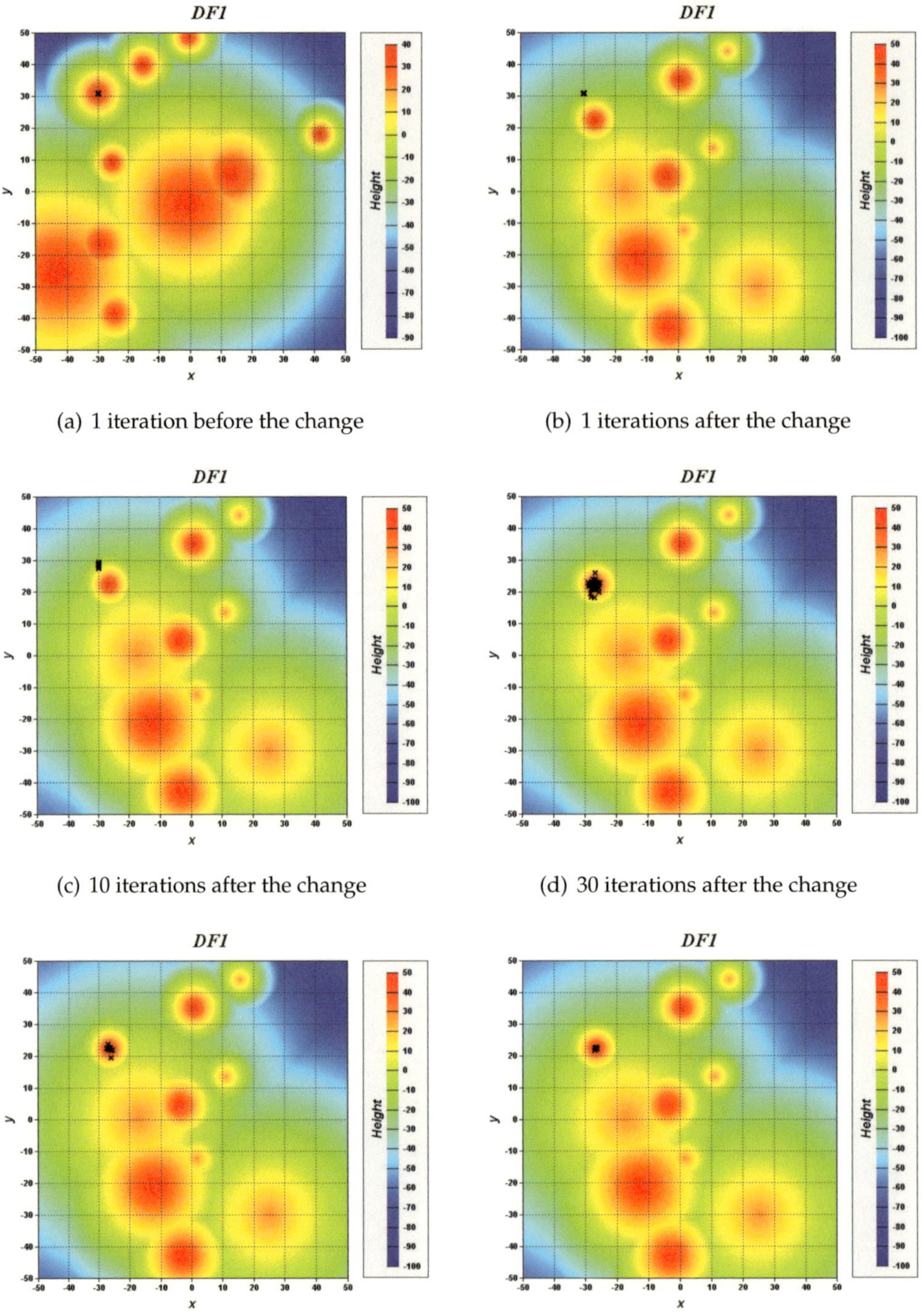

(a) 1 iteration before the change

(b) 1 iterations after the change

(c) 10 iterations after the change

(d) 30 iterations after the change

(e) 50 iterations after the change

(f) 100 iterations after the change

Fig. 7. Positions of the particles for the *Clan PSO-L 3x18* in a dynamic environment.

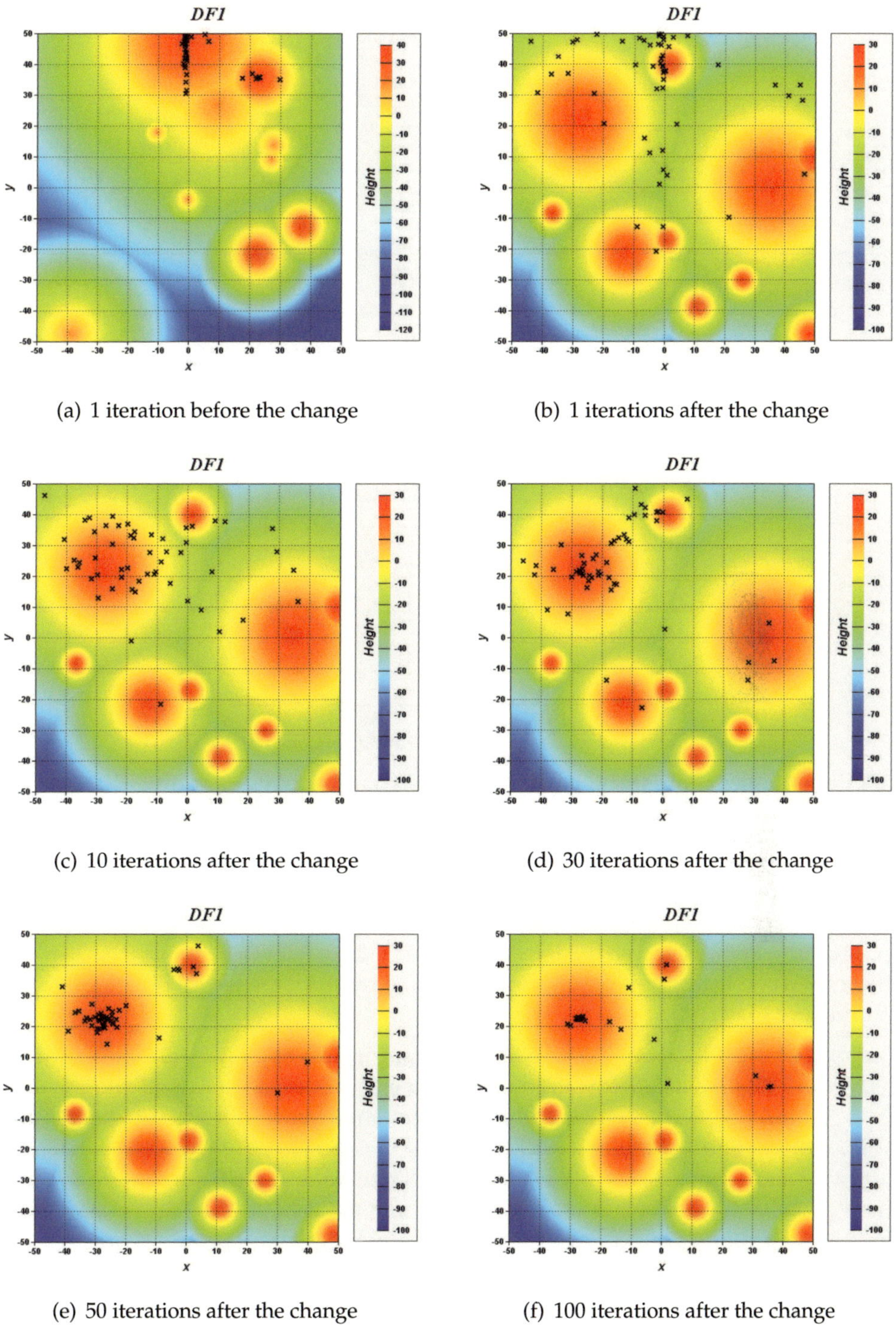

(a) 1 iteration before the change

(b) 1 iterations after the change

(c) 10 iterations after the change

(d) 30 iterations after the change

(e) 50 iterations after the change

(f) 100 iterations after the change

Fig. 8. Positions of the particles for the *Volitive Clan PSO-L 3x18* in a dynamic environment.

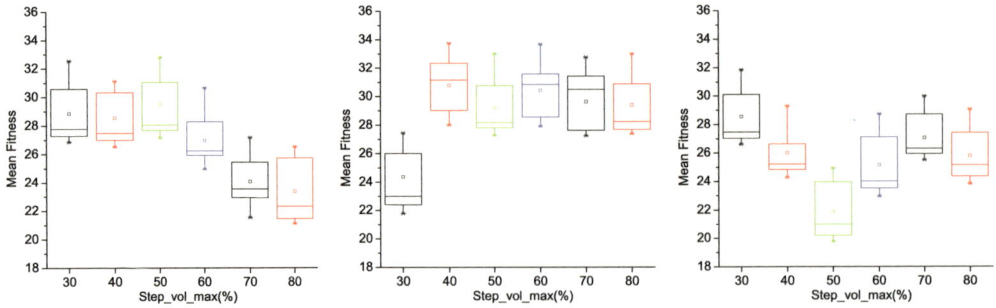

(a) $decay_{vol} = 0\%$ (b) $decay_{vol} = 5\%$ (c) $decay_{vol} = 10\%$

Fig. 9. Box plot of *Volitive Clan PSO 3x18* in the last iteration in high severity environment.

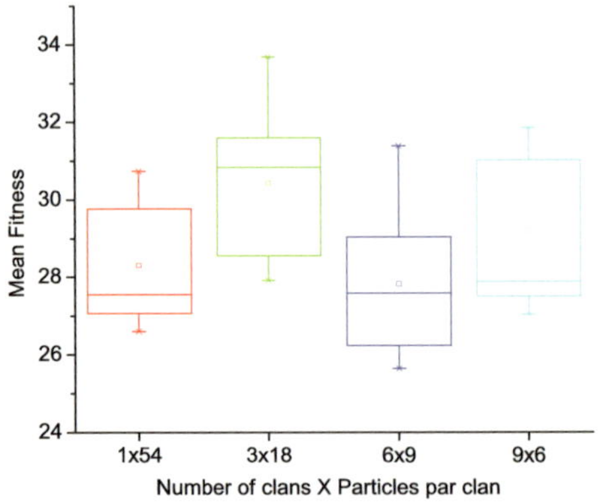

Fig. 10. Performance comparison between different number of clans and particles per clan with $decay_{vol} = 5\%$ and $step_{vol\_max} = 60\%$.

reinitialization process slightly mitigated the overall performance. It probably occurs because the mutation causes information loss. Furthermore, it indicates that the volitive operator can generate enough diversity for the presented case. The *Volitive Clan PSO* achieved slightly better results when compared to the *Volitive PSO*. The *PSO-G* improves its performance significantly when using the reinitialization, but the results were worse than the *Volitive PSO* and the *Volitive Clan PSO*.

Figure 12 and Tables 1(a) and 1(b) present the results for the experiments with 10 dimensions and 50 peaks. The results are similar to the ones with 10 dimensions and 10 peaks. Again, the *PSO-G* improves its performance with the reinitialization and achieved results similar to the *Volitive PSO* and the *Volitive Clan PSO*. Nevertheless, the *PSO-G* was dependent on the reinitialization to generate diversity, in this case all reinitialized particles loose their memories (*i.e.* the $\vec{P}_{best_i}$). On the other hand, the *Volitive PSO* and the *Volitive Clan PSO* are not dependent on the reinitialization. Thus, in these algorithms the information acquired previously is not totally lost.

The Table 3 shows the processing time in seconds running 10.000 iterations. The *Charged PSO* reached the smallest processing time. Nevertheless, the processing time among all algorithms are not so different.

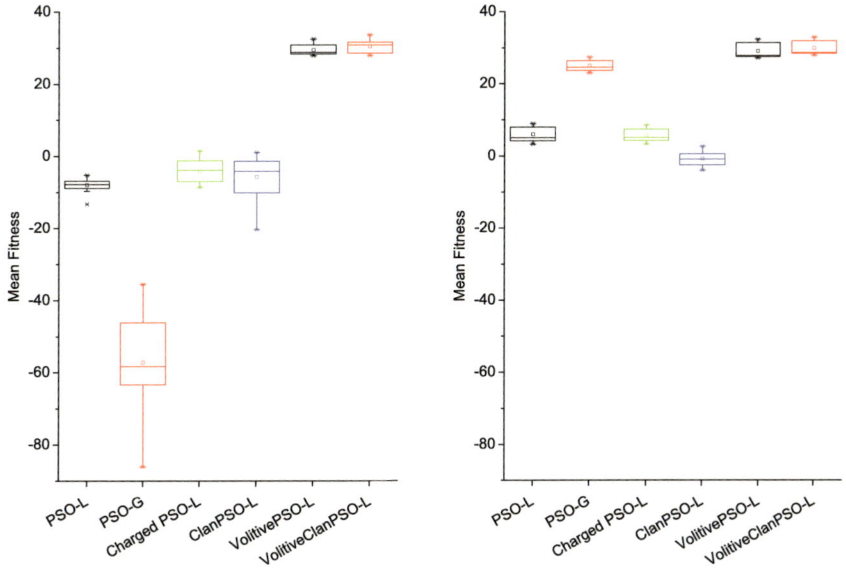

(a) Without reinitialize particles after an environment change

(b) Reinitializing 50% of particles after an environment change

Fig. 11. Mean Fitness comparison between five algorithms in environment with 10 dimensions and 10 peaks.

(a) High severity.

Algorithm	Mean	Standard deviation
PSO-L	-7.886	1.589
PSO-G	-57.240	12.699
ChargedPSO-L	-4.175	2.856
ClanPSO-L	-5.740	5.437
VolitivePSO-L	29.496	1.453
VolitiveClanPSO-L	30.430	1.732

(b) High severity with initialization of 50% of particles.

Algorithm	Mean	Standard deviation
PSO-L	6.001	2.022
PSO-G	24.924	1.484
ChargedPSO-L	5.573	1.672
ClanPSO-L	-0.813	1.816
VolitivePSO-L	28.953	2.009
VolitiveClanPSO-L	29.762	1.854

Table 1. Mean fitness in the last iteration with 10 dimensions and 10 peaks - mean and standard deviation after 10,000 iterations.

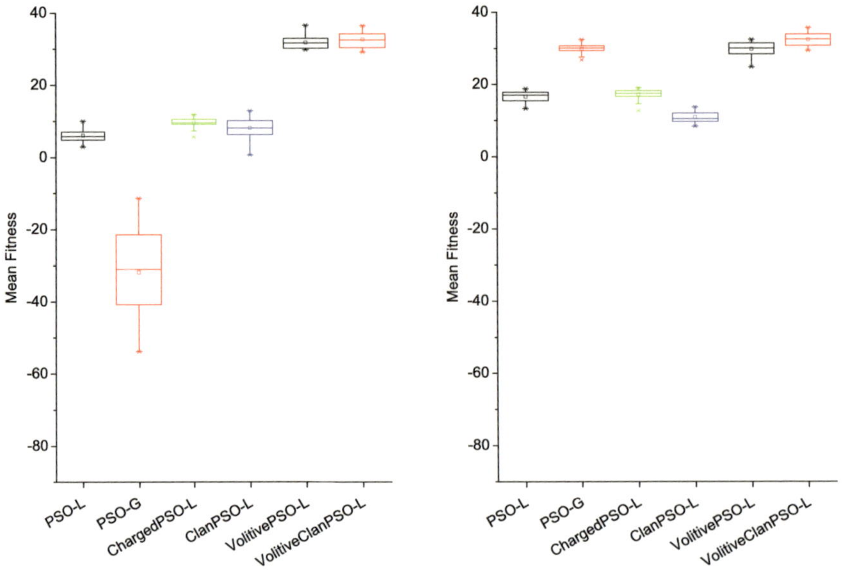

(a) Without reinitialize particles after an environment change

(b) Reinitializing 50% of particles after an environment change

Fig. 12. Mean Fitness comparison between five algorithms in environment with 10 dimensions and 50 peaks.

(a) High severity.

Algorithm	Mean	Standard deviation
PSO-L	6.082	1.693
PSO-G	-31.905	11.588
ChargedPSO-L	9.658	1.375
ClanPSO-L	8.098	3.210
VolitivePSO-L	31.769	1.682
VolitiveClanPSO-L	32.545	2.119

(b) High severity with initialization of 50% of particles.

Algorithm	Mean	Standard deviation
PSO-L	16.587	1.532
PSO-G	29.947	1.3557
ChargedPSO-L	17.261	1.416
ClanPSO-L	10.865	1.601
VolitivePSO-L	29.807	2.163
VolitiveClanPSO-L	32.372	1.958

Table 2. Mean fitness in the last iteration with 10 dimensions and 50 peaks - mean and standard deviation after 10,000 iterations.

Algorithm	Mean	Standard deviation
PSO-L	11.323 s	0.934
PSO-G	8.545 s	0.253
ChargedPSO-L	7.570 s	0.673
ClanPSO-L	9.433 s	0.387
VolitivePSO-L	11.613 s	0.218
VolitiveClanPSO-L	10.022 s	0.244

Table 3. Processing time of the algorithms in 10 dimensions and 10 peaks - mean and standard deviation after 10,000 iterations.

10. Conclusions

In this chapter we presented a new *PSO*-based approach capable to handle dynamic problems. We achieved this by incorporating the volitive operator in the *Clan PSO*. Our approach is capable to generate diversity without use particles reinitialization. Thus, it does not totally loose information about the environment whenever a change occurs. Actually, the reinitialization of the particles was detrimental for our approach.

We believe that the fast convergence of the *PSO* and the ability of the volitive operator to self-regulate the granularity of the search were responsibly for the success in dealing with dynamic problems. The volitive operator contributes either for diversity and convergence by expanding or shrinking the swarm, then this is another feature that improved the performance of either *PSO* and *Clan PSO*. For all experiments, the *Volitive Clan PSO* outperforms *PSO*, *Clan PSO*, *Charged PSO* and slighly outperforms the *Volitive PSO*.

11. References

Bastos Filho, C. J. a., de Lima Neto, F. B., Lins, A. J. C. C., Nascimento, A. I. S. & Lima, M. P. (2009). A novel search algorithm based on fish school behavior, *2008 IEEE International Conference on Systems, Man and Cybernetics*, IEEE, pp. 2646–2651.

Bastos-Filho, C. J. A., Lima-Neto, F. B., Sousa, M. F. C. & Pontes, M. R. (2009). On the Influence of the Swimming Operators in the Fish School Search Algorithm, *SMC* pp. 5012–5017.

Blackwell, T. & Bentley, P. (2002). Dynamic Search with Charged Swarms, *Proceedings of the Genetic and Evolutionary Computation Conference* pp. 19–26.

Carlisle, A. & Dozier, G. (2002). *Applying the particle swarm optimizer to non-stationary environments*, Phd thesis, Auburn University, Auburn, AL.

Carvalho, D. F. & Bastos-Filho, C. J. A. (2009a). Clan particle swarm optimization, *International Journal of Intelligent Computing and Cybernetics* 2: 197–227.

Carvalho, D. F. D. E. & Bastos-Filho, C. J. A. (2009b). Clan Particle Swarm Optimization, *International Journal Of Intelligent Computing and Cybernetics* pp. 1–35.

Cavalcanti-Júnior, G. M., Bastos-Filho, C. J. A., Lima-Neto, F. B. & Castro, R. M. C. S. (2011). A hybrid algorithm based on fish school search and particle swarm optimzation for dynamic problems, *in* Y. Tan (ed.), *Proceedings of the International Conference on Swarm intelligence*, Lecture Notes in Computer Science, Springer-Verlag, Berlin, Heidelberg, pp. 543–552.

Leonard, B. J., Engelbrecht, A. P. & van Wyk, A. B. (2011). Heterogeneous Particle Swarms in Dynamic Environments, *IEEE Symposium on Swarm Intelligence - SIS, IEEE Symposium Series on Computational Intelligence - SSCI* pp. 9–16.

Morrison, R. & De Jong, K. (1999). A test problem generator for non-stationary environments, *Proceedings of the Congress on Evolutionary Computation* pp. 2047–2053.

Morrison, R. W. (2003). Performance Measurement in Dynamic Environments, *GECCO Workshop on Evolutionary Algorithms for Dynamic Optimization Problems* pp. 5–8.

Shi, Y. & Eberhart, R. (1998). A modified particle swarm optimizer, *Evolutionary Computation Proceedings, 1998. IEEE World Congress on Computational Intelligence., The 1998 IEEE International Conference on* pp. 69–73.

6

Inverse Analysis in Civil Engineering: Applications to Identification of Parameters and Design of Structural Material Using Mono or Multi-Objective Particle Swarm Optimization

M. Fontan[1], A. Ndiaye[2], D. Breysse[3] and P. Castéra[2]
[1]*Ecole Normale Supérieure de Cachan, LMT - CNRS UMR 8535 - Department of Mechanical Engineering Cachan,*
[2]*INRA, I2M, USC 927, Talence,*
[3]*Univ. Bordeaux, I2M, UMR 5295, Talence,*
France

1. Introduction

Many engineering applications suffer from the ignorance of mechanical parameters. It is particularly true when soil model is necessary to assess soil behaviour [Meieret *al.*, 2008]. Nevertheless, it is not always efficient to directly assess the values of all the parameters in the case of soil mechanics. Considering structural mechanics, [Li et *al.*, 2007] also worked to propose an optimal design of a truss pylon respecting the stress constraints of the elements but it is not an easy task to solve considering the number and loading of the structure. Inverse analysis is an efficient solution to reach these aims. This technique becomes more and more popular thanks to the increase of the computing capabilities. Computing costs have decreased and allow to handle complex optimization problems through meta heuristic methods for example to identify the solution of the problem like the mechanical parameters of a behaviour model of a soil [Fontan et *al.*, 2011, Levasseur et *al.*, 2008], to define the best section of the beams composing a truss structure or to optimize wood-plastic composite mechanical properties designed for decking and taking into account the environmental impact during the life cycle of the product [Ndiaye et *al.*, 2009]. The literature about inverse analysis is very rich and it covers many application fields like management or mechanical science as attesting the table number 1 in [Fontan et *al.*, 2011] which presents several civil engineering applications (this table is not presented there). Most of the authors mentioned in this paper used the concept of inverse analysis to identify parameters either in structural mechanics [Li et *al.*, 2007, Fontan 2011] or soil mechanics [Meier et *al.*, 2008, Levasseur et *al.*, 2008]. They were just using different mechanical models (analytical or numerical) or different algorithms to solve their problem (PSO, descent gradient, ant colony, genetic algorithm, etc.). Inverse analysis is based on the simple concept of solving an equation to find the n values X_n respecting equation 1, with M: the mechanical model corresponding to the real behaviour of the analysis and Y_m: the m measurement carried out on site.

$$Y_m = M(X_n) \quad (1)$$

Solving this problem is mechanically difficult due to (a) the accuracy of the measurements X_n which contain observational error, (b) the number of measurement data - it is necessary to respect the following relation m > n to identify a single value otherwise, a front of solutions will be identified -, (c) the accuracy of the mechanical model M. We consider that the accuracy of the model is well known. The nature of the model can be either analytical or numerical using the finite element method (FEM) as it will be explained in the following sections. One of the main problems during the development of inverse analysis is the limitation of use regarding the algorithm in charge of solving these equations. Classical algorithms like Descent Gradient, Cholesky, Lower Upper method are efficient for perfect data, which is not the case in engineering. Usual algorithms have often a limited efficiency because of local minima and observational errors on field data. This justifies the use of meta-heuristic algorithms that are capable of overcoming the presence of local minimum and to converge towards the solution of the problem. In this chapter, we will present two different applications based on the inverse analysis using the PSO algorithm. The first application is the identification of structural parameters like stiffnesses of a continuous beam laying on three elastic supports through the resolution of an objective function. The second work is about a resolution of contradictory multi-objective functions. The next section will present the principles of the inverse analysis and the PSO. The following section is about the one objective function work, including a discussion about the various sources of errors that can strongly impact the accuracy of the parameter identification. The last part is about the work focused on a multi-objective resolution.

2. Principle of inverse analysis and particle swarm optimization

The principle of the direct inverse analysis is to find the most appropriate values X_n to find the data Y_m through a mechanical model M. This method is not always efficient due to the presence of noise on data that can strongly impact the result. Then, an indirect inverse analysis is more appropriate. In this case, the objective is to minimize the error between the real data Y_m^{real} and predicted data $Y_m^{predicted}$ obtained through a mechanical model, cf. defined equation 2. Thus, the new objective is to minimize the objective function $F_{objective}$, cf. equation 3, finding the appropriate parameters to identify X_n with $Y^{predicted}$. In the case of multi-objective functions, several functions $F^i_{objective}$ are minimized simultaneously in order to reach an optimal compromise.

This approach is an indirect inverse analysis where the impact of the metrology, which defines Y_m^{real} data, is strongly impacting the accuracy of the identification of parameters. So as to solve this difficult NP-complete Problem, meta-heuristic algorithms are very efficient [Kennedy, 1995]. The PSO is a powerful algorithm quickly converging to the solution of the problem [Kaveh 2009] where local minima are then not such an important problem unlike when using a descent gradient algorithm. This advantage is also an inconvenient because of the lack of capabilities to correctly explore the n dimensions of research space containing the parameters to identify. Another advantage is the small number of parameters to choose beforehand so as to run the algorithm, which means that the knowledge of the user is not another source of error during the identification process. Besides, several comparison tests were carried out between different meta-heuristics and the PSO algorithm was considered as being one of the most efficient in terms of accuracy and time cost computing [Fan 2006, Hammouche 2010].

$$Y_m^{predicted}=(M\ (Xn))_m \tag{2}$$

$$\min\left\{F_{objective}(X_n)\right\} = \min\left\{\frac{\sum_{i=1}^{m}\left(1-\left(\frac{Y_i^{predicted}}{Y_i^{real}}\right)\right)}{m}\right\} \tag{3}$$

2.1 Particle swarm optimization (PSO)

Particle swarm optimization (PSO) is a swarm intelligence technique developed by Kennedy and Eberhart (1995). This technique, inspired by flocks of birds and shoals of fish, has proved to be very efficient in hard optimization problems. The swarm is composed of particles, a number of simple entities, randomly placed in the search space of the objective function. Each particle can interact with members of the swarm that are its social neighbourhood. It can evaluate the fitness at its current location in the search space, it knows its best position ever visited and the best position of its social neighbourhood. It determines its movement through the search space by combining these information, and moving along with the corresponding instantaneous velocity. A particle position is better than another one if its objective function is better; (better means smaller than if it is a minimization problem and greater than if it is a maximization problem).

The social neighbourhood of a given particle influences its trajectory in the search space. The two most commonly used neighbourhood topologies are the *fully connected* topology named g_{best} topology and the *ring* topology named l_{best} topology [Kennedy and Mendes, 2002]. In the *fully connected* topology the trajectory of each particle is influenced by the best position found by any particle of the swarm as well as their own past experience. Usually the *ring* topology neighbourhood comprises exactly two neighbours, every particle is connected to its two immediate neighbours, one on each side with toroidal wrapping. With a *fully connected* topology the swarm converges quickly on the problem solution but is vulnerable to the attraction of local optima, while, with *ring* topology, it better explores the search space and is less vulnerable to the attraction of local optima. Various neighbourhood topologies have been investigated in [Kennedy, 1999; Kennedy and Mendes, 2002; Mendes et *al.*, 2004] (fig.1). The main conclusion was that the difference in performance depends on the topology implemented for a given objective function, with nothing suggesting that any topology was generally better than any other [Poli et *al.*, 2007].

If the objective function is n dimensional, the position and velocity of any particle can be represented as a vector with n components. Starting with the velocity vector, $v_p = (v_{p,1}, \ldots, v_{p,n})$, each component, $v_{p,i}$, is given by equation (4). For the position vector $x_p = (x_{p,1}, \ldots, x_{p,n})$, each component $x_{p,i}$ is given by equation (5).

$$v_{p,i}(t+1) = \omega\, v_{p,i}(t) + c_1 r_1 (p_{p,i}(t) - x_{p,i}(t)) + c_2 r_2 (g_{p,i}(t) - x_{p,i}(t)) \tag{4}$$

$$x_{p,i}(t+1) = x_{p,i}(t) + v_{p,i}(t+1) \tag{5}$$

where $x_{p,i}(t)$ is the ith component of the position of the particle i and $v_{p,i}(t)$ the ith component of its velocity; $p_{p,i}$ is the i_{th} component of the best position ever visited by the ith particle; $g_{p,I}$ is the i_{th} component of the best position ever visited by the neighbourhood of the particle; $\omega$is called inertia weight, it is used to control the impact of the previous history of velocity on the current one; r_1 and r_2 are uniformly distributed random numbers between 0 and 1; c_1 and c_2 are positive acceleration constants. The formula (4) is used for each dimension of the objective function, for each particle and synchronously at time step for all the particles of the swarm.

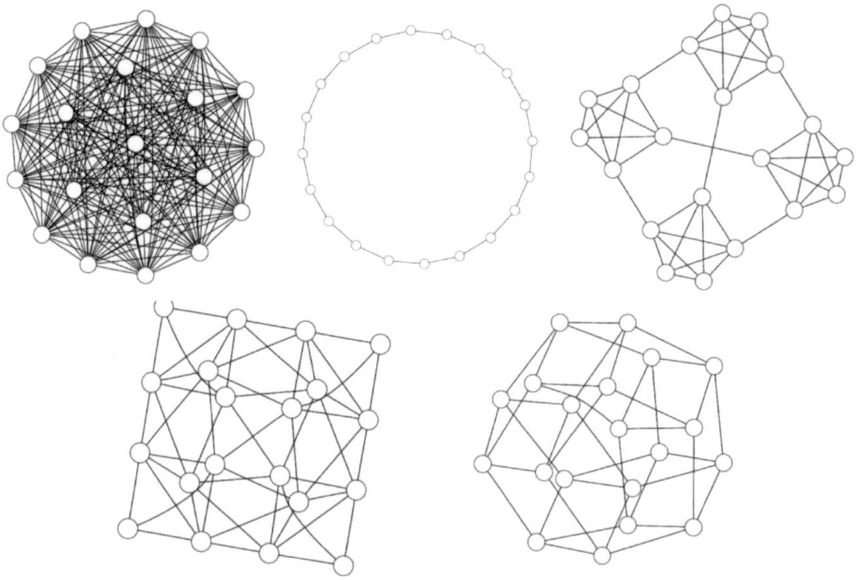

Fig. 1. Illustration of neighbourhood topologies from [Mendes et al., 2004]:
Fully connected (All), *Ring*, *Four clusters*, *Pyramid* and *Square*.

2.2 Discrete binary Particle Swarm Optimization (DPSO)

Kennedy and Eberhart (1997) have introduced a discrete binary version of PSO (DPSO) that operates on binary variables (bit, symbol or string) rather than real numbers. The difference between the PSO and DPSO definitions is in the velocity updating rules where the position updating rule $x_{p,i}(t+1)$ (7) is based on a logistic function (6). The introduction of DPSO extends the use of PSO to optimization of discrete binary functions as well as functions of continuous and discrete binary variables at the same time.

$$S(v_{p,i}(t+1)) = \frac{1}{1+e^{-v_{p,i}(t+1)}} \tag{6}$$

$$\begin{aligned} x_{p,i}(t+1) &= 1 \quad \text{if } \varphi < S(v_{p,i}(t+1)) \\ &= 0 \quad \text{otherwise} \end{aligned} \tag{7}$$

Where φ is an uniformly distributed random number between 0 and 1

Michaud et *al.* (2009), to be able to handle the optimization of functions including more than two discrete variables, have generalised the discrete binary version of PSO to a discrete *n*-ary version of PSO (8).

$$\begin{aligned} x_{p,i}(t+1) &= n_k \quad \text{if } \varphi_{k-1} < S(v_{p,i}(t+1)) \\ &= n_l \quad \text{if } \varphi_{l-1} < S(v_{p,i}(t+1)) \le \varphi_l \quad \text{with } 1 < l \le k-1 \\ &= n_1 \quad \text{if } \varphi_1 \ge S(v_{p,i}(t+1)) \end{aligned} \tag{8}$$

where φ_1, ... φ_{k-1} are strictly ordered uniformly distributed random numbers between 0 and 1

3. Application to structural problems

This section presents the results of the work carried out on a continuous beam laying on three elastic supports. A numerical code were developed using real data (synthetic data in the case of numerical analysis), a FE model of the structure as the mechanical model, and the PSO. The flowchart of the code is presented figure 2. As it was explained above, the code combined (a) a mechanical model of the structure (numerical or analytical), (b) a field data generator and (c) a particle swarm optimisation algorithm (PSO) to iteratively minimize the distance between field data and predicted data. This work had been realized on both a numerical case and at real scale case. The influence of the metrology had been studied by changing either the number of measurement data to identify the three stiffnesses, or the level of noise of sensors, or the localization of the sensors on the beam. The developed code using the PSO succeeds to estimate the stiffnesses with accuracy according the different sources of errors taking into account during the experiences. More synthetic experiences were carried out to identify the different sources of errors by using this code that can impact the accuracy of the identification process as:

- error from the accuracy of location sensors,
- error from the sensors placements,
- error from the optimization algorithm used during the identification process,
- the sensitivity of the unknown parameters to the field data.

Both numerical and real experiences were carried out to validate the methodology and to highlight the influence of the input data (here displacements data) on the quality of identification. A general numerical frame was developed, combining different tools and methods (inverse analysis, FEM, PSO). The efficiency in terms of CPU time of the PSO to converge towards the solution of the problem allows the integration of a FE model of the structure without any problem. A second part of this work focussed on the different sources of error that may alter the accuracy of the parameters identification process. It is shown on two structures, a continuous beam bearing on three elastic supports, cf. fig. 3, and a half frame structure, cf. fig. 4, that four points strongly impact the parameter identification. Several experiences were carried out, considering different metrology set, i.e. by modifying either the number of sensors, or their accuracy or their location on the structure. Several recommendations are mentioned to help engineers to prepare as best as possible their metrology set in order to do an identification of parameters using the inverse analyse concept with the PSO.

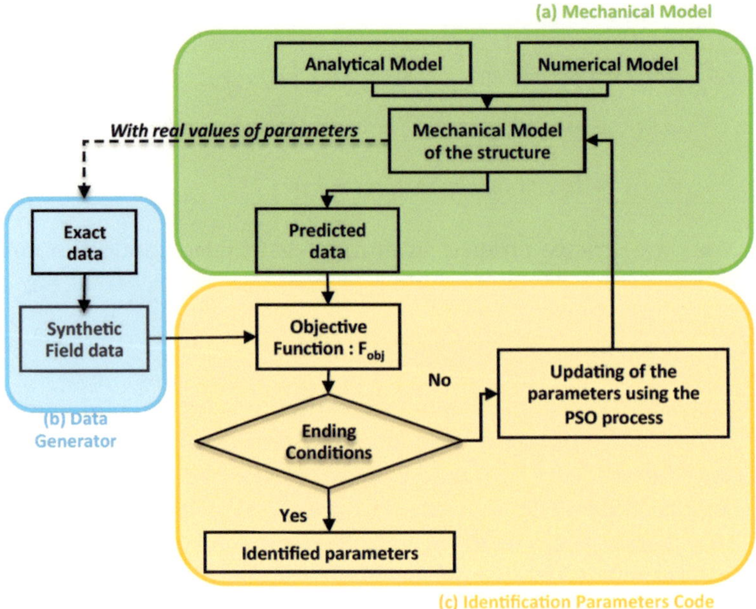

Fig. 2. Flowchart of code based on the concept of the inverse analysis.

3.1 Framework and objectives of both synthetic and real experiences

Concerning numerical experience, the following work relies on either numerical model using the finite element (FE) software Castem©, or analytical model. This means that "field data" are also fully synthetic. In order to reproduce what happens on field data with real sensors, introducing some noise disturbs the original "true" values that are first generated, using a controlled random process. The result is then synthetic "noised" data at each location where a sensor can be located. It is from these "noised" data that the inversion process is carried out. The main advantage of the synthetic simulation is that, the "true" values being also known, it is always possible to quantify the quality of the estimation (i.e. distance between "true" and estimated values), making possible detailed analysis of errors sources. Using exact data u_{exact} obtained from the mechanical model and a random coefficient β generates the synthetic field data, u_{insitu}, cf. Equation10. This coefficient models the magnitude of the error of measurement, which depends on the accuracy of the sensors. It is assumed to be normally distributed with a zero mean, and a given standard error ε (the various values of ε are: 0% or 1% or 3% or 5%), cf. Equation9 that simulates sensors of different quality. Those errors should cover all the sources of errors and uncertainties concerning the measurement process either due to the device, or to the other causes (environmental conditions, electronic noise, etc.). The errors arising on different sensors are assumed to be uncorrelated. As soon as ε exist, it is impossible for F_{obj} to converge towards zero [Fontan et *al.*, 2011].

$$u_{insitu} = u_{exact} * (1+ \beta) \quad (9)$$

$$\beta = N(0, \varepsilon) \quad (10)$$

The real experience was carried out on a quite similar structure with the numerical model of the beam bearing a three elastic support. The main difference is due to the integration of several components so as to model the effect of the soil structure interaction. These structures are described section 3.1.1.

3.1.1 Presentation of the studied structures

The first numerical example is that of a continuous beam bearing on three elastic supports, cf. fig. 3 and named STR1. It models a wooden beam bearing on three elastic supports, with two equal spans L_i = 1.35 m which has also been the support of a "physical experience" in the same research program, not detailed here [Hasançebi et *al.*, 2009 and Li et *al.*, 2009]. The section is a square 7.50 x 7.50 cm^2. The beam is assumed to be homogenous and the Young's modulus is equal to 10 GPa. A 50 daN/m load is uniformly distributed all along the beam. The parameters that must be identified from the measurements are the stiffnesses of the three elastic bearings (modelled as Winkler springs), whose true values (known in this synthetic model) are respectively: k_1 = 28726 daN/m, k_2 = 9575 daN/m, k_3 = 2209 daN/m. The true values of the support stiffnesses result in a large settlement on the third bearing (bearing 1 is the stiffer and bearing 3 is the softer). Ten measurements of displacement were extracted to generate the synthetic field data. The abscissas of those ten displacements are given Table 1. Four metrology sets, called CM_i are given at Table 1. Those metrology sets are created to stress either the number of sensors, or their localisation on the beam for a same number. This first example will be used in order to study the influence of the number, accuracy or localisation of the sensors on the accuracy of the parameters identification.

The second numerical structure is a half frame, cf. fig. 4., named STR2. The column is embedded at its foot whereas the beam is articulated. The beam is 4.00m long and the column is 5.00 m high (H). The section of the beam is an IPE270, (inertia I_{beam}= 5790 cm^4) and the column is a HEA340 (inertia I_{column}= 27700 cm^4). The beam and the column are made of standard steel (Young modulus E = 210 GPa). A distributed load q = 500 daN/m, is vertically applied on the beam whereas a horizontal concentrated load (F_{lat} = equals 1000 daN) which is applied on the column at its two thirds. The parameters to identify are the flexural stiffnesses of the beam EI_{beam} and of the column EI_{column}. The metrology set is made of six displacements sensors. Three sensors are evenly distributed on the beam and the others on the column, cf. fig. 4. The analytical relationships giving the displacements for each sensor have been explicated as functions of E, I_{beam}, I_{column}, q, F_{lat}, L and H using the beam theory.

Concerning the real experience, cf. fig. 5, a continuous wooden beam of 3.00 m long is bearing on three different supports (*Pinus pinaster*, square section 7.50x7.50 cm2, Young's modulus equals 10 GPa). This structure is named STR3. The distance between supports is 1.35 m. Each support is made of a transverse beam, or Secondary Beam, SB. Varying the span of the SB comes to vary the support stiffness. Each SB lies on a wooden plate, which relies on its four sides on a fully rigid concrete support. This physical model reproduces the main patterns of a bridge deck (the continuous beam) bearing on foundations (the beams

SB) lying on a deformable soil mass (here modelled by the wooden plate). This three-component system has some complexity, typical of the soil-structure interaction:

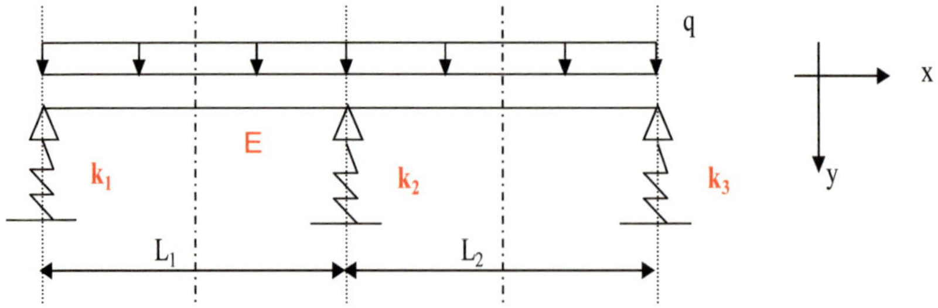

Fig. 3. Continuous beams bearing on three elastics supports with a distributed load, k_i and E_i are the unknown parameters.

Metrology set	x1 = 0.00	x2 = 0.45	x3 = 0.65	x4 = 0.90	x5 = 1.30	x6 = 1.35	x7 = 1.40	x8 = 1.80	x9 = 2.25	x10 = 2.70
CM1	o	o	o	o	o	o	o	o	o	o
CM2		o			o					
CM3	o				o					o
CM4		o	o	o						

Abscissa (m) of the used sensors function to the metrology set

(shaded) Abscissa of a sensor positioned at the abscissa of an elastic support

o Used sensor for a metrology set

Table 1. Positions of sensors used during the identification process function to the metrology set.

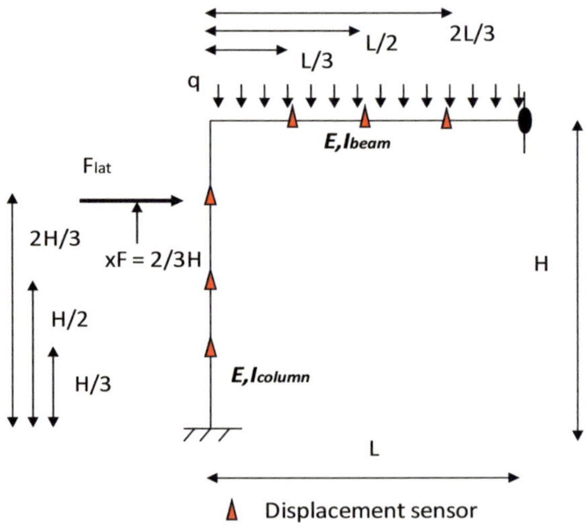

Fig. 4. Half truss structure with its loads; EI_{beam} and EI_{column} are the unknown parameters.

Fig. 5. Experimental device reproducing the soil-structure interaction for a two-span continuous beam.

a. the supports of the SB can move, because of the loading and the flexibility of the plate support,
b. because the supports of the primary beam are not rigid, the value of the external load transferred to each of these three supports depends on their stiffness (i.e. of their displacement.

3.1.2 Presentation of the objectives to reach by experience

Two kinds of numerical structures and one real structure have been studied to reach several objectives and to highlight several points: firstly, the feasibility of the identification process using the PSO as an efficient tool and, secondly to clearly identify the sources of errors which occur during an identification process.

The real experiment, applied on STR3, focused on the identification of mechanical parameters and studied the impact of the localisation of used sensors. Indeed, the goal of the numerical experiments was to study the influence of:

- the noise induced by the meta-heuristic algorithm applied on STR1,
- the noise measurement applied on STR1,
- the impact of the interaction of the parameters to identify applied on STR2.

For each numerical experiment, the identification process is repeated 20 times. Those simulations are using 20 sets of noise data as it is explained in the following section. The average of the identified parameters (20 values per parameter per experiment), their standard deviation and their coefficient of variation (CV) are calculated. The ending conditions of the identification process are either (a) the maximum number of iterations is fixed at 35, it has been shown in [Fontan et *al.*, 2011] that increasing the number of iterations is not efficient in terms of gain about the F_{objec} in this case, or (b) the threshold of the F_{objec} is fixed at 10^{-5}. As soon as the F_{objec} value is below this threshold, the identification process automatically stops.

3.2 Results of the identification process: real experience

The real experimental tests use three different support sets so that the length of the SB are the following according the three configurations studied:

- configuration 1 : l_{SB1} = 0.50m, l_{SB2} = 0.50m and l_{SB3} = 0.50m,
- configuration 2 : l_{SB1} = 0.30m, l_{SB2} = 0.90m and l_{SB3} = 1.30m,
- configuration 3 : l_{SB1} = 0.20m, l_{SB2} = 0.50m and l_{SB3} = 1.30m,

A 3D finite element model, 3DFEM, presents the global experience fig. 6. This 3DFEM helps to estimate the equivalent stiffnesses of the elastic support of the main beam considering the association of the stiffnesses of the SB and the plate as a Winkler spring of which stiffness by support is unknown. The fig. 7 gives the displacements measured during the experimental tests for each support set (illustrated by the points), whereas the displacements obtained with 3DFEM for each support set is illustrated by the continuous curve. The good correlation between measurements and simulations confirms the good quality of the 3DFEM model and justifies both a priory estimation of the equivalent stiffness by support and the limits of the space research using for the PSO.

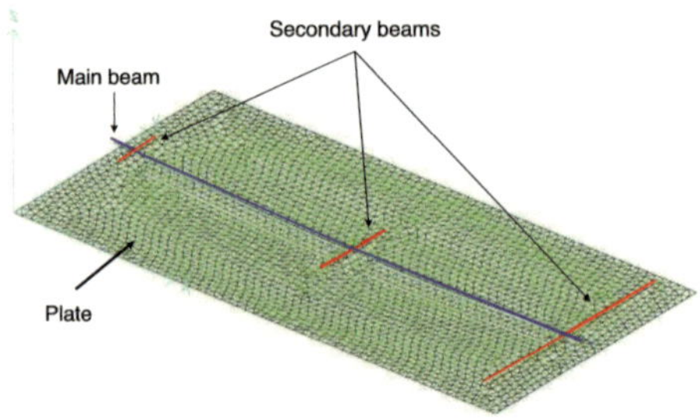

Fig. 6. FE model of the physical model with the main beam bearing on SB and the wood plate.

Then, it was possible to constrain the research domain for the equivalent stiffnesses k_i between 0 and 2 MN/m. The physical model is used with the distributed load and for the three configuration of support sets defined above. The vertical displacements are measured on all sensors. Thus the IdP software is used, where the PSO is combined to a 2DFEM mechanical model presented fig. 8. So as to analyse the influence of the number and location of sensors, the efficiency of the identification process is compared by considering three possible sensor sets:

- Set A: three sensors (n°1, n°5 and n°9, cf. Table 2), located on the three supports,
- Set B: ten sensors (n°1 to n°10, cf. Table 2) regularly spaced all along the beam,
- Set C: three sensors (n°3, n°5 and n°7, cf. Table 2), concentrated in the left span.

The value of the objective function at convergence (well above 10^{-12}) is due to the measurement noise. The stiffnesses presented in Tables 3–5 are identified by the software for the three respective sensor sets (A, B and C). For each support set, each Table compares, for the three supports sets, identified values with "reference values" obtained with the 3DFEM (Av. means average and s.d. means standard deviation). The identification process (PSO combined with the mechanical model) was repeated ten times for each case (support set x sensor set), keeping the same input data (measurements). Since the PSO has some random dimension, the values obtained as a final solution differ from one simulation to another.

The tables provide the average value and the standard deviation calculated from these 10 simulations. Let us consider first the results obtained for sensor set B (using data from all 10 sensors for inversion). All simulations converge towards similar values, leading to a small standard deviation. In addition, the identified values are close to the "reference values", which confirms the ability of the process to correctly identify the unknown parameters. The small difference between reference and identified values is not a problem when one reminds that the former cannot be considered as the "true" solution (it is only a good indicator of the range of the true solution). These results confirm the efficiency of the identification process. When comparing the results of Table 4 with those of Table 5, it can be seen that the sensor sets A and B lead to almost the same results. This shows that using three well-located sensors can be sufficient. It is not the case for Set C, which shows some limits for identifying the stiffnesses on external supports 1 and 3. This confirms, on a practical application, that the location of sensors has a high influence on the quality of the identification.

	x1	x2	x3	x4	x5	x6	x7	x8	x9	x10
Abscissa (m)	0.015	0.15	0.60	0.91	1.05	1.58	1.94	2.40	2.90	3.00

Table 2. Abscissa of the sensors used during the real experience.

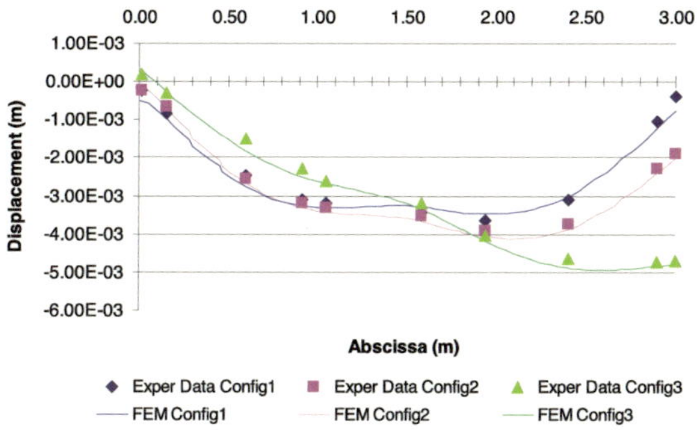

Fig. 7. Experimental displacements measured and obtained by 3D-FEM for the different support sets.

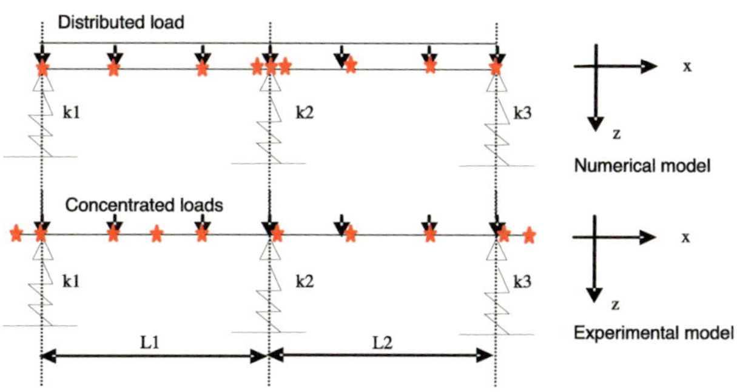

Fig. 8. Localisation of the sensors used in both numerical and physical models.

	Identified stiffness'						3D FEM		
	k_1 (MN/m)		k_2 (MN/m)		k_3 (MN/m)		k_1	k_2	k_3
	Av.	s.d.	Av.	s.d.	Av.	s.d.	(MN/m)	(MN/m)	(MN/m)
Support set 1	2.586	0.08	0.372	0.02	0.792	0.02	0.652	0.405	0.600
Support set 2	1.874	0.09	0.346	0.01	0.162	0.01	1.521	0.366	0.214
Support set 3	1.799	0.08	0.429	0.04	0.073	0.01	1.455	0.419	0.092

Table 3. Identified equivalent stiffnesses using sensors from set C.

	Identified stiffness'						3D FEM		
	k_1 (MN/m)		k_2 (MN/m)		k_3 (MN/m)		k_1	k_2	k3
	Av.	s.d.	Av.	s.d.	Av.	s.d.	(MN/m)	(MN/m)	(MN/m)
Support set 1	0.726	0.05	0.401	0.02	0.681	0.02	0.652	0.405	0.600
Support set 2	1.549	0.06	0.371	0.01	0.251	0.03	1.521	0.366	0.214
Support set 3	1.372	0.06	0.449	0.03	0.089	0.00	1.455	0.419	0.092

Table 4. Identified equivalent stiffnesses using sensors from set A.

	Identified stiffness'						3D FEM		
	k_1 (MN/m)		k_2 (MN/m)		k_3 (MN/m)		k_1	k_2	k3
	Av.	s.d.	Av.	s.d.	Av.	s.d.	(MN/m)	(MN/m)	(MN/m)
Support set 1	0.689	0.00	0.398	0.00	0.721	0.00	0.652	0.405	0.600
Support set 2	1.602	0.00	0.381	0.00	0.198	0.00	1.521	0.366	0.214
Support set 3	1.333	0.04	0.433	0.02	0.089	0.02	1.455	0.419	0.092

Table 5. Identified equivalent stiffnesses using sensors from set B.

3.3 Sources of errors impacting the accuracy of the identification process: Synthetic experience

Concerning synthetic experience, the following works relies on either numerical using the finite element (FE) software Castem©, or analytical model.

3.3.1 Error from the meta-heuristic algorithm

Twenty identification processes were carried out without any noise applied on field data (i.e. considering perfect measurements). These tests were applied on structure 1 or STR1 using the CM_1 metrology set, cf. Table 1. This case corresponds to a perfect case with a high number of sensors, evenly distributed and no measurement error. The convergence curve of the best particle of the swarm is presented Figure 9 for one simulation. The three elastic stiffnesses were correctly identified but the identified parameters show slight variations for each of the 20 simulations. The results are presented in Table 6.

		Results of the identification		
	Reference	Average	Standard Dev.	C.V.
k_1 (daN/m)	28726.2	28725.67	31.92	1.11E-03
k_2 (daN/m)	9575.2	9574.64	2.68	2.80E-04
k_3 (daN/m)	2209.7	2209.67	5.41	2.45E-03

Table 6. Statistical analysis of the identified parameters using exact field data, structure 1, metrology set CM_1.

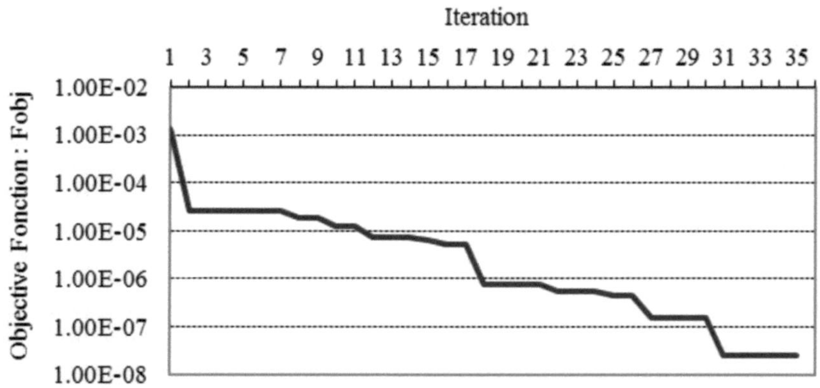

Fig. 9. Convergence curve of F_{objec} during an IdP process using exact field data.

The average value of each unknown parameter is very close to the reference but the standard deviation in not zero, which means that all solutions are not identical, even in this perfect case. Some scatter due to the meta-heuristic algorithm affects the identification process. However this scatter remains small. In real cases, it will be overshadowed by other error sources that will be studied now.

3.3.2 Sensors with measurement noise

In this section, the three elastic stiffnesses are identified on structure 1, STR1, using the metrology set CM_1. The objective is to show how noisy data impact the accuracy of the predicted parameters. Several values of ε (1%, 3% and 5%) were used to noise the field data. 20 identification processes with a different noise for each identification were carried out. The results are given in Table 7. The average, standard deviation and coefficient of variation C.V. illustrate the impact of noise on the accuracy of the processes. The larger the ε coefficient is, the wider the scatter appears to be coherent. It can be also noticed that a random noise from a normal distribution with a zero mean, and a varying standard error ε = 5% does not impact so much the prediction of the identified parameters: the error on the average of 20 simulations is about 1% and the C.V. is between 1 and 7% for this metrology set made of 10 sensors evenly distributed. The loss of accuracy is linear with the standard deviation of the random error, cf. table 7 and figure10. The accuracy of the predicted parameters is linearly correlated with the accuracy of the sensors.

	Noise ε	Reference	Results of the identification: Average	Error on average (%)	Standard Dev.	C.V.
k_1 (daN/m)	1%	28726.2	28769.23	0.15	379.97	1.32E-02
k_2 (daN/m)	1%	9575.2	9604.43	0.31	78.43	8.17E-03
k_3 (daN/m)	1%	2209.7	2206.21	-0.16	26.6	1.21E-02
k_1 (daN/m)	3%	28726.2	28960.58	0.82	972.11	3.36E-02
k_2 (daN/m)	3%	9575.2	9599.53	0.25	174.73	1.82E-02
k_3 (daN/m)	3%	2209.7	2204.8	-0.22	87.36	3.96E-02
k_1 (daN/m)	5%	28726.2	28593.17	-0.46	1421.14	4.97E-02
k_2 (daN/m)	5%	9575.2	9618.48	0.45	366.62	3.81E-02
k_3 (daN/m)	5%	2209.7	2226.67	0.77	143.67	6.45E-02

Table 7. Statistical analysis of the identified parameters using noised field data, structure 1, metrology set CM_1.

3.3.3 Dependence between unknown parameters

The studied structure is here the structure 2, STR2, i.e. the half truss structure presented at section 3.1.1. Let us assume that one must identify the Young Modulus E, the inertia of the column I_{column} and the inertia of the beam, I_{beam}. Four different levels of noise on field data (ε = 0% (perfect data), then ε = 1%, 3% and 5%) are considered and simulations are repeated 20 times. The results are presented in Figures 11and 12and Table 8.The first result is that one obtains a front of solutions, since it is not possible to uncouple the weight of E from that of inertia: for the same product EI_i, there exists an infinite number of acceptable pairs $\{E, I_i = (EI_i)/E = k/E\}$ satisfying the same criteria. In order to estimate the sensitivity of the identified parameters to the field data, the sensibility of the displacement to stiffnesses was calculated. EI_{column} or EI_{beam} are varied in the [-50%; +50%] range and the displacement is calculated on 3 points of the beam, and on three points of the column, cf. fig. 4. Only displacements perpendicular to the main axis of the element are calculated.

	Exact field data: Average (MN.m²)	Standard Dev. (MN.m²)	C.V.		Noisy field data with ε = 1%: Average (MNm²)	Standard Dev. (MN.m²)	C.V.
EI_{beam}	12.16	0.01	5.87E-04	EI_{beam}	12.18	0.1	7.85E-03
EI_{column}	58.15	0.1	1.76E-03	EI_{column}	59.34	4.81	8.11E-02
	Noisy field data with ε = 3%: Average (MN.m²)	**Standard Dev. (MN.m²)**	**C.V.**		**Noisy field data with ε = 5%: Average (MN.m²)**	**Standard Dev. (MN.m²)**	**C.V.**
EI_{beam}	12.25	0.21	1.75E-02	EI_{beam}	12.11	0.29	2.38E-02
EI_{column}	61.96	8.4	1.36E-01	EI_{column}	57.53	8.27	1.44E-01

Table 8. Statistical analysis of the identified parameters using noised field data, structure 3.

The results confirm that only some field data are sensitive to the stiffness variations. The stiffness variation of the column inertia (reversely beam) has only a negligible influence on beam (reversely column) displacements. Thus, during the identification process, the magnitude of the errors on sensors localized on the beam will not impact the column because a lack of sensibility, and reversely. A more detailed analysis Table 9 shows that sensitivity of column displacement to column parameters is slightly larger than the same for the beam. The sensitivity has been calculated as the ratio between the variation of the displacements at the studied point with the variation of the stiffness. Those results show that the displacements of the column are more sensitive to a variation of the stiffness of the column that for the beam and explain why the scatter of the identified stiffnesses EI_{column}fig.12 is more important that the scatter of the identified stiffnesses EI_{beam}. Indeed,

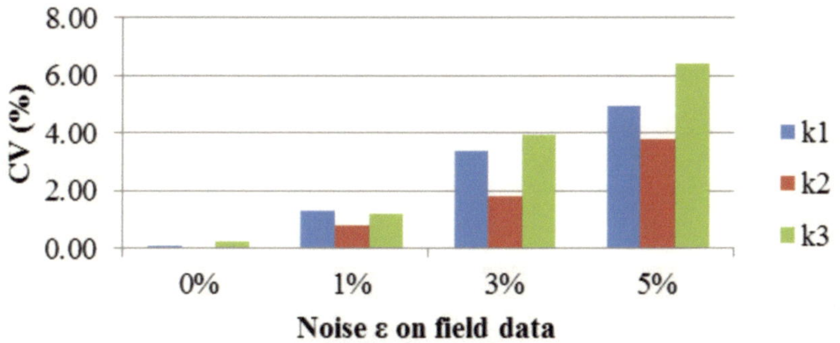

Fig. 10. Illustration of the noise on field data and the dispersion of identified parameters k_i, Structure 1, CM_1.

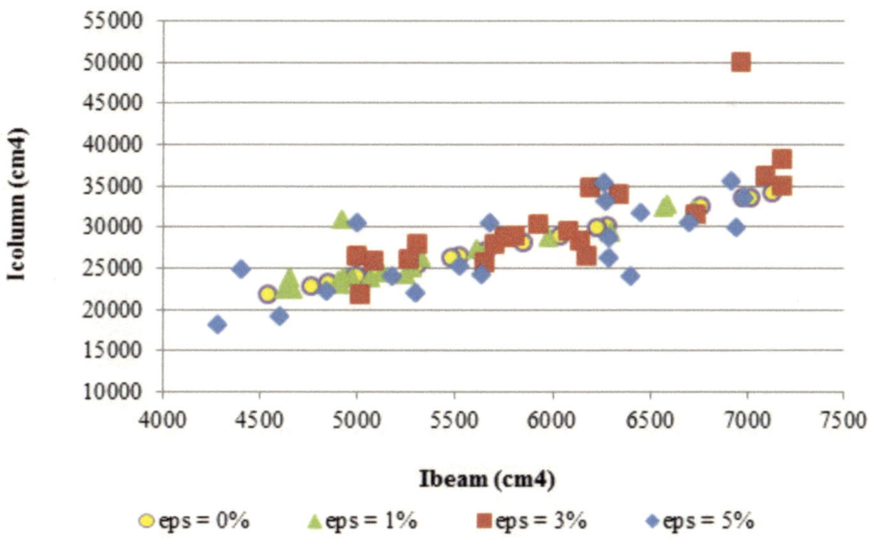

Fig. 11. I_{beam} and I_{column} identified for varying magnitude of noise on field data, applied on the half truss structure

when field data on the column are noised, the inertia of the column to identified have to be badly identified from the reference value regards the magnitude of the noise. That result focuses how chosen of both the nature and the localisation of the field data regards the parameters to identified is important on the accuracy of the identification process.

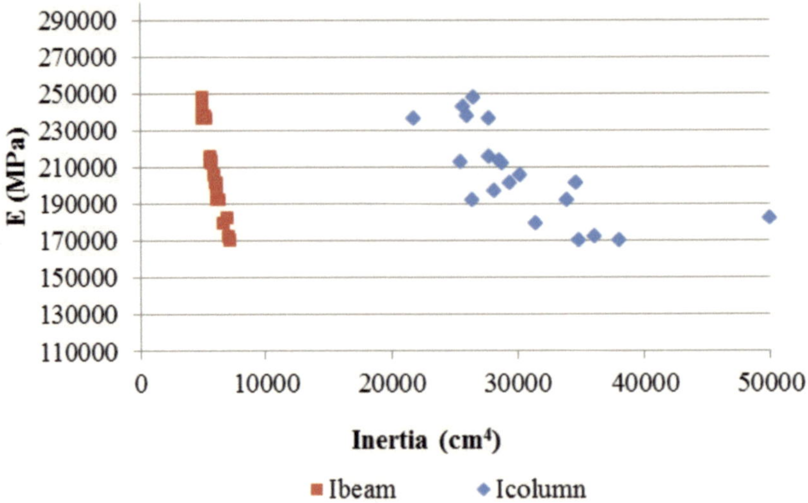

Fig. 12. Inertia and Young Modulus identified, structure 2, noised with $\varepsilon = 3\%$.

	$u_{column1}$	$u_{column2}$	$u_{column3}$	u_{beam1}	u_{beam2}	u_{beam3}
Variation of the stiffness EI_{column}	-2,09	-2,09	-2,09	-0,04	-0,03	-0,02
Variation of the stiffness EI_{beam}	0,21	0,24	0,31	-1,80	-1,87	-1,90

Table 9. Sensitivity of the displacement on several points of the structure to the variation of the stiffnesses.

4. Application to eco conception

Taking into account environmental impact criteria in the preliminary eco-design of semi-products or of full functional units is becoming more and more an issue for industry. It implies going through a life cycle analysis (LCA) that is now the international standard to evaluate such impacts. It is in fact the only way to compare the environmental impact of different products that fulfil the same function; and this, from the production of raw materials to the final destination. The fact that it is necessary to know the life cycle of a product makes it difficult to use the LCA during the preliminary eco-design stage. One way to tackle the problem would be to focus on one of the stages of the life cycle of the product and to consider it as independent from the other stages.

The design process will be different if we are trying to: i) improve the environmental characteristics of a product while disturbing as little as possible its production process, ii) optimize the environmental impact of a product defined by end-use performances without restricting oneself to a particular process. The first case, frequent with manufacturers, being guided by the manufacturing process, can make it impossible to meet both the technical and the environmental requirements in a given manufacturing scheme. The second approach, which is more prospective and open, is guided by the end-use properties that are required, and therefore can be tackled either in seeking an environmental optimum in a search space that is constrained by functional specifications or through a multi-objective optimization.

The second approach is closer to conventional preliminary design. However, as multi-objective optimization does not provide a single solution, but a set of possible solutions satisfying the design criteria among which the designer will be able to choose according to additional constraints, both approaches will be considered as preliminary (eco) design.

The example that is presented here concerns the preliminary design of an outdoor decking taking into account its environmental profile (first approach). The initial choice was of a wood-plastic composite, this choice allowing the use of industrial by-products in a constrained search space. The optimum of the required properties will be obtained by multi-objective optimization.

4.1 A multi-objective optimization problem

Design by multi-objective optimization implies simultaneous optimization of various contradictory objectives like it is illustrated below.

If we take a simple example consisting in minimizing simultaneously the two following functions: $f_1(x) = x_1$ and $f_2(x) = x_2/ax_1$, the improvement of the first objective, $f_1(x)$, comes with a degradation of the second objective $f_2(x)$). This contradiction expresses the fact that there does not exist an optimal solution regarding the two objectives, there are only optimal compromises.

With this example we see that for a minimal f_1 and thus x_1 the lowest possible, we need the lowest possible x_2 to minimize f_2. In addition, the absolute minimum f_2 is obtained with x_1 the highest possible and x_2 the lowest possible. It is the taking into account of this contradiction between minimization of f_1 and minimization of f_2 that introduces the notion of compromise whether one favours f_1 or f_2. We see that from a purely algebraic point of view x_1 cannot be null (division by zero). This observation introduces the fact that there is often a certain amount of constraints that must be met by the objective functions and/or their variables. These are also called parameters, optimization variables or design variables. The constraints that are specifications of the problem limit the search spaces of the parameters and/or the determining, for example, bottom or top values. A general multi-objective optimization problem includes a set of k objective functions of n decision variables (parameters) constrained by a set of m constraint functions. It can be defined as below:

Optimize $\vec{f} = \left[f_1(\vec{x}), f_2(\vec{x}), \rightleftharpoons, f_k(\vec{x})\right]$

subject to $g_i(\vec{x}) \leq 0 \quad for \quad i = 1, \rightleftharpoons, m$and $h_j(\vec{x}) = 0 \quad for \quad j = p+1, \rightleftharpoons, p$

where $\vec{x} = (x_1, x_2, \rightleftharpoons, x_n) \in \Re^n$ is the vector of decision variables,

$f_i : \Re^n \rightarrow \Re \; for \;\; i = 1, \rightleftharpoons, k$ are the objective functions and

$g_i, h_j : \Re^n \rightarrow \Re \; for \; i = 1, \rightleftharpoons, m \; and \; j = 1, \rightleftharpoons, p$ are the constraint functions of the problem

A compromise will be said optimal if every improvement of an objective induces degradation of another objective. A compromise whose objectives can be improved is not optimal. It is said to be dominated by at least another compromise, which is the one obtained after improvement of its objective functions. The optimal compromises are located on a front, named Pareto front (fig.13). The Pareto Dominance can be defined as below:

$\vec{u}=(u_1,\rightleftharpoons,u_n)$ is said to dominate $\vec{v}=(v_1,\rightleftharpoons,v_n)$ (denoted $\vec{u}\prec\vec{v}$) if and only if $\forall i\in\{1,\rightleftharpoons,k\},u_i\le v_i\ and\ \exists j\in\{1,\rightleftharpoons,k\},u_j<v_j$

A solution is Pareto optimal if and only if it is not dominated by any other solution [Van Veldhuizen et *al.*, 2000; Reyes-Sierra et *al.*, 2006 ; Zitzler et *al.*, 2000]. A Pareto optimal solution, a vector of decision variables $\vec{x}=(x_1,x_2,\rightleftharpoons,x_n)\in\Re^n$, can be defined as below [Castéra et *al.*, 2010]:

$$\exists\vec{x}\in\Re^n\wedge\nexists\vec{x}'\in\Re^n:\forall q\in\{1,\rightleftharpoons,k\},f_q(\vec{x}')\le f_q(\vec{x})\ \wedge\ f_q(\vec{x}')<f_q(\vec{x}) \qquad (11)$$

The presence of a Pareto front, thus a set of optimal non-equivalent solutions, allows the choice of an optimal solution with regard to economical of functional criteria, which are external to the solved problem of multi-objective optimization.

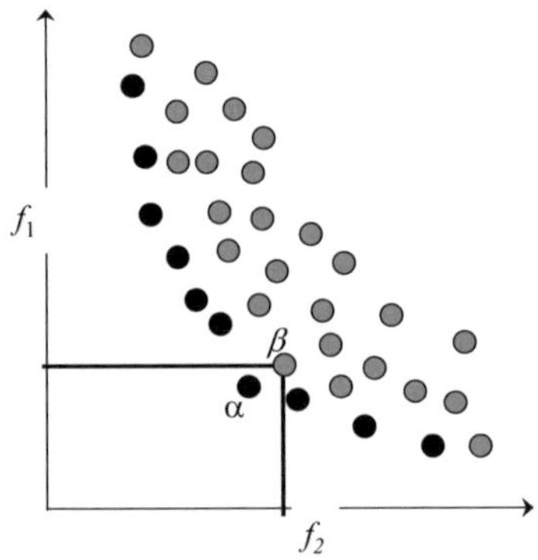

Fig. 13. The Pareto front is constituted by the plain dots, the objective functions f_1 and f_2 at point β can still be improved to reach point α; therefore point β is dominated by at least point α.

We will illustrate the multi-objective particle swarm optimization for the design of a wood-plastic composite decking with three objectives [Michaud et *al*, 2009]. In this example, the optimization focuses on the creep, swelling, and exhaustion of abiotic resources functions. The design variables are mainly characteristics of raw materials such as timber particle sizes and chemical or thermal timber changes.

5. The wood-plastic composite preliminary eco-design problem

The wood-plastic composites (WPC) initially developed in North America for recycling materials - plastics and papers - they also enable a significant reduction of the plastic coming from the petrochemical industry. There is thus in their development both a definite economic advantage and a potential environmental interest. Nevertheless when decking is used outdoor, these products exhibit a certain amount of weakness points and contradictions: in order to allow a homogeneous extrusion and to prevent the material from becoming too fragile, a minimal quantity of thermoplastic (about 30 percent in the case of a PEHD/wood composite) is necessary. In addition, chemical additives are included in the formula in order to improve compatibility between the two components; one being polar and the other apolar.

The WPC preliminary eco-design requires first that the designer solves a multi-objective optimization problem. Usually one of the three strategies below is used:

- optimization of one objective with constraints from the others, which leads to a single solution;
- optimization of a weighted function including the different objectives, which leads to a single solution;
- Pareto optimization, which leads to a set of optimal compromises between the objectives that is well distributed in the space of solutions.

The population based search approaches- genetic algorithm (GA), ant colony (AC), particle swarm optimization (PSO), etc…- are well adapted to the Pareto optimization with more or less efficiency. The PSO technique, like other evolutionary techniques, finds optima in complex optimization problems. Like GA, the system is initialized with a population and searches for optima by updating generations. However, unlike GA, PSO has no evolution operators such as crossover and mutation. PSO while traversing the search space is focused on the optimum, whereas GA explores the search space and then takes more time to find the optimum. In the WPC preliminary eco-design the main objective is to find the relevant optima to be able to choice an optimum with regard to economical of functional criteria; knowing that completely different composite formulations lead to equivalent composites in reference to the objective functions. Multi-objective PSO technique is specially and fully suitable for this problem.

5.1 The wood-plastic composite preliminary eco-design modelling

The modelling of WPC for decking application preliminary eco-design has required a multidisciplinary team (physicists and computer scientists). The modelling process consisted in: generating knowledge by some experiments, collecting knowledge generated and those from the literature and building up the influence graphs of relationships between the problem variables (fig.14). The three objectives considered in the preliminary eco-design of wood-plastic composite (creep, swelling and exhaustion of fossil resources functions) have been identified as critical weak points of the product [Michaud et *al.*, 2009]. From an environmental point of view, exhaustion of fossil resources is, with the greenhouse effect, the weak point of this material. We will recall their definition in order to highlight the algorithmic nature of these functions.

The creep function (*def*)

The creep function, $def(t_{ref})$, is an empirical non linear power function that has been fitted to bending experimental results. The magnitude of creep deformation is related to the elastic compliance $1/E$. The kinetics of creep deformation is related to the viscosity of the composite, ν. The fiber size distribution parameter k_{GRAN} used in equation (13) is a discrete variable that can take three different values between 0.3 (random) and 1 (unidirectional)

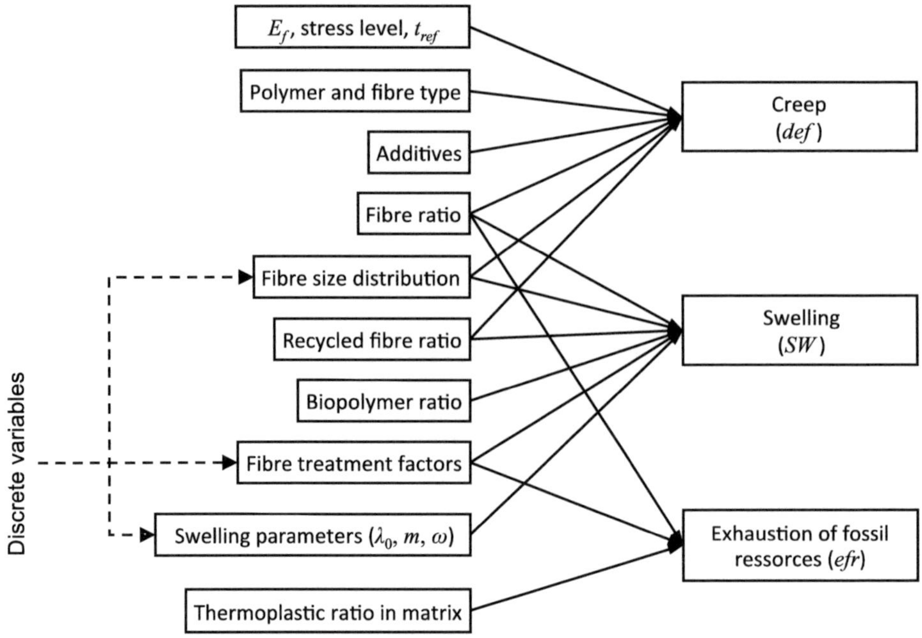

Fig. 14. The influence graph of relationships between the decision variables and the objectives.

with an intermediate value calculated at 0.69 (partially oriented) – see Michaud *et* al, *op.cit.*, whereas the other variables used in the equations (12), (13) and (14) are continuous. In fact the *def* function (equation 12), in its developed formula has an algorithm form due to the conditions on the discrete k_{GRAN}.

$$def(t_{ref}) = \frac{A\left(\frac{\sigma_0}{\sigma_{MOR}}\right) \cdot t_{ref}^{\;\frac{N \cdot e^{\left(\frac{\sigma_0}{\sigma_{MOR}}\right)}}{\nu}}}{E} \tag{12}$$

Where A and N are fitted parameters of the creep function model, σ_0 is applied stress, σ_{MOR} is modulus of rupture of the composite material, t_{ref} is the time to reach a limit state deflection, E is the modulus of elasticity and ν is the apparent viscosity of the composite at room temperature. E and ν are calculated through a simple mixture law, as shown in equations (13) and (14). These equations reveal the main optimization variables, *i.e.* material properties, volume fractions and fibre orientation.

$$E = \lambda_m(\alpha_{bio}E_{bio} + (1-\alpha_{bio}-\alpha_{add})E_m) + \lambda_{add}E_{add} + (k_{GRAN}).(1-\lambda_m-\lambda_{add})E_f \tag{13}$$

$$\nu = \lambda_m(\alpha_{bio}\nu_{bio} + (1-\alpha_{bio})\nu_m) + \lambda_{add}\nu_{add} + (1-\lambda_m-\lambda_{add})\nu_f \tag{14}$$

see table 10 for the meaning of other variables.

x_j	Description	Main relations
$x_1 = \lambda_f$	Fiber ratio in composite formulation	$0 \leq x_1 \leq 1$ and $x_1 = x_1 (x_4 + x_5 + x_6)$
$x_2 = \lambda_{add}$	Additives ratio in composite formulation	$0 \leq x_2 \leq 1$
$x_3 = \lambda_m$	Matrix ratio in composite formulation	$0 \leq x_3 \leq 1$, $x_3 = 1 - x_1 - x_2$ and $x_3 = x_3 (x_7 + x_8 + x_9)$
$x_4 = \alpha_f$	Fiber ratio in Fiber component	$0 \leq x_4 \leq 1$ and $x_4 + x_5 + x_6 = 1$
$x_5 = \alpha_{frec}$	Recycled Fiber ratio in Fiber component	$0 \leq x_5 \leq 1$
$x_6 = \alpha_{reinf}$	Other reinforcement ratio in Fiber component	$0 \leq x_6 \leq 1$
$x_7 = \alpha_m$	Thermoplastic ratio in matrix component	$0 \leq x_7 \leq 1$ and $x_7 + x_8 + x_9 = 1$
$x_8 = \alpha_{bio}$	Biopolymer ratio in matrix component	$0 \leq x_8 \leq 1$
$x_9 = \alpha_{trec}$	Recycled thermoplastic ratio in matrix	$0 \leq x_9 \leq 1$
x_{10} = gran	Fiber size distribution factor	discrete variable $x_{10} = \{1, 2, 3\}$
$x_{11} = k_t$	Fiber treatment factor	discrete variable $x_{11} = \{0, 1, 2, 3\}$
x_{12}	Viscoelastic properties of constituents	E, n

Table 10. Variables $X = \{x_1, x_2, \ldots, x_{12}\}$ related to the composite formulation.

Water swelling function (*SW*)

The swelling function due to water absorption, *SW*, is defined by equation (15). It expresses the fact that the swelling of the composite is the sum of the swelling deformations of all hygroscopic components present in the composite and accessible to water, *e.g.* wood, biopolymers…. The part representing the swelling of the fibres vanishes when the fibres are not accessible to water (below a given percolation threshold λ_0). In addition the swelling capacity of wood fibres can be changed by thermal or chemical wood modification, which is expressed in equation (15) by the discrete variable k_t that can take three different values (low, medium or high effect). The *SW* function is also an algorithm: there are conditions on the discrete variables (k_t, m and ω) and on the threshold variable λ_0.

$$\begin{aligned} SW &= (1-\alpha_{f_{rec}}(1-k_{fr}))k_t(1-e^{-m.\lambda_f^{\omega+1}})\lambda_f SW_f + \alpha_{bio}\lambda_m SW_m \quad \text{if } \lambda_f + \alpha_{bio}\lambda_m \geq \lambda_0 \\ &= \alpha_{bio}\lambda_m SW_m \quad \text{otherwise} \end{aligned} \tag{15}$$

where

λ_0 is the percolation threshold; k_{fr} is the user defined coefficient for influence of recycled fiber onto swelling; k_t is the user defined coefficient for influence of treatment onto swelling; m, ω, SW_f and SW_m are swelling function parameters.

See table 10 for the meaning of other variables.

Exhaustion of fossil resources function (*efr*)

The exhaustion of fossil resources function, efr, is defined as an addition of two factors (equation 16): one for fibres used and one for the non-renewable part of the polymer if the polymer is a blend.

$$efr = a_1.\lambda_f + a_2.(1-\alpha_{bio})(1-\lambda_f) \quad (16)$$

where the coefficient a_1 represents the impact of fiber processing and treatment on the exhaustion of fossil resources, and the coefficient a_2 reflects the impact of non renewable thermoplastic and additives production and processing. Other factors have an impact on *efr*, such as consumption of non-renewable energy during composite assembly, production of additives... For simplification they have not been considered. Normally a_2 is expected to be higher than a_1. The balance between the two coefficients influences the environmental optimization.

See table 10 for the meaning of other variables.

5.2 Application of the MOPSO algorithm

In the design of wood-plastic composite (WPC), the creep and swelling functions are conflicting: the swelling of the composite growth when the creep decreases with the rate of fibers (wood). The MOPSO deals with such conflicting objectives; even if the representation of each objective is an algorithm and thus with a high number of functions. In our WPC preliminary design we have three objective functions with two of them represented each by an algorithm utilizing several variables.

Dealing with continuous and discrete variables

The equations (5) and (8) are used as *position* updating rule of respectively real and discrete variables. The equation (4) is used as *velocity* updating rule for all variables. During the optimization process, the real variables converge to their optima according to the objective functions, whereas each discrete variable randomly traverses its space of definition and consequently its best solution is identified. Due to the discrete variables, the solution space of the multi-objective optimization problem is discontinuous (fig. 15)

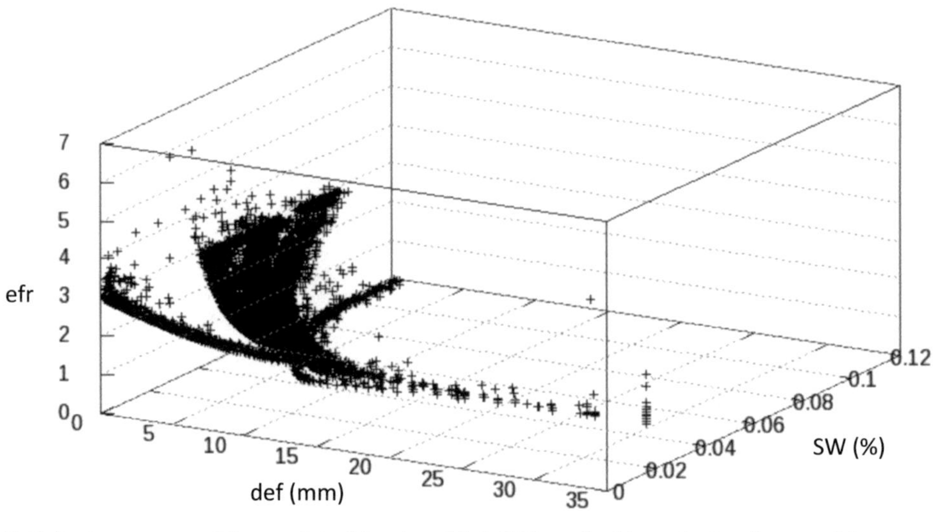

Fig. 15. Solution space of the multi-objective (def, SW and efr) optimization problem determined from a MOPSO of 1000 generations of 30 particles.

Multi-objective optimization

In this work we have applied the MOPSO method described in [Alvarez-Benitez et *al.*, 2005]. In this method only the *fully connected* topology is used to calculate the position of each particle for each objective function and then the Pareto dominance test is applied to each particle regarding the particle's positions stored in the *extended memory*. If the position of a particle dominates some particle's positions in the *extended memory*, the position of the particle is stored in the *extend memory* and the ones dominated are discarded from the *extended memory*. We used, as end condition of the optimization process, a given maximum number of iterations. Of course the swarm is randomly initialized and the number of its particles is given. The Pareto front is constituted by the particle's positions in the *extended memory* at the end of the optimization process.

The efficiency of the optimization is hardly influenced by the constant parameters ω, c_1 and c_2 in the equation (4). Such parameters have to be experimentally adapted to each optimization problem. For our problem the parameters ω, c_1 and c_2 have been respectively settled to 0.63, 1.45 and 1.45 (fig. 16).

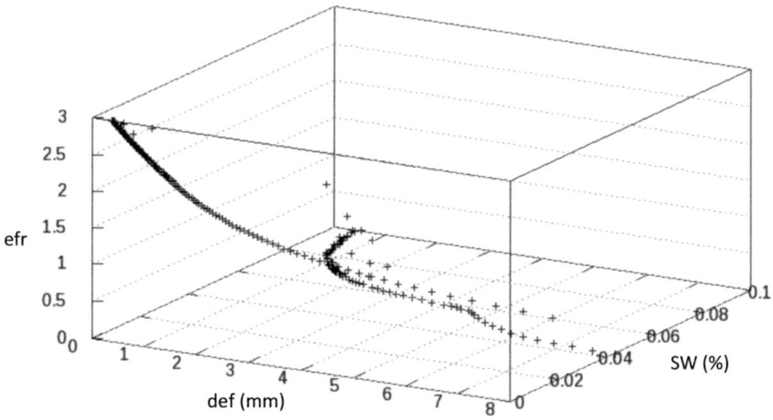

Fig. 16. The Pareto front of the multi-objective (def, SW and efr) optimization problem determined from a MOPSO of 1000 generations of 30 particles.

6. Results and discussion

Stability of the Pareto front

The Pareto front is stable regarding the swarm size and the number of generations of particles (number of iterations used as end-condition of the optimization process) [Ndiaye et *al.* 2009]. For a given swarm size, the number of particles in the Pareto front increases with the increasing number of generation of particles according to an affine law, but the shape of the front remains the same (fig. 17a); and for a given number of generation of particles, the number of particles in the Pareto front increases with the increase of the swarm size (fig. 17b).The size of the Pareto front can be rather large and therefore the swarm size and the number of iterations should be fitted in order to obtain a reasonable front size.

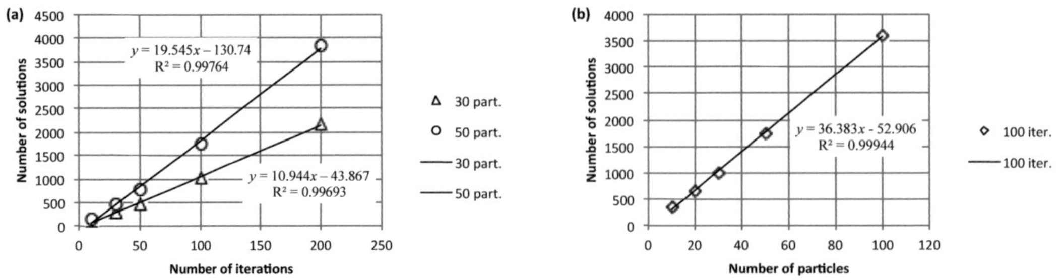

Fig. 17. Stability of the Pareto front: a) constant number of particles,
b) constant number of iterations [Ndiaye et *al.*, 2009].

Analysis of MOPSO solutions on composite formulations

Two solutions very close in the Pareto front can refer to two completely or slightly different composite formulations. Table 11 illustrates two kinds of differences:

- The values of decision variables of the solutions (*a*) and (*b*) are completely different: the solution (*a*) contains a low rate of plastic (36%) without biopolymer, randomly oriented short fibers with 9% of recycled ones and a high treatment level; the solution (*b*) contains a high plastic content (59%) with 39% of biopolymer thermoplastic, randomly oriented short fibers with 2% of recycled ones and a high treatment level. These two solutions are rather equivalent regarding the objective functions values: for (*a*) 1mm/3%/4.67 for creep/swelling/efr and 1.9mm/3%/4.10 for (*b*).
- The values of decision variables of the solutions (*c*) and (*d*) are slightly different: the solution (*c*) contains a slightly high rate of plastic (46%) with 44% of biopolymer, unidirectionally oriented short fibers without recycled ones and a high treatment level; the solution (*d*) contains a high plastic content (57%) with 48% of biopolymer thermoplastic, unidirectionally oriented short fibers without recycled ones and a high treatment level. These two solutions are rather equivalent regarding the objective functions values: for (*a*) 1mm/3%/3.68 for creep/swelling/efr and 1.4mm/3%/3.67 for (*d*).

These results show a significant gap for raw materials content and underline the power of such optimization process offering new possibilities of preliminary design.

Solution	λ_m (%)	a_{bio} (%)	*GRAN*	a_{frec} (%)	k_t	Creep (mm)	Swelling (%)	efr
a	33	0	2	9	2	1.0	3	4.67
b	59	39	2	2	2	1.9	3	4.10
c	46	44	3	0	2	1.0	3	3.68
d	57	48	3	0	2	1.4	3	3.67

Table 11. Examples of solutions in the Pareto front.

A large number of solutions

The number of MOPSO solutions on composite formulations depends on the ratios between the components and their desired precision. The number of solutions grows in function with the precision of ratios between the components using a logarithm-like law. It starts at 1500 solutions for a precision of 2 (the lowest possible precision) to more than 5000 for a precision greater than 5 (fig.18). The matrix ratio in composite formulation generates a peak of solutions around 75% for any precision of ratio. This large number of solutions makes them difficult to handle. One solution is to take into account, in the system process, the user of the system so he could fix the precision of ratios, and for each ratio, its desired range; the latter being included in the domain of validity of the variable representative of the ratio. For example if you want to formulate a wood-plastic composite with a matrix ratio lying between 30% and 40% without biopolymer, it is sufficient to restrict the range of the variable representative of the matrix ratio (λ_m) between 0.3 and 0.4 and the one representative of the biopolymer ratio in matrix component (α_{bio}) between 0.0 and 0.0. In this case the number of solutions in the Pareto front fall down to 20.

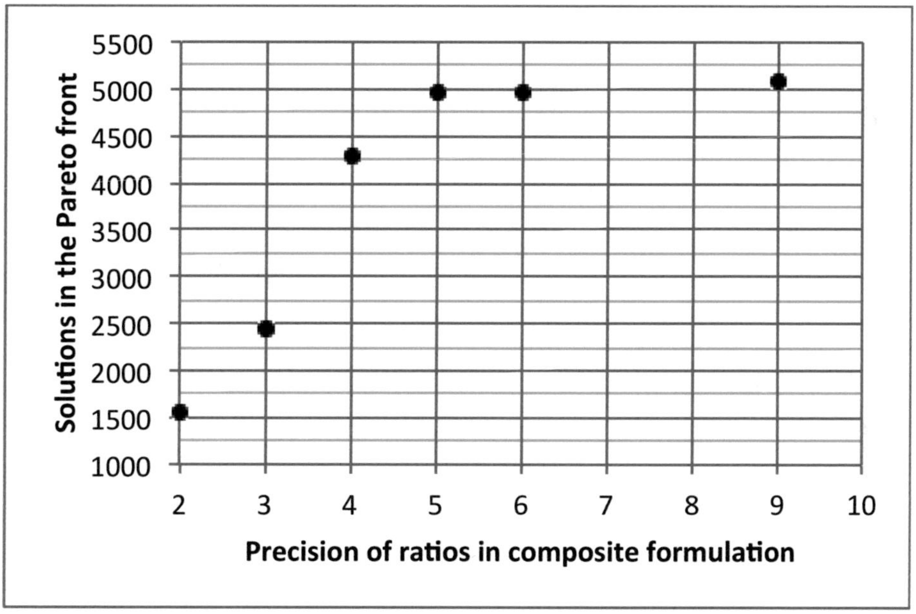

Fig. 18. The influence of the precision of ratios in composite formulation on the number of solutions in the Pareto front.

7. Conclusion

This chapter described two examples of the civil engineering field in which PSO has been used. The first case is a structural problem when the second is a material problem. In both cases, the advantage of PSO have been highlighted:

- The PSO algorithm is blind to the real physics, and can be easily adapted to a wide variety of engineering problem. The main issue is the definition of a relevant objective function, which describes the goal to reach (mimic the physical field measurement at best in the first case, minimize a multi-objective function in the second one).

- The PSO can be used either for mono-objective or for multi-objective problems. The quick convergence of the PSO to the solution of the problem and its capabilities to be blind to local minimum shows that this algorithm is particularly appropriate for solving such kind hard optimisation problems.
- Thanks to its simplicity of use, the PSO can be combined with more sophisticated computations (like for instance finite element computations, which are used, as a "slave code", in the direct model).
- Moe practically, significant results have been obtained in the engineering field:
- the first case has shown the impact of the relations between parameters to identify on the accuracy of the identification using the PSO. These examples focused on the several points to take into account (a) metrology set (i.e. number and locations), and (b) either the sensitivity of the field data on the parameters to identify or the independence between parameters to identify.
- the second case has shown the easiness of handling the multi-objective particle swarm optimization (MOPSO) method and its interest in preliminary eco-design. The method provides a set of "interesting" solutions among which the designer will be able to refine the design process, introducing for instance processes, availability of raw materials and economic viability. There is no restriction on the number of objectives, provided their expressions and interactions can be clearly defined. We have used a MOPSO algorithm based on an extended memory technique to calculate a stable Pareto front for three objective functions: creep, swelling and exhaustion of fossil resources in the context of the environmental optimization of the wood-plastic composite. The creep and swelling functions are in fact algorithms using in the same time continuous and discrete variables. A flexible and multiplatform (Unix, Windows and Mac osx) computer program has been developed.

8. References

Alvarez-Benitez, J. E., R. M. Everson and J. E. Fieldsend (2005). "A MOPSO Algorithm Based Exclusively on Pareto Dominance Concepts. Evolutionary Multi-Criterion Optimization, Guanajuato, Mexico. Lecture Notes in Computer Science(Issue): 459-473, Springer.

Castéra, P., A. Ndiaye, C. Delisée, C. Fernandez and J. Malvestio (2010). "Élaboration d'un isolant thermique et acoustique à base végétale : du concept à sa réalisation." Revue des composites et matériaux avancés 20(3): 315-334.

Fan S.K., Liang Y.C., Davin A., Zahara E., "A genetic algorithm and a particular swarm optimizer hybridized with Nelder-Mead simplex search", Computers & industrial engineering, Vol. 50, 2006, p. 401-425.

Fontan M., Ndiaye A., Breysse D., Bos F., Fernandez C., "Soil Structure Interaction: Parameters Identification using Particle Swarm Optimization", Computers and Structures, Vol.89, 2011, p.1602-1614.

Hammouche K., Diaf M., Siarry P., "A comparative study of various meta heuristic techniques applied to the multilevel thresholding problem", Engineering applications of Artificial Intelligence., Vol. 23, 2010, p. 676-688.

Hasançebi O, Carbas S, Dogan E, Erdal F, Saka MP. Performance evaluation of meta heuristic search techniques in the optimum design of real size pin jointed structures. Comput Struct 2009;87:284–302.

Kaveh A, Talatahari S. Particle swarm optimizer, ant colony strategy and harmony search scheme hybridized for optimization of truss structures. Comput Struct 2009;87:267–83.

Kennedy, J. (1999). Small worlds and mega-minds: effects of neighborhood topology on particle performance. In Proceedings of the IEEE congress on evolutionary computation (pp. 1931–1938). Piscataway: IEEE.

Kennedy, J. and R. C. Eberhart. 1997. "A discrete binary version of the particle swarm algorithm," Proceedings of the World Multiconference on Systemics, Cybemetics and lnformatics, Piscataway, NI. pp. 4104- 4109.

Kennedy, J. and R. Eberhart (1995). "Particle swarm optimization". IEEE International Conference on Neural Networks. Part 1 (of 6) 4(Issue): 1942-1948, IEEE.

Kennedy, J., and Mendes, R. (2002). Population structure and particle swarm performance. In Proceedings of the IEEE congress on evolutionary computation (CEC) (pp. 1671–1676), Honolulu, HI. Piscataway: IEEE.

Levasseur S., Malecot Y., Boulon M., Flavigny E., "Soil parameter identification using a genetic algorithm", Int. J. Numer. Anal. Meth. Geomech., Vol. 32, 2008, p. 189-213.

Li L.J., Huang Z.B., Liu F., Whu Q.H., "A heuristic particle swarm optimizer for optimization of pin connected structures", Computers and Structures, Vol. 85, 2007, p. 340-349.

Li LJ, Huang ZB, Liu F. A heuristic particle swarm optimization method for truss structures with discrete variables. Comput Struct 2009;87:435–43.

Meier J., Schaedler W., Borgatti L., Corsini A., T. Schanz, "Inverse parameter identification technique using PSO algorithm applied to geotechnical modeling", Journal of Artificial Evolution and Applications, doi:10.1155/2008/574613, 2008.

Mendes, R., J. Kennedy and J. Neves (2004). The Fully Informed Particle Swarm: Simpler, Maybe Better. IEEE Transactions of evolutionary computation, 8(4): 204-210.

Michaud, F., P. Castéra, C. Fernandez and A. Ndiaye (2009). "Meta-heuristic Methods Applied to the Design of Wood-Plastic Composites, with Some Attention to Environmental Aspects." Journal of Composite Materials 43(5): 533-548

Ndiaye A., Castéra P., Fernandez C., Michaud F., "Multi-objective preliminary ecodesign", Int. J Interact Des Manuf., Vol. 3, 2009, p.237-245.

Poli, R., J. Kennedy and T. Blackwell (2007). "Particle swarm optimization: An overview." Swarm Intelligence 1(1): 33-57.

Reyes-Sierra, M. and C. Coello Coello (2006). "Multi-Objective Particle Swarm Optimizers: A Survey of the State-of-the-Art." International Journal of Computational Intelligence Research 2(3): 287-308.

Van Veldhuizen, D., G. Lamont, "Multiobjective Evolutionary Algorithms: Analyzing the State-of-the-Art", Evolutionary Computation, vol. 8, n° 2, 2000, p. 125-147.
Zitzler E., Deb K. and Thiele L., "Comparison of Multiobjective Evolutionary Algorithms: Empirical Results", Evolutionary Computation, vol. 8, n° 2, 2000, p. 173-195.

7

Firefly Meta-Heuristic Algorithm for Training the Radial Basis Function Network for Data Classification and Disease Diagnosis

Ming-Huwi Horng[1], Yun-Xiang Lee[2], Ming-Chi Lee[1] and Ren-Jean Liou[3]
[1]*Department of Computer Science and Information Engineering, National Pingtung Institute of Commerce*
[2]*Department of Computer Science and Information Engineering, National Cheng Kung University*
[3]*Department of Computer and Communication, National Pingtung Institute of Commerce*
Taiwan

1. Introduction

The radial basis function (RBF) network is a type of neural network that uses a radial basis function as its activation function (Ou, Oyang & Chen, 2005). Because of the better approximation capabilities, simpler network structure and faster learning speed, the RBF networks have attracted considerable attention in many science and engineering field. Horng (2010) used the RBF for multiple classifications of supraspinatus ultrasonic images. Korurek & Dogan (2010) used the RBF networks for ECG beat classifications. Wu, Warwick, Jonathan, Burgess, Pan & Aziz (2010) applied the RBF networks for prediction of Parkinson's disease tremor onset. Feng & Chou (2011) use the RBF network for prediction of the financial time series data. In spite of the fact that the RBF network can effectively be applied, however, the number of neurons in the hidden layer of RBF network always affects the network complexity and the generalizing capabilities of the network. If the number of neurons of the hidden layer is insufficient, the learning of RBF network fails to correct convergence, however, the neuron number is too high, the resulting over-learning situation may occur. Furthermore, the position of center of the each neuron of hidden layer and the spread parameter of its activation function also affect the network performance considerably. The determination of three parameters that are the number of neuron, the center position of each neuron and its spread parameter of activation function in the hidden layer is very important.

Several algorithms had been proposed to train the parameters of the RBF network for classification. The gradient descent (GD) algorithm (Karayiannis, 1999) is the most popular method for training the RBF network. It is a derivative based optimization algorithm that is used to search for the local minimum of a function. The algorithm takes steps proportional to negative of the gradient of function at the current situation. Many global optimization methods had been proposed to evolve the RBF networks. The genetic algorithm is a popular method for finding approximate solutions to optimization and search problems. Three genetic operations that are selection, crossover and mutation, of the main aspects of GA evolve the optimal solution form an initial population. Barreto, Barbosa & Ebecken (2002) used the real-code genetic algorithm to decide the centers of hidden neurons, spread and bias parameters by minimizing the mean square error of the desired outputs and actual outputs. The particle swarm optimization is a swarm intelligence technique, first introduced by Kennedy & Eberhart (2007), inspired by the social behavior of bird flocks or fish schools. The computation of the PSO algorithm is dependent on the particle's local best solution (up to the point of evaluation) and the swarm's global best solution. Every particle has a fitness value, which is evaluated by the fitness function for optimization, and a velocity which directs the trajectory of the particle. Feng, (2006) designed the parameters of centers, the spread of each radial basis function and the connection weights as the particle, and then applied the PSO algorithm to search for the optimal solution for constructing the RBF network for classification. Kurban & Besdok, (2009) proposed an algorithm by using artificial bee colony algorithm to estimate the weights, spread, bias and center parameters based on the algorithm. This chapter concluded the ABC algorithm is superior to the GA, PSO and GD algorithms.

The firefly algorithm is a new swarm-based approach for optimization, in which the search algorithm is inspired by social behavior of fireflies and the phenomenon of bioluminescent communication. There are two important issues in the firefly algorithm that are the variation of light intensity and formulation of attractiveness. Yang (2008) that simplifies the attractiveness of a firefly is determined by its brightness which in turn is associated with the encoded objective function. The attractiveness is proportional to their brightness. Furthermore, every member x_i of the firefly swarm is characterized by its bright I_i which can be directly expressed as an inverse of a cost function for a minimization problem. Lukasik & Zak (2009) applied the firefly algorithm for continuous constrained optimization. Yang (2010) compared the firefly algorithm with the other meta-heuristic algorithms such as genetic and particle swarm optimization algorithms in the multimodal optimization. These works had the same conclusions that the algorithm applied the proposed firefly algorithm is superior to the two existing meta-heuristic algorithms.

In this chapter, a firefly algorithm of the training of the RBF network is introduced and the performance of the proposed firefly algorithm is compared with the conventional algorithms such as conventional GD, GA, PSO and ABC algorithms on classification problems from the UCI repository. Furthermore, the receiver operating characteristic analysis is used to evaluate the diagnosis performance of medical datasets. Some conclusions are made in the final section.

2. Radial basis function network

The neural network are non-linear statistical data modeling tools and can be used to model complex relationships between inputs and outputs or to find patterns in a dataset. The radial basis function network is a popular type of network that is very useful for pattern classification (Bishop, 1995). A radial basis function (RBF) network can be considered a special three-layered network shown in Fig 1.

The input nodes pass the input values x to the internal nodes that construct the hidden layer. Each unit of hidden layer implements a specific activation function called radial basis function. The nonlinear responses of hidden nodes are weighted in order to calculate the

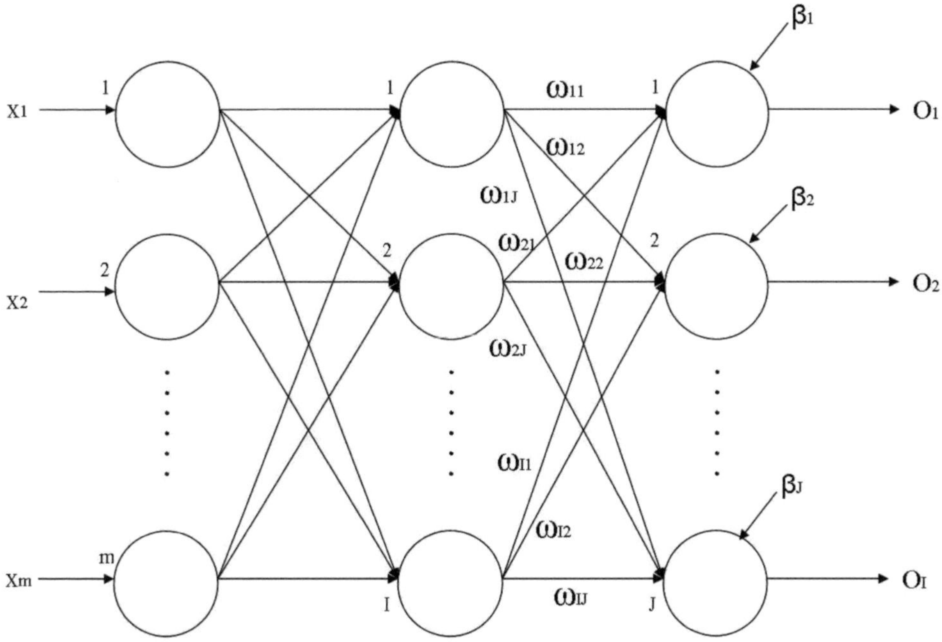

Fig. 1. The structure of radial basis function network

final outputs of network in the output layer. The input layer of this network has m units for m dimensional input vectors. The input units are fully connected to I hidden layer units, which are in turn fully connected to the J output layer units, where J is the number of output layer. Each neuron of the hidden layer has a parameter mean vector called center. Figure 1 shows the detailed structure of an RBF network. Each input data x with m dimensions, x= $(x_1, x_2, ..., x_m)$, are located in the input layer, which broadcast to hidden layer. The hidden layer has I neurons and each neuron compute the distance between the centers and the inputs. Each activation function of the neuron in hidden layer is chosen to be Gaussians and is characterized by their mean vectors c_i and its spread parameter α_i (i=1,2,...,I). That is, the activation function $\phi(x)$ of the ith hidden unit for an input vector **x** is given by:

$$\phi_i(x) = exp[-\alpha_i \cdot \|\text{x-}c_i\|^2] \tag{1}$$

The ϕ_i affects the smoothness of the mapping, thus, the output value of the neuron j of output layer $\overline{y_j}$ for training sample x, are given by $o(x)$ in (2).

$$o(x_i) = (o_1, o_2, ..., o_J)$$
$$o_j = \sum_{h=1}^{I} w_{hj}\phi_i(x_i) + \beta_j \tag{2}$$

The weights, w_{ij} (i=1,2,...,I., j=1,2,...,J), is the i-th node of output of hidden layer that transmitted to j-th node of the output layer, and β_j is the bias parameter of the j-th node of output layer determined by the RBF network training procedure. In practice, the training procedure of RBF is to find the adequate parameters w_{ij} , α_i , β_i and c_i such that the error metrics such as the mean square error (MSE) is minimum.

$$MSE(\mathrm{w}, \alpha,\beta,\mathrm{c}) = \frac{1}{N}\sum_{k=1}^{N}\left\|d(x_k) - o(x_k)\right\|^2 \tag{3}$$

where $d(x_i)$ and $o(x_i)$ is denoted to the desired output vector and actual output vector for training sample x_i . In (3), the N is the number of the training samples.

3. Training algorithms: GD, GA, PSO, ABC and FA

This section gives brief descriptions of training algorithms of RBF network that include the gradient descent algorithm (GD), the genetic algorithm (GA), the particle swarm optimization (PSO) algorithm and the artificial colony bee (ABC) algorithm.

3.1 Gradient Descent (GD) algorithm

GD is the derivative based optimization algorithm (Karayiannis, 1999)that is used to search for the local minimum of a function. The algorithm takes steps proportional to negative of the gradient of function at the current situation with given the parameters α_i and assumed all β_i are equal to 0. In general, the output of a RBF network can be written in the following form.

$$\overline{O} = (o_1, o_2, \ldots, o_J) = \begin{bmatrix} w_{11} & w_{12} & \cdot & \cdot & w_{1J} \\ w_{21} & w_{22} & \cdot & \cdot & w_{2J} \\ \cdot & \cdot & \cdot & \cdot & \cdot \\ \cdot & \cdot & \cdot & \cdot & \cdot \\ w_{I1} & w_{I2} & \cdot & \cdot & w_{IJ} \end{bmatrix} \cdot \begin{bmatrix} exp[-\alpha_1 \cdot \|\mathrm{x}\text{-}c_1\|^2] \\ exp[-\alpha_2 \cdot \|\mathrm{x}\text{-}c_2\|^2] \\ \\ \\ exp[-\alpha_I \cdot \|\mathrm{x}\text{-}c_I\|^2] \end{bmatrix} \tag{4}$$

and

$$O = \mathrm{W} \cdot \mathrm{H} \tag{5}$$

where the weight matrix is represented as W and the ϕ matrix is the H matrix, respectively. The GD algorithm can be implemented to minimize the MSE term defined as the equation (3) based on the following equations.

$$w_{ij} = w_{ij} - \eta \frac{\partial MSE}{\partial w_{ij}} \tag{6}$$

$$c_i = c_i - \eta \frac{\partial MSE}{\partial c_i} \tag{7}$$

where the η is the parameter of learning rate.

3.2 Genetic Algorithm (GA)

Genetic algorithm (Goldberg, 1989) inspired by the evolutionary biology is a popular method for finding approximate solutions to optimization and search problems. In the genetic algorithm, a population of strings called chromosomes which encode candidate solutions to an optimization problem, evolves toward better solutions. The evolution usually starts from a population of randomly generated individuals and happens in generations. In each generation, the fitness of every individual in the population is evaluated, multiple individuals are stochastically selected from the current population based on their fitness, and modified by recombined and possibly randomly mutated to form a new population. The new population is then used in the next iteration of the algorithm. Commonly, the algorithm terminates when either a maximum number of generations has been produced, or a satisfactory fitness level has been reached for the population. If the algorithm has terminated due to a maximum number of generations, a satisfactory solution may or may not have been reached. The three genetic operations that are selection, crossover and mutation, of the main aspects of GA evolve the optimal solution form an initial population. Barreto, Barbosa & Ebecken (2002) used the real-code genetic algorithm to decide the centers of hidden neurons, spread and bias parameters by minimizing the MSE of the desired outputs and actual outputs.

3.3 Particle Swarm Optimization (PSO) algorithm

The particle swarm optimization (PSO) first introduced by Kennedy & Eberhart (1995), is a swarm optimization method that optimizes a problem by iteratively trying to improve candidate solutions called particles. The improvement of candidate particles with *D* dimension in the PSO algorithm is dependent on the particle's local best solution, $P_l^t = (p_{l1}^t, p_{l2}^t, ..., p_{lD}^t)$ (up to the point of evaluation) and the swarm's global best solution $p_g^t = (p_{g1}^t, p_{g2}^t, ..., p_{gD}^t)$ at the iteration t. Every particle has a fitness value, which is evaluated by the fitness function for optimization, and a velocity which directs the trajectory of the particle. The *D*-dimensional position for particle *i* can be at the iteration *t* represented as $x_i^t = (x_{i1}^t, x_{i2}^t, ..., x_{iD}^t)$. Like to the position, the velocity of particle *i* can be described as $v_i^t = (v_{i1}^t, v_{i2}^t, ..., v_{iD}^t)$. The movements of particles *i* at the $t+1$ iteration are followed as the Eq. [8] and [9].

$$v_{id}^t = v_{id}^{t-1} + c_1 r_1 (P_{id}^t - x_{id}^t) + c_2 r_2 (p_{gd}^t - x_{id}^t) \quad d = 1,2,..,D \tag{8}$$

$$x_{id}^t = x_{id}^{t-1} + v_{id}^t \quad d = 1,2,..,D \tag{9}$$

where c_1 indicates the cognition learning factor; c_2 indicates the social learning factor, and r_1 and r_2 are random numbers between (0, 1). Feng (2006) designed the parameters of centers, the spread of each radial basis function and the connection weights as the particle, and then applied the PSO algorithm to search for the optimal solution for constructing the RBF network for classification.

3.4 Artificial Bee Colony (ABC) algorithm

The artificial bee colony (ABC) algorithm was proposed by the Kurban and Besdok, (2009) applied it to train the RBF network. In the ABC algorithm, the colony of artificial bees contains three groups of bees: employed bees, onlookers and scouts. The employed bees bring loads of nectar from the food resource to the hive and may share the information about food source in the dancing area. These bees carry information about food sources and share them with a certain probability by dancing in a dancing area in the hive. The onlooker bees wait in the dances area for making a decision on the selection of a food source depending on the probability delivered by employed bees. The computation of probability is based on the amounts of the food source. The other kind of bee is scout bee that carries out random searches for new food sources. The employed bee of an abandoned food source becomes a scout and as soon as it finds a new food source it becomes employed again. In other words, the each search cycle of the ABC algorithm contains three steps. First, the employed bees are sent into their food sources and the amounts of nectar are evaluated. After sharing this information about the nectar, onlooker bees select the food source regions and evaluating the amount of nectar in the food sources. The scout bees and then chosen and sent out to find the new food sources.

In the ABC algorithm, the position of a food source z_i represents a possible solution to the optimization problems and the amount of nectar in a food source corresponds to the fitness $fit(z_i)$ of the corresponding solution z_i. In the training RBF network, a solution z_i is made up of the parameters of weights, spread, bias and vector centers of RBF network. The number of employed or onlooker bees is generally equal to the number of solutions in the population of solutions. Initially, the ABC algorithm randomly produced a distributed initial population *P* of *SN* solutions, where *SN* denoted the number of employed bees or onlooker bees. Each solution z_i $(i=1,2,\ldots,SN)$ is a *D*-dimensional vector. Here *D* is the number of optimization parameters. In each execution cycle, *C* (*C=1, 2,…, MCN*), the population of the solutions is subjected to the search processes of the employed, the onlooker and scout bees. An employed bee modifies the possible solution depending on the amount of nectar (fitness vale) of the new source (new solution) by using the Eq. (10).

$$z_{ij} = z_{ij} + rand(-1,1)(z_{ij} - z_{kj}) \tag{10}$$

Where $k \in \{1,2,.....,SN\}$ but $k \neq i$ and $j \in \{1,2,.....,D\}$ are randomly selected indexes. *rand(a, b)* is a random number between *[a, b]*.

If there is more nectar in new solution is than that in the precious one, the bee remembers the new position and forgets the old one, otherwise it retains the location of the previous one. When all employed bees have finished this search process, they deliver the nectar information and the position of the food sources to the onlooker bees, each of whom chooses a food source according to a probability proportional to the amount of nectar in that food source. The probability p_i of selecting a food source z_i is determined using the following Eq. (11).

$$p_i = \frac{fit(z_i)}{\sum_{i=1}^{SN} fit(z_i)} \tag{11}$$

In practical terms, any food source z_i,(*i*=*1,2,…,SN*) sequentially generates a random number between [0, 1] and if this number is less than p_i, an onlooker bee are sent to food source z_i and produces a new solution based on the equation (9). If the fitness of the new solution is more than the old one, the onlooker memorizes the new solution and shares this information with other onlooker bees. Otherwise, the new solution will be discarded. The process is repeated until all onlookers have been distributed to the food sources and produces the corresponding new solution.

If the position of food source can not be improved through the predetermined number of "*limit*" of bees, then the food resource z_i is abandoned and then the employed bee becomes a scout. Assume that the abandoned source is z_i and $j \in \{1,2,....,D\}$, then the scout discovers a new food source to be replaced with z_i. This operation can be defined as in (12).

$$z_{ij} = z_{min}^j + rand(0,1)(z_{max}^j - z_{min}^j) \tag{12}$$

where the z_{min}^j and z_{max}^j are the upper bound and upper bound of the *j*-th component of all solutions. If the new solution is better than the abandoned one, the scout will become an employed bee. The selection of employed bees, onlooker bees and scouts is repeated until the termination criteria have been satisfied.

3.5 Firefly Algorithm

Firefly algorithm (FA) was developed by Xin-She Yang at Cambridge University in 2008. In the firefly algorithm, there are three idealized rules: (1) all fireflies are unisex so that one firefly will be attracted to other fireflies regardless of their sex; (2) Attractiveness is proportional to their brightness, thus for any two flashing fireflies, the less brighter one will move towards the brighter one. If there is no brighter one than a particular firefly, it will move randomly. As firefly attractiveness one should select any monotonically decreasing function of the distance $r_{i,j} = d(x_j, x_i)$ to the chosen *j*-th firefly, e.g. the exponential function.

$$r_{i,j} = \|x_i - x_j\| \tag{13}$$

$$\beta \leftarrow \beta_0 e^{-\gamma r_{i,j}} \tag{14}$$

where the β_0 is the attractiveness at $r_{i,j} = 0$ and γ is the light absorption coefficient at the source.

The movement of a firefly *i* is attracted to another more attractive firefly *j* is determined by

$$x_{i,k} \leftarrow (1-\beta)x_{i,k} + \beta x_{j,k} + u_{i,k} \tag{15}$$

$$u_{i,k} = \sigma(rand1 - \frac{1}{2}) \tag{16}$$

The particular firefly x_i with maximum fitness will move randomly according to the following equation.

$$x_{i^{max},k} \leftarrow x_{i^{max},k} + u_{i^{max},k}, \text{ for k=1,2,...,c}$$

$$u_{i^{max},k} = \sigma(rand2 - \frac{1}{2}) \tag{17}$$

when $rand1$, $rand2$ are random vector whose each element obtained from the uniform distribution range from 0 to 1; (3). The brightness of a firefly is affected or determined by the landscape of the fitness function. For maximization problem, the brightness I of a firefly at a particular location x can be chosen as $I(x)$ that is proportional to the value of the fitness function.

4. Training RBF network using firefly algorithm

The individuals of the fireflies include the parameters of weights (w), spread parameters (α), center vector (c) and the bias parameters (β). The mean vector c_i of the i-th neuron of hidden layers is defined by $c_i = (c_{i1}, c_{i2}, ..., c_{im})$, therefore, the parametric vector t_i of each of fireflies with $IJ + I + mI + J$ parameters is expressed as:

$$t_i = (w_{11}^i,\ w_{12}^i, ..., w_{IJ}^i,\ \alpha_1^i, \alpha_2^i, ..., \alpha_I^i, \mathrm{c}_{11}^i, \mathrm{c}_{12}^i, ..., \mathrm{c}_{1\mathrm{m}}^i, ..., c_{I1}^i, \mathrm{c}_{I2}^i, ..., \mathrm{c}_{Im}^i, \beta_1^i, \beta_2^i, ... \beta_m^i, ..., \beta_J^i)$$

In fact, each of fireflies can represent a specific RBF network for classification. In our proposed FF-based training algorithm, the optimum vectors t_i of firefly of specific trained RBF network can maximize the fitness function defined in the Eq. (18).

$$f(t_i) = \frac{1}{1 + MSE} = \frac{1}{1 + \frac{1}{N}\sum_{k=1}^{N} \left\| d(x_k) - o(x_k) \right\|^2} \tag{18}$$

where $d(x_i)$ and $o(x_i)$ are denoted to the desired output vector and actual output vector for training sample x_i of RBF network designed by parametric vector t_i. The N is the number of the training samples. Figure 2 shows the pseudo codes of this proposed algorithm and the steps of the proposed algorithm are detailed described as follows.

Step 1. (Generate the initial solutions and given parameters)

In this step, the initial population of m solutions are generating with dimension $IJ + I + mI + J$, denoted by the matrix D.

$$D = [t_1, t_2, ..., t_n]$$

$$t_i = (w_{11}^i,\ w_{12}^i, .., w_{IJ}^i,\ \alpha_1^i, \alpha_2^i, .., \alpha_I^i, \mathrm{c}_{11}^i, \mathrm{c}_{12}^i, .., \mathrm{c}_{1\mathrm{m}}^i, .., c_{I1}^i, \mathrm{c}_{I2}^i, ..., \mathrm{c}_{Im}^i, \beta_1^i, \beta_2^i, .., \beta_m^i, .., \beta_J^i) \tag{19}$$

where the values of weights (w) and centers (c) are assigned between -1 and 1, and the values of the spread and bias parameters α and β range from 0 to 1. Furthermore, the step will assign the parameters of firefly algorithm, that are σ, β_0, the maximum cycle number (MCL) and γ. Let number of cycle l to be 0.

Step 2. Firefly movement

In step 2, each solution t_i computes its fitness value $f(t_i)$ as the corresponding the brightness of firefly. For each solution t_i, this step randomly selects another one solution t_j with the more bright and then moves toward to t_j by using the following equations.

$$r_{i,j} = \left\| t_i - t_j \right\| = \sqrt{\sum_{k=1}^{IJ+I+mI+J} (t_{i,k} - t_{j.k})^2} \tag{20}$$

$$\beta = \beta_0 e^{-\gamma r_{i,j}} \tag{21}$$

$$t_{i,k} = (1-\beta)t_{i,k} + \beta t_{j,k} + u_{j,k},\ k=1,2,\dots,\ IJ + I + mI + J \tag{22}$$

where $u_{j,k} \sim U(0,1)$ is a randomly number ranged form 0 to 1 and the $t_{i,k}$ is the *k*-th element of the solution t_i.

Step 3. (Select the current best solution)

The step 3 selects the best one from the all solutions and defines as x_i^{max}, that is,

$$\begin{aligned} i^{max} &= arg\,\max_i f(t_i); \\ x_i^{max} &= arg\,\max_{x_i} f(t_i); \end{aligned} \tag{23}$$

Step 4. (Check the termination criterion)

If the cycle number l is equal to the *MCL* then the algorithm is finished and output the best solution x_i^{max}. Otherwise, l increases by one and randomly walks the best solution x_i^{max} then go to Step 2. The best solution x_i^{max} will randomly walk its position based the following equation.

$$t_{i^{max},k} \leftarrow t_{i^{max},k} + u_{i^{max},k},\ k = 1,2,\dots,IJ + I + mI + J \tag{24}$$

where $u_{i^{max},k} \sim U(0,1)$ is a randomly number ranged from 0 to 1.

5. Experimental results and discussion

The platform used to develop the five training algorithm included the gradient descent (GD), genetic algorithm (GA), particle swarm optimization (PSO), artificial bee colony algorithm (ABC) and the firefly algorithm (FF) is a person computer with following features: Intel Pentium IV 3.0 GHZ CPU, 2GB RAM, a Windows XP operating system and the Visual C++ 6.0 development environment. In experiments, learning parameter of GD is selected as $\eta = 0.01$. The used parameters of GA, PSO, ABC and FF algorithms are given at Tables 1, 2, 3 and 4, respectively. In order to obtain the classification results without partiality, the following data set are used: Iris, Wine, Glass, Heart SPECTF and Breast cancer (WBDC) listed in Table 5, taken from the UCI machine repository (Asuncion, 2007).

In order to avoid the feature values in greater numeric ranges from dominating those in smaller numeric range, the scaling of feature is used, that is the range of each feature value can be linearly scaled to range [-1, 1]. Furthermore, the 4-fold method is employed in experiments, thus, the dataset is split into 4 parts, with each part of the data sharing the same proportion of each class of data. Three data parts is applied in the training process, while the remaining one is used in the testing process. The program is run 4 times to enable each slice of data to take a turn as the testing data. The percentage of correct classification of this experiment is computed by summing the individual accuracy rate for each run of testing, and then dividing the total by 4.

Firefly Algorithm

Input:

$f(x)$, $x=[t_1,t_2,....,t_m]$, t_i is the i-th firefly (solution) in the solution space with x the fitness function $f(t_i)$, $t_i=[t_{i,1},t_{i,2},....,t_{i,IJ+I+mI+J}]$, any of fireflies is a $IJ+I+mI+J$-dimensional vector, and the given parameters m, α, β_0, iteration number l and γ.

Output:

The best solution x_i^{max} with the largest fitness value.

for $i=1$ to m do
  $t_i \leftarrow generate\_InitialSolutions()$;
 iter=0;
Repeat
  $i^{max} = \arg\max_i f(t_i)$;
  $t_i^{max} = \arg\max_{t_i} f(t_i)$;
for $i=1$ to m do
  for $j=1$ to m do
   if $f(x_j) < f(x_i)$ then
  $\{ r_{i,j} \leftarrow distance(x_i, x_j)$; $\beta \leftarrow \beta_0 e^{-\gamma r_{i,j}}$;
   $\mu_i \leftarrow generate\_random\_vector()$;
   for $k=1$ to $IJ+I+mI+J$ do
    $t_{i,k} \leftarrow (1-\beta)t_{i,k} + \beta t_{j,k} + u_{i,k}$; }
 $\mu_i^{max} \leftarrow generate\_random\_vector()$;
 for $k=1$ to $IJ+I+mI+J$ do
 $\{ t_{i^{max},k} \leftarrow t_{i^{max},k} + t_{i^{max},k}$;}
 iter++;
 Until (iter< l)

Fig. 2. The pseudo-code of the firefly algorithm for the training the RBF network

Parameter	Parameter value
Number of iteration	1000
Number of individuals	50
Selection type	Roulette
Mutation type	Uniform
Mutation ratio	0.05
Crossover type	Single point
Crossover ratio	0.8

Table 1. The used parameters of GA

Parameter	Value
Number of particles	50
Velocities randomly	[0.0, 1.0]
Number of iterations	1000
Cognitive coefficient C1	2.1
Cognitive coefficient C2	2.0

Table 2. The used parameters of PSO

Parameter	Value
Number of the initial solutions	50
Limit	100
MCN	1000

Table 3. The used parameters of ABC

Parameter	Value
Attractiveness β_0	1.0
Light absorption coefficient γ	1.0
Number of fireflies	50
Iteration number	1000
σ	0.1

Table 4. The used parameters of Firefly algorithm

Dataset	**Class Number**	**Attributes number**	**Number of patterns**
Iris	3	4	150
Wine	3	13	178
Glass	2	9	214
Heart SPECTF	2	22	267
Breast WDBC	2	30	569

Table 5. The used datasets in this study

Qasem & Shamsuddin (2011) uses three indices to evaluate the performance of trained RBF network using the different algorithms. The three performance indices are:

The percent of correct classification (PCC) is used as the measure for evaluating the trained RBF network.

$$PCC = \frac{\text{correct classification samples}}{\text{total samples}} \times 100 \tag{25}$$

The mean square error (MSE) on the data set is used to act as the performance index shown in (3) where $o(x_k)$ and $d(x_k)$ are the actual output and the desired output and N is the number of data paris in all dataset.

$$MSE = \frac{1}{N}\sum_{k=1}^{N} \|d(x_k) - o(x_k)\|^2 \tag{26}$$

The complexity index shows in (27) that is the sum of squared weights which is based on the concept of regularization and represents the smoothness of the RBF network.

$$Complexity = \frac{1}{2}\sum_{i=1}^{I}\sum_{j=1}^{J} w_{ij}^2 \tag{27}$$

5.1 Classification evaluation

One of the most important issues of designing the RBF network is the number of neurons in the hidden layer. Thus, we implement the RBF networks which have 1 neuron to 8 neurons for comparison, and each dataset is running 10 times based on 4-flod cross-validation. The average percentage and the corresponding standard derivation defined as the Eq. (25) of the designed RBF network by different algorithms are listed in Tables 6-10.

	The number of neuron of hidden layer						
	2	3	4	5	6	7	8
GD	75.33 ± 6.09	81.33 ± 5.89	84.67 ± 4.98	88.00 ± 5.12	89.33 ± 4.34	90.00 ± 4.21	89.33 ± 3.13
GA	84.66 ± 6.78	89.33 ± 6.88	90.00 ± 5.42	90.67 ± 4.65	92.00 ± 4.52	94.00 ± 3.45	91.67 ± 2.87
PSO	86.67 ± 4.23	92.21 ± 4.01	93.67 ± 3.32	94.00 ± 2.89	94.67 ± 2.34	95.45 ± 2.55	97.33 ± 1.78
ABC	87.33 ± 4.31	92.00 ± 3.97	94.67 ± 3.14	93.33 ± 2.69	94.67 ± 2.65	94.21 ± 2.47	96.14 ± 2.67
FF	**87.33 ± 2.13**	**93.33 ± 2.23**	**94.00 ± 2.98**	**94.00 ± 1.45**	**94.67 ± 1.23**	**96.14 ± 1.43**	**97.33 ± 1.02**

Table 6. The average PCC and standard deviation results of the Iris dataset using different algorithm.

	The number of neuron of hidden layer (sec)						
	2	3	4	5	6	7	8
GD	70.79 ± 6.53	74.16 ± 5.43	76.97 ± 6.32	79.21 ± 4.32	84.83 ± 3.89	88.96 ± 3.91	90.76 ± 3.23
GA	89.53 ± 5.23	88.65 ± 3.42	92.13 ± 3.56	90.45 ± 2.21	93.82 ± 2.34	95.35 ± 1.98	94.98 ± 1.64
PSO	90.52 ± 4.32	91.57 ± 3.29	92.13 ± 2.89	93.82 ± 2.45	94.38 ± 2.43	94.70 ± 1.98	95.35 ± 2.31
ABC	94.76 ± 4.06	95.45 ± 3.61	96.57 ± 3.41	95.10 ± 2.54	95.47 ± 3.14	96.70 ± 2.15	97.82 ± 2.51
FF	**94.76 ± 3.21**	**96.01 ± 2.87**	**97.45 ± 2.67**	**98.07 ± 2.23**	**97.82 ± 2.45**	**97.94 ± 1.86**	**98.07 ± 1.22**

Table 7. Statistical average PCC results of the Wine dataset using different algorithms

	The number of neuron of hidden layer						
	2	3	4	5	6	7	8
GD	64.49 ± 6.58	65.89 ± 7.14	68.69 ± 7.25	74.30 ± 5.21	78.51 ± 4.52	86.92 ± 3.25	93.39 ± 2.58
GA	69.62 ± 5.54	75.23 ± 4.25	85.05 ± 3.25	86.92 ± 3.98	89.25 ± 4.15	90.65 ± 3.24	92.25 ± 2.68
PSO	**89.16 ± 5.28**	**94.29 ± 4.68**	**92.25 ± 3.78**	**95.79 ± 4.12**	**95.79 ± 3.81**	**97.19 ± 2.45**	**98.48 ± 2.17**
ABC	92.25 ± 5.14	92.25 ± 4.21	92.25 ± 4.87	94.39 ± 4.51	95.79 ± 3.53	95.79 ± 2.26	98.48 ± 2.97
FF	92.25 ± 6.12	92.25 ± 3.91	94.39 ± 3.24	94.39 ± 4.18	94.39 ± 3.10	95.79 ± 2.19	97.19 ± 1.97

Table 8. Statistical average PCC results of the Glass dataset using different algorithms.

	The number of neuron of hidden layer						
	2	3	4	5	6	7	8
GD	61.42 ± 5.25	63.29 ± 5.65	68.91 ± 4.25	77.91 ± 3.95	78.65 ± 5.24	84.26 ± 3.24	88.37 ± 3.25
GA	60.67 ± 4.26	71.53 ± 4.64	79.40 ± 4.06	89.14 ± 4.58	88.39 ± 3.25	89.14 ± 2.85	92.13 ± 2.14
PSO	71.53 ± 4.52	72.23 ± 3.79	85.39 ± 3.14	86.52 ± 3.95	88.39 ± 2.52	88.76 ± 4.19	92.88 ± 2.53
ABC	74.16 ± 3.25	76.40 ± 3.21	85.39 ± 3.51	88.39 ± 3.28	89.14 ± 3.84	92.13 ± 2.91	95.18 ± 3.29
FF	**74.16 ± 3.69**	**79.40 ± 4.15**	**85.39 ± 4.09**	**88.39 ± 2.85**	**89.51 ± 3.12**	**95.18 ± 2.17**	**95.18 ± 1.56**

Table 9. Statistical average PCC results of the Heart SPECT dataset using different algorithms.

	The number of neuron of hidden layer						
	2	3	4	5	6	7	8
GD	75.92 ± 8.45	80.49 ± 6.78	85.59 ± 5.62	87.52 ± 5.67	88.05 ± 6.17	89.98 ± 4.78	91.21 ± 3.56
GA	84.44 ± 6.87	85.59 ± 5.97	93.50 ± 4.21	94.20 ± 4.54	93.85 ± 3.91	96.49 ± 3.21	98.36 ± 3.67
PSO	93.32 ± 5.34	93.59 ± 4.98	94.38 ± 3.76	95.08 ± 4.19	96.49 ± 3.27	97.19 ± 2.98	98.36 ± 2.65
ABC	93.84 ± 6.10	94.37 ± 4.12	95.78 ± 3.84	96.49 ± 3.61	95.85 ± 4.14	96.49 ± 3.19	98.49 ± 3.14
FF	**93.32 ± 4.78**	**93.59 ± 4.98**	**95.78 ± 3.23**	**96.13 ± 3.43**	**97.19 ± 2.87**	**98.49 ± 2.57**	**99.72 ± 1.87**

Table 10. Statistical average results of the WDBC dataset using different algorithms.

These tables reveal that GD is the worst because the gradient descent algorithm is a traditional derivative method which traps at local minima. Furthermore, unlike the other four algorithms, as the number of neurons increases, the correct classification rates of the network designed by GD algorithm increase accordingly. In other words, the usage of bio-inspired algorithms is more robust than traditional GD algorithms. The Table 6 and 7 are the classification results of the Iris and Wine datasets, which are three-class classification problems. In Table 6, we find the fact that the results of the deigned RBF networks using the PSO, ABC and FF are not significantly difference but are superior to the results using GA. In Table 7, the results of ABC and FF algorithms are better than the results of the GA and PSO algorithms. These results may reveal that the GA and PSO algorithms need more number of initials or more execution iterations for searching the optimal parameters of the radial basis function network. Tables 8-10 are the classification results of the Glass, Heart SPECTF and WDBC datasets, which are two-class classification problems. We also find that the results designed by the PSO, ABC and FF algorithms are better than the result of GA algorithm. The better results of each of the three tables are the usages of PSO, ABC and FF, but, the differences between them are not indistinct from these tables.

5.2 The analysis of complexity and mean square error

Generally speaking, the complexity of trained RBF network with a large number of hidden nodes is larger but its corresponding mean square error is smaller. In experiments, The Figs. 3-7 recorded the mean square error and complexity of each trained RBF network based the Eq. (23) and (24). These figures clearly appear the phenomenon that the GD is the worst because of the largest mean square error with the same complexity among all algorithms.

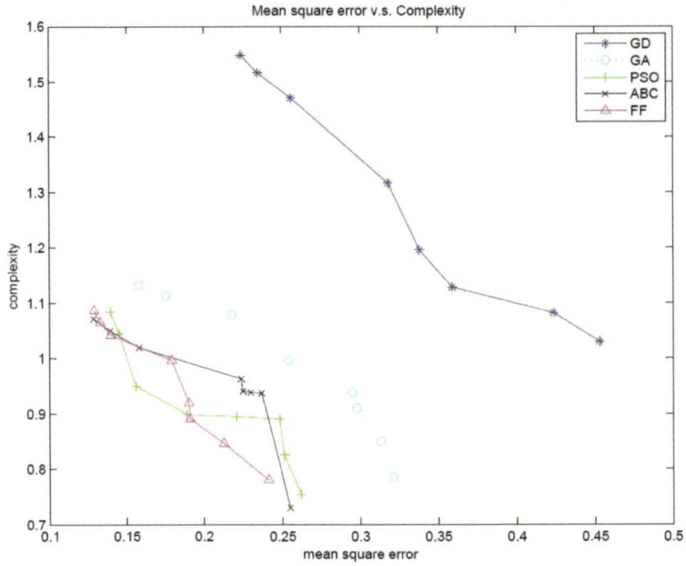

Fig. 3. The mean square error versus complexity of the classification of the Iris dataset.

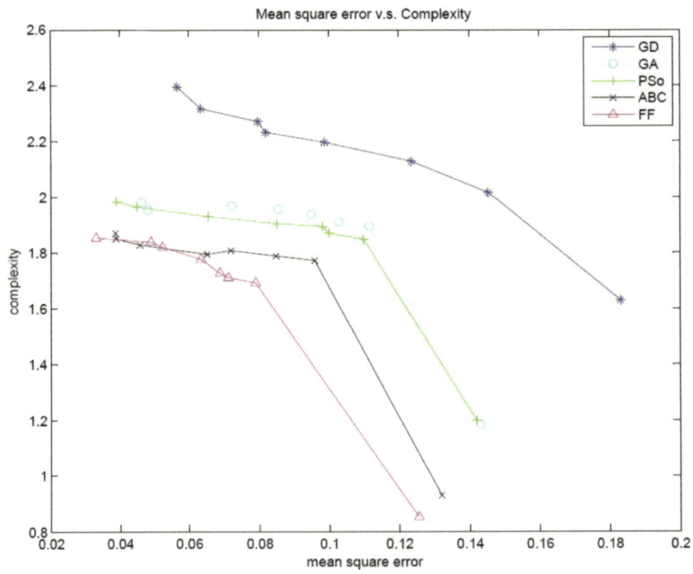

Fig. 4. The mean square error versus complexity of the Wine classification.

Figure 3 shows the relationship between the complexity and mean square error in training the RBF networks of Iris dataset. These figures appear that the results of PSO, ABC and FF are superior to the GD. The Fig. 4 show the results of ABC and FF algorithm are superior to the results of GD and PSO in the training the RBF networks for Wine dataset. The Fig. 5 show the best is the result designed by PSO algorithm. The Fig. 7 demonstrates the best are the usages of the FF, however, the results of GD, PSO, ABC and FF do not clearly differentiate form the results of Fig. 6.

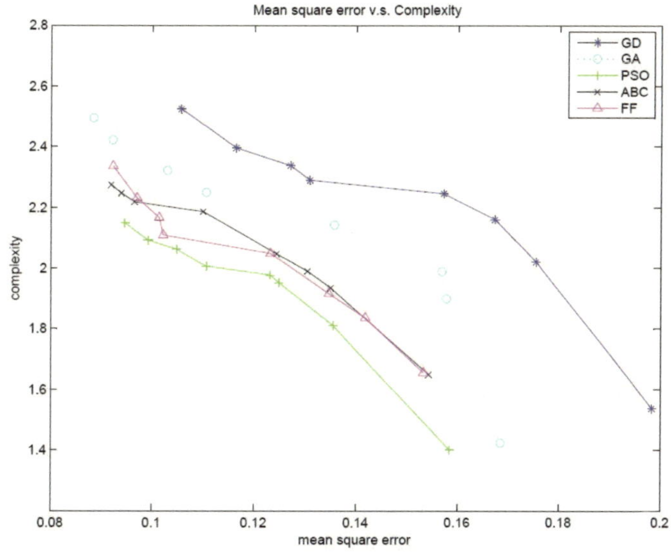

Fig. 5. The mean square error versus complexity of the Glass classification.

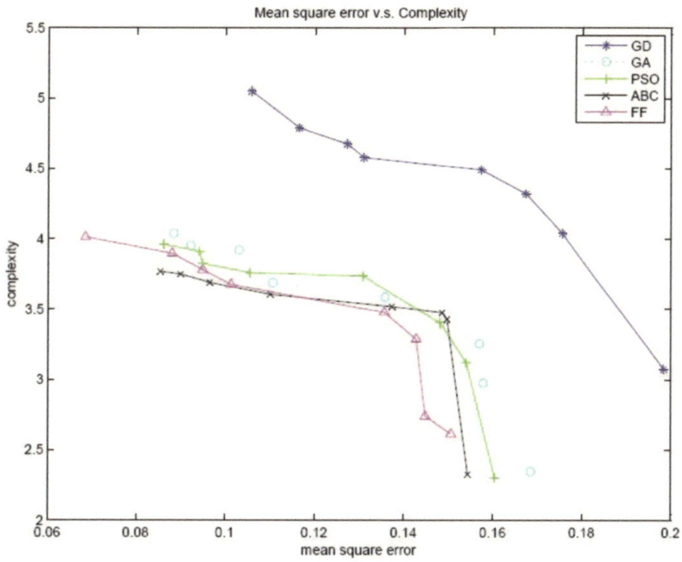

Fig. 6. The mean square error v.s. complexity of the Heart SPECT classification.

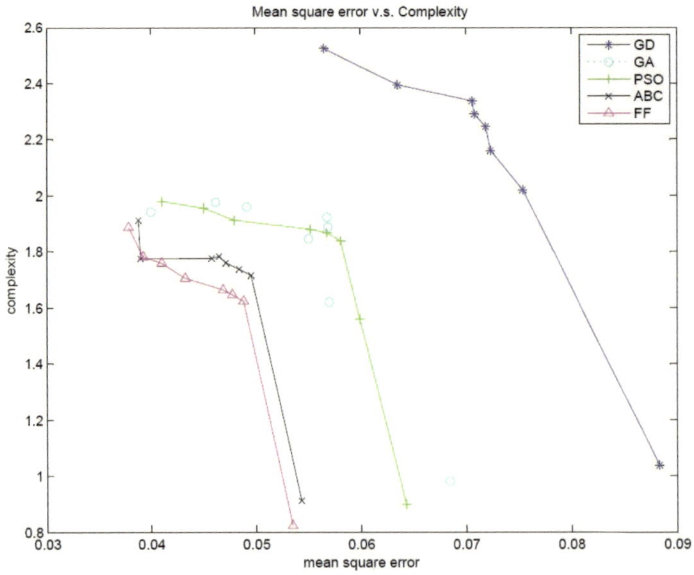

Fig. 7. The mean square error v.s. complexity of the WDBC classification.

5.3 Receiver operating characteristic analysis

The receiver operating characteristics analysis is a graphical curve is a tool for two-class classification problems that gives the evaluation of the predictive accuracy of a logistic model. The curve displays the relationship of the true positive rate (sensitivity) and the false positive rate (1-specificity) within a range of cutoffs. The sensitivity is a measure of accuracy for predicting events that is equal to the true positive/total actual positive; nevertheless, the specificity is a measure of accuracy for predicting nonevents that is equal to the true negative/total actual negative of a classifier. The area under curve (AUC) is an important index for evaluating the performance of classification. In general, the high AUC represents to good performance in the classification problems. The classifications of the two Heart SPECTF and Breast WDBC datasets listed Table 5 are two-class problems of the medical diagnosis that are suitable for this analysis. The SPECT dataset generated from describes diagnosing of cardiac single proton emission computed tomography images. The database of 267 SPECT image sets (patients) with 22 binary attributes was processed to extract features that summarize the original SPECT images and each of the patients is classified into two categories: normal (negative) and abnormal (positive). The Wisconsin Diagnostic Breast Cancer (WDBC) dataset was collected from Dr. William H. Wolberg of Wisconsin University. The dataset includes 567 data samples with 30 continuous attributes that are divided into 357 benign (negative) and 210 malignant (positive). In order to take one step ahead for analyzing the capability of classifications by using the five algorithms, the average of sensitivity and the average specificity of the receiver operating characteristic (ROC) analysis by using the SPECTF and WDBC datasets under the eight hidden nodes of trained RBF network are listed in the Table 11; and further, the corresponding AUC of ROC analysis with varied the bias parameters also listed in this table. In this table we find that the usage of ABC algorithm can have better capability in the classification of the SPECT dataset, however, the FF algorithm is best in the classification of WDBC dataset. The average computation times of classifying the Heart SPECT dataset in 4-fold cross validation by using the GD, GA, PSO, ABC and FF are 0.21, 429.67, 103.76, 123.67 and 98.21 seconds, however, the average computation times of classifying the Breast dataset in 4-fold cross validation by using the GD, GA, PSO, ABC and FF are 0.24, 513.23, 161.84, 189.59 and 134.91 seconds

Algorithms	Heart SPECTF Database			Breast (WDBC) Database		
	Sensitivity	Specificity	AUC	Sensitivity	Specificity	AUC
GD	0.8868	0.8727	0.789	0.9151	0.8868	0.854
GA	0.9198	0.9273	0.896	0.9811	0.9860	0.944
PSO	0.9292	0.9010	0.902	0.9858	0.9832	0.961
ABC	**0.9528**	**0.9454**	**0.941**	0.9953	0.9832	0.975
FF	0.9321	0.9367	0.932	**1.0000**	**0.9944**	**0.984**

Table 11. Area under curve (AUC) of ROC analysis of RBF network with eight hidden nodes. (The best results are highlighted in bold)

6. Conclusions

In this chapter, the firefly algorithm has been applied to train the radial basis function network for data classification and disease diagnosis. The training procedure involves selecting the optimal values of parameters that are the weights between layer and the output layer, the spread parameters, the center vectors of the radial functions of hidden nodes; and the bias parameters of the neurons of the output layer. The other four algorithms that are gradient descent (GD), genetic algorithm (GA), particle swarm optimization (PSO) and artificial bee colony algorithms are also implemented for comparisons. In experiments, the well-known classification problems such as the iris, Wine, Glass, heart SPECT and WDBC datasets, obtained from UCI repository had been used to evaluate the capability of classification among the five algorithms. Furthermore, the complexity and trained error also be discussed form experiments conducted in this chapter. The experimental results show that the usage of the firefly algorithm can obtain the satisfactory results over the GD and GA algorithm, but it is not apparent superiority to the PSO and ABC methods form exploring the experimental results of the classifications of UCI datasets. In order to go a step further for talking over the capability of classification among the five algorithms, the receiver operating characteristic (ROC) analysis are applied for this objective in classification of the heart SPECT and WDBC datasets. The experimental results also appear that the use of firefly algorithm has satisfactory in the high sensitivity, high specificity and bigger AUC in the corresponding ROC curves in WDBC dataset, however, the differences between ABC, PSO and firefly algorithms are not significant. The experimental results of this chapter reveal that the swarm intelligence algorithms, such as the particle swarm optimization, the artificial bee colony algorithm and the firefly algorithm are the good choices to search for the parameters of radial basis function neural network for classifications and disease diagnosis.

7. Acknowledgment

The authors would like to thank the National Science Council, ROC, under Grant No. NSC 100-2221-E-251-012 for support of this work.

8. References

Asuncion A. &, Newman D. (2007), UCI Machine Learning Repository. URL:http:// www. ics.uci.edu/~mlearn/MLRepository.html.

Barreto, Ada.M.S., Barbosa, H.J.C & Ebecken, N.F.F. (2002). Growing Compact RBF Networks Using A Genetic Algorithm, *In Proceedings of the VII Brazilian Symposium on Neural Networks*, pp. 61-66.

Bishop, C.M. (1995). Neural Networks for Pattern Recognition, Oxford, Clarendon Press.

Feng H.M. (2006), Self-generating RBFNs Using Evolutional PSO Learning, *Neurocomputing*, Vol. 70, pp. 241-251.

Feng, M.H. & Chou, H.C. (2011). Evolutional RBFNs Prediction Systems Generation in the Applications of Financial Time Seriies Data. Expert Systems with Applications, Vol. 38, 8285-8292.

Goldberg, David E. (1989). Genetic Algorithm in Search Optimization and Machine Learning, *Addison Wesley*.

Horng, M.H. (2010). Performance Evaluation of Multiple Classification of the Ultrasonic Supraspinatus Image by using ML, RBFNN and SVM Classifier, *Expert Systems with Applications*, 2010, Vol. 37, pp. 4146-4155.

Karayiannis, N.B. (1999). Reformulated Radial Basis Function Neural Network Trained by Gradient Descent. *IEEE Trnas. Neul Netw.*, Vol. 3, No, 10, pp. 657-671.

Kennedy J. & Eberhart, R. C. (1995). Particle Swarm Optimization, *In the Proceedings of the IEEE International Conference on Neural networks*. pp.1942-1948.

Korurek, M. & Dogan, B. (2010). ECG Beat Classification Using Particle Swarm Optimization and Radial Basis Function Network. *Expert Systems with Application*, Vol. 37, pp. 7563-7569.

Kurban T. & Besdok, E. (2009). A Comparison of RBF Neural Network Training Algorithms for Inertial Sensor based Terrain Classification, *Sensors*, Vol..9, pp. 6312-6329.

Lukasik, S. & Zak S. (2009). Firefly Algorithms for Continuous Constrained Optimization, *Computional Collective Intelligence, Semantic Web, Social Networks and Multigent Systems, Lecture Notes in Computer Sciences*, Vol. 5796, pp.97-106.

Ou, T. T., Oyang Y. J. & Chen C. Y. (2005). A Novel Radial Basis Function Network Classifier with Centers Set by Hierarchical Clustering. , *In Proceedings of the international joint conference on neural network, (IJCNN '05)*, Vol. 3, pp.1383-1388.

Qasem S.N. & Shamsuddin S.M. (2011). Radial Basis Function Network Based on Time Variant Multi-objective Particle Swarm Optimization for Medical Diseases Diagnosis. *Applied Soft Computing*, Vol. 11, pp. 1427-1438.

Wu, D., Warwick, K., Ma, Z., Gasson, M. N., Burgess, J. G., Pan, S. & Aziz, T. (2010). A Prediction of Parkinson's Disease Tremor Onset Using Radial Basis Function Neural Networks, *Expert Systems with Applications*, Vol .37, pp.2923-2928.

Yang X.S. (2010). Firefly Algorithm, Stochastic Test Functions and Design Optimization, *Int. J. Bio-inspired Computation*, No.2, Vol. 2, pp. 78-84.

Yang, X.S. (2008). Nature-inspired Metaheuristic Alogirthms. Frome; Luniver Press. ISBN 2008.

8

Under-Updated Particle Swarm Optimization for Small Feature Selection Subsets from Large-Scale Datasets

Victor Trevino and Emmanuel Martinez
Tecnológico de Monterrey, Campus Monterrey, Cátedra de Bioinformática
México

1. Introduction

Feature selection is the process of choosing a subset of features from the original larger set that are related to a certain outcome, such as disease type, dose, income, and time to event. The use of feature selection procedures is almost compulsory and complex in biology and medicine because the generation of massive datasets is nowadays common for many state-of-the-art technologies such as transcriptomics, proteomics, metabolomics, and genomics where a single, conventional, and relatively cheap experiment may yield the measurement of several thousands of features per sample (Hieter and Boguski, 1997; Sauer et al., 2005). In such cases, feature selection is used to reduce complexity and large computational costs, as well as to improve pattern recognition accuracy, data interpretability and hypothesis generation (Shen et al., 2008; Vapnik, 1998; Guyon et al., 2002).

Filter, embed, and wrapper methods have been proposed for feature selection (Neumann et al., 2005; Guyon and Elisseeff, 2003; Saeys et al., 2007). Filter methods, also known as univariate methods, apply a rule to every feature ignoring any other feature. The filter consists of a classical statistical test such a t-test, a ranking procedure such a signal-to-noise ratio, or an empirical permutation test as the evaluation procedure (Saeys et al., 2007; Golub et al., 1999). The search engine is composed of a model selection procedure such as forward and backward elimination strategies or a procedure that choose top features by a threshold. Embed methods couple the evaluation rule to the search, for example, by using the loadings vector associated to a component in Principal Component Analysis (Carzaniga et al., 2007), or by using the weight vector from Support Vector Machines (Guyon and Elisseeff, 2003; Guyon et al., 2002). Wrapper methods utilize independently a search engine and an evaluation procedure to choose good feature combinations. The search engine is guided depending on the evaluation of feature combinations. Because of the independency in the implementation of the search engine and the evaluation procedures, wrapper methods are highly attractive as a general tool for many types of datasets.

Although in large datasets the number of features related to an outcome could be high, there are some reasons why one would like to design a predictive model containing a small feature subset. The models that contain many variables tend to over-fit the data (Occam's razor) and to be more complex, difficult to interpret, expensive, and hard to implement in practice. For example, in a clinical test, assessing a large number of indicators is complex, tedious, and more expensive than testing only a handful of indicators. We have previously shown that models containing around 10-20 features can be found in functional genomics data (Trevino and Falciani, 2006; Martinez et al., 2010).

Particle Swarm Optimization (PSO) is a recent and very successful wrap-based search engine (Eberhart et al., 2001). However, standard implementations for feature selection fail or their performance is severely affected in selecting small feature subsets from large datasets (see section 3.1 for some grounds). For these reasons, some authors have adapted the standard binary PSO (sbPSO) presented by (Eberhart et al., 2001) implementing ad-hoc algorithms to overcome the dataset size problem (Wang et al., 2007; Chuang et al., 2008; Xu et al., 2007; Takahashi Monteiro and Yukio, 2007; Bello et al., 2007; Alba et al., 2007). Nevertheless, these implementations are mainly focused on maximizing the evaluation accuracy and little or no consideration is done to minimize the number of features selected (for an exception see (Alba et al., 2007)).

In this paper, we propose a wrapper feature selection method based on PSO named Under-Updated Particle Swarm Optimization (uuPSO) designed to efficiently select small feature subsets from large-scale functional genomics data. For illustrative purposes, we used a 10-fold-cross-validation error estimation coupled within a nearest centroid classifier as the evaluation procedure in five large datasets. We focused on selecting small feature subsets at maximum accuracy from functional genomics data that hopefully will help in designing cheap and easy to implement clinical assays. We show that our algorithm is capable of selecting the most relevant genes. We also demonstrate that uuPSO is able to find alternative models that could not be found with univariate or ranking methods such as SVM-RFE.

The remainder of the paper is organized as follows. Section 2 describes PSO methodology and the standard feature selection algorithm. Section 3 describes the rationale of the implemented procedures in uuPSO to improve the selection of small feature subsets. Section 3 also includes the datasets used and the experiments performed to show their effects. Section 4 describes and interprets the results of each experiment. Section 5 provides a general discussion and practical advices for the selection of parameter values. Finally, section 6 includes a summary and concluding remarks.

2. Background

2.1 Particle Swarm Optimization

Recalling, PSO is an optimization technique inspired in social behavior observed in nature (Eberhart et al., 2001). PSO algorithm starts by creating a swarm of particles placed randomly in the solution landscape. The swarm explores the solution landscape guided by particle leaders. Particle leaders are those particles better placed in the solution landscape. This is achieved using a goodness function whose input is the particle position. The leadership can be global attracting all particles, or local pulling only neighboring particles. If the new goodness function evaluation results in higher values than those of the leaders, leadership is changed. Thus, particles will update their position depending on their own experience following global and local bests but attempting being better on their way. The process of updating all particle positions and velocities is called *epoch* in the PSO paradigm. The position of a particle is updated as

$$x_{id}(t) = x_{id}(t - 1) + v_{id}(t) \quad (1)$$

where i is the i-particle of the swarm, d is the space dimension, t is the epoch, v is the velocity, and x_{id} is the position of the i-particle in the dimension d. All $x_{id}(0)$ are set randomly. The velocity of a particle i for dimension d is defined as

$$v_{id}(t) = w * v_{id}(t - 1) + r_1 * c_1 * (p_{ld} - x_{id}(t - 1)) + r_2 * c_2 * (p_{gd} - x_{id}(t - 1)) \quad (2)$$

where p_{gd} is the position of the best particle in the dimension d, p_{ld} is the position of the local best particle in the dimension d, w is used as an inertial value, r_1 and r_2 are positive random numbers, and c_1 and c_2 are local and global weights respectively (commonly summing 4). The local best is commonly designated as the best of the c neighbors in the swarm array. When a particle i has changed its position x_i, the evaluation function will determine whether it is the new global or local best depending on the goodness compared to the swarm best goodness or the goodness of the c neighbor particles respectively. Note that for the global best particle only the inertial term will be actually used because p_{ld} and p_{gd} will be both i cancelling both terms. To avoid this, an elitism scheme is usually used, which consists on ignoring the global best particle from the update procedure.

2.2 Binary PSO for feature selection

The common implementation for feature selection using PSO, known as standard binary PSO (sbPSO), simply sets the maximum dimension as the total number of features, then employs the value of v_{id} to decide whether the feature d for particle i is selected. This is achieved by the use of a sigmoid function s (Eberhart et al., 2001):

$$\text{if } r_{id} < s(v_{id}(t)) \text{ then } x_{id}(t) = 1; \text{ else } x_{id}(t) = 0$$

$$s(v_{id}) = 1/(1 + exp(-v_{id})) \quad (3)$$

where r_{id} is a random number drawn from a uniform distribution between 0 and 1. In this way, the goodness function would use only the selected features for the evaluation (those whose $x_{id}(t) = 1$). In practice, v_{id} is limited between the range $[-v_{max}; v_{max}]$ where v_{max} is usually 4. This establishes practical limits for the sigmoid function and helps to change direction faster. Also, the inertial w is gradually changed during the course of the procedure, e.g. from 0.9 in early epochs to 0.4 in late epochs.

2.3 Others implementations for feature selection using PSO

Some authors have proposed modifications to sbPSO algorithm in order to improve performance in terms of search and evaluation capabilities (Chuang et al., 2008; Xu et al., 2007; Wang et al., 2007; Takahashi Monteiro and Yukio, 2007; Bello et al., 2007). However, these implementations are mainly focused in maximizing the evaluation accuracy. Little or no consideration is done to minimize the number of features selected (Alba et al., 2007). Therefore, in most of these methods a large number of features were selected (Chuang et al., 2008; Xu et al., 2007). Others implementations are more difficult to review in the context of small feature subset selection because datasets used contained only around a hundred features (Takahashi Monteiro and Yukio, 2007; Wang et al., 2007). One of the adaptations that attempted to control the number of selected features was introduced by (Xu et al., 2007) defining a parameter f to bias the random decision for activating features as follows:

$$\text{if } r_{id} + f < s(v_{id}(t)) \text{ then } x_{id}(t) = 1; \text{ else } x_{id}(t) = 0$$

In this way, high values of f would tend to turn off most of the variables. The experiments from (Xu et al., 2007) using $f = 0.45$ resulted in models containing from 60 to 120 features which still seems too high for our purposes. However, this adaptation provides the concept of activating a smaller number of features by changing the selection decision.

A great effort to select small feature subsets was introduced by (Wang et al., 2007) in which only a subset of x_{id} was updated. They used a unique velocity per particle v_i which roughly means how many x_{id} bits should be changed. If v_i is less than or equal to x_g (the number of different variables of x_{id} from the best global particle), v_i bits are randomly changed different from those of x_g. If v_i is greater than x_g, x_g is copied to x_i (the complete particle) and v_i - x_g bits are also swapped to explore neighboring space. If v_i is close to zero this would mean that the particle is approaching to a stable and optimal solution whereas high values of v_i would indicate poor fitting and large navigation distances. Although the authors tested datasets containing less than a hundred features, this work is a milestone because it introduces the concept of updating only a subset of dimensions rather than all dimensions. Other adaptation of PSO replaces the concept of PSO velocity by a complex crossover operator resembling genetic algorithms rather than to PSO (Alba et al., 2007).

3. Methods

In this section, we describe the adaptations to sbPSO in order to select small feature subsets from massive datasets such as gene expression data. The parameters introduced in these adaptations are intended to show the effects of our adaptations rather than to burden the exquisite simplicity of the PSO algorithm. Finally, the datasets used for the experiments are mentioned and the values of parameters employed are listed.

3.1 Initialization

sbPSO has been successful in a variety of feature selection problems (Eberhart et al., 2001). However, the performance in accuracy, feature selection, and computation time of sbPSO is inadequate when data consists of thousands of variables, which is common for functional genomics data. In the sbPSO, the random initialization of v_{id} and x_{id} would select 50% of the features just by chance. This issue affects drastically the performance and goodness in some aspects. First, the performance of multivariate methods (classification or regression) that would be inevitably part of the goodness function depends on the number of features and matrix operations such as inversions. This would consume unnecessary CPU time. Second, the error estimation consists of the evaluation of these multivariate methods several times, such as the cross-validation methods worsening the CPU time consumption. Third, given that particles velocities depend on the global and local best, which will contain a large number of features selected, several epochs would be needed to decrease the number of selected features from thousands to a handful by the standard PSO selection. Fourth, the overall goodness could be decreased by the overload of selected features that might not be related to the predictor. This could confuse multivariate methods generating random effects.

For these reasons, our first proposal is to control the number of active features in the initialization procedure. To achieve this, we used a predefined constant b, which specifies the number of random features that will be initialized to 1 (x_{ib} = 1). This procedure is independent of the initialization of v_{id}, which is random in all dimensions as usual.

3.2 Updates

If initialization as stated in previous section is used alone, it would not have long-term effects because v_{id} is initialized as random, so updates in further epochs will reset initial x_{id} values. Thus, we included an adaptation to limit the total number of v_{id} updates, which is controlled by a user-specified parameter u. In order to choose which features will be updated, we thought that particles should maintain the essence of the PSO algorithm, that particles should follow the global and local best expecting to be better on their way. So, to manage this, a candidate list of updates is formed for each particle i. This list is populated from the union of the active features (x_{id}) for particle i, the active features from global best g, and those from local best l. In addition, the candidate list also considers e random updates, which is presented in the next paragraph as "innovation". Finally, only u random features are updated from the candidate list generated. In this way, particles can even fly in direction of the global best and local best, although slower than in sbPSO, still leaving some room for innovation to fulfill the expectation of being even better. In social terms, as in the original PSO paradigm, this could be interpreted as if a particle cannot make an effort to imitate all the features of the best particle (global and local) at the same time, sometimes it will imitate certain features and in other occasions it will imitate another. This constrained imitation seems, by common sense, a reasonable social behavior.

3.3 Innovation

In sbPSO, innovation is the combined result of updating all dimensions and the random decision of activating a feature. However, considering only the first two adaptations described so far, we would update only u dimensions chosen from the particle itself, the local best and global best. Consequently, the universe of updatable x_{id} would be limited to the initial random activation. If some features were not initially activated within the swarm population, those features would never be explored. For instance, for a swarm population of 50 and an initial activation of 5 features, there will be at most 250 updatable features for the entire swarm. This number seems scarce compared to the functional genomics datasets we are focusing on, which may contain thousands of features. In addition, global best would be stuck since it has no way to update other features. Hence, the swarm could converge quickly to a poor local optimum. For these reasons, we introduced a mechanism to control how many random features will be included in the candidate list of updates per particle, managed by a parameter e. In the PSO social terms, this would mean that imitation of the best particles is combined with a sense of uniqueness, hopefully surpassing those best particles. To show the effects of innovation, we ran some experiments varying e.

3.4 Number of selected features

The adaptations shown above do not ensure that the number of selected features will be small. Although the constrained number of updates would limit over-activation, activation might change freely during the course of the epochs. Therefore, we introduced another adaptation to keep the number of selected features within a range. We set n as the minimum number of active features and m as the maximum. After updating, if the number of active features a is larger than m, then a-m randomly chosen features are turned off. On the contrary, if a is less than n, n-a randomly chosen features are turned on, which would provide other mechanism for innovation.

3.5 Under-updated Particle Swarm Optimization algorithm

Considering the adaptations described in previous paragraphs, the uuPSO pseudo-code algorithm to maximize the Goodness function is shown in Algorithm 1. The algorithm can be easily thought as a generalization of sbPSO. If the total number of features is k, setting $b = k / 2$, $u = k$, $n = 1$, and $m = k$ should behave as sbPSO.

```
Initialize v_id randomly;
// Adaptation 3.1
q = draw b features;
for (j in q) { x_ij(0) = 1; }
epoch = 0;
while (epoch < limit or Goodness(p_gd) > goal) {
        epoch = epoch + 1;
        for (i=1 to number of particles) {
                if (Goodness(x_i) > Goodness(p_g)) then p_g = x_i;
                if p_g != x_i OR NOT Elitism then p_l = x_i;
                for (j in the indexes of neighbors) {
                        if (Goodness(x_j) > Goodness(p_l)) then p_l = x_j;
                }
// Adaptation 3.2
                candidates = union(active(x_i), active(p_l), active(p_g));
                innovation = draw e features not present in candidates;
                candidates = union(candidates, innovation);
                toupdate  = draw u  features from candidates;
                for (d in toupdate) {
                        v_id (t) = w * v_id (t - 1) + r_1 * c_1 * ( p_ld - x_id (t - 1)) + r_2 * c_2 * ( p_gd - x_id (t - 1))
                        if v_id(t) > v_max then v_id(t) = v_max;
                        if v_id(t) < -v_max then v_id(t) = -v_max;
                        if r_id < s(v_id(t)) then x_id(t) = 1 else x_id(t) = 0
                }
// Adaptation 3.3
                while (active(x_i) < n) {
                        q  = draw one feature not active(x_i);
                        x_iq(t) = 1; }
                while (active(x_i) > m) {
                        q  = draw one feature not active(x_i);
                        x_iq(t) = 0; }
        }
}
```

Algorithm 1. Under-Updated Particle Swarm Optimization Algorithm.

3.6 Datasets

In this paper we focused on the selection of small subsets of features from large-scale datasets. In this context, we mainly used two datasets generated using microarray data from breast cancer and leukemia that had been previously reported and studied in a similar fashion (Trevino and Falciani, 2006). For comparison with other PSO algorithms, we also used other three datasets in order to show overall effects and the generality of our adaptations (see Table 1).

Dataset	*Molecular Data*	*Features*	*Classes*	*Samples per class*
Breast Cancer	mRNA Rosetta	2,920	2	44 No metastases, 34 metastases
Leukemia Yeoh	mRNA Affymetrix	2,435	5	27 E2A-PBX, 79 TEL, 64 Hyp+50, 20 MLL, 43 T
Leukemia Golub	mRNA Affymetrix	7,219	2	47 AML, 25 ALL
Colon Cancer	mRNA Affymetrix	2,000	2	40 Tumor, 22 Normal
Ovarian Cancer	Proteomics	15,154	2	162 Tumor, 91Normal

Table 1. Datasets considered for this study.

The breast cancer (BC) dataset was originally developed and published by van't Veer et al. (2002) obtained from the gene expression taken from 44 patients with no metastases developed within the first five years, and 34 patients positive for metastases within the first five years. Data were normalized as described in the original publication. Genes with a p-value larger than 0.001 were filtered out (confidence level that a gene's mean ratio is significantly different from 1). Finally, the data used consisted of a matrix of 2,920 features (genes) * 78 samples and a binary vector indicating the state of metastases. It is worth mentioning that some of the best multivariate-selected classifiers published for this dataset lie at around 80% accuracy whereas the univariate-selected classifiers lie at around 65% ((Trevino and Falciani, 2006), supplementary material). Thus, this dataset is considered a difficult dataset.

The leukemia-golub dataset (Golub et al., 1999) contains 72 bone marrow samples that correspond to two types of leukemia: 47 Acute Myeloid Leukemia (AML) and 25 Acute Lymphoblastic Leukemia (ALL). It was obtained from an Affymetrix high-density oligonucleotide microarray that includes 7129 genes.

The colon cancer dataset was obtained from the expression levels of 2000 genes using Affymetrix oligonucleotide microarrays (Alon et al., 1999). The genes correspond to 40 tumor and 22 normal colon tissue samples. Data were quantile-normalized before processing (Bolstad et al., 2003).

The leukemia-yeoh (LY) dataset was developed by (Yeoh et al., 2002) using Affymetrix microarrays, and describes the gene expression profile of 327 acute lymphoblastic leukemia patients representing 7 different disease sub-classes. In this paper, we have selected the five largest classes: E2A-PBX, Hyp+50, MLL, T, and TEL. These sub-classes include respectively 27, 64, 20, 43, and 79 samples. Data have been filtered to eliminate the most invariant genes. The standard deviation and difference between maximum and minimum expression values were calculated for each gene. The genes were ranked by these values and selected if they were within the top 15%. Finally, the dataset used consisted of 2,435 features (genes) * 233 samples and a string label indicating the sample sub-class. Although this dataset compromise 5 classes, it is considered an easy dataset because there are several features correlated to classes (Yeoh et al., 2002) and both univariate and multivariate searches have found models around 98% accuracy ((Trevino and Falciani, 2006), supplementary material).

The ovarian cancer dataset consists of proteomic spectral data from serum (Petricoin et al., 2002).This dataset comprises on 15,154 mass/charge (M/Z) identities obtained from 91 normal individuals and 162 ovarian cancers. Data were quantile normalized before processing. A summary of the datasets used is listed by cancer type or author in Table 1.

3.7 Experiments

As explained in previous paragraphs, we tested the algorithm varying the controlling parameters. For each combination of parameters, we ran the uuPSO algorithm 100 times and the goodness and active features of the global best was monitored during 1000 epochs. No other termination criteria were active. The median of the 100 runs for each epoch is reported. If not stated, the values of the parameters used were $b = 10$, $n = 10$, $m = 10$, $u = 10$, $e = 10$, *elitism* = true. The standard PSO parameters used were $v_{max} = 4$, $w = 0.9\text{-}0.0005\text{*epoch}$ (corresponding to an initial $w = 0.9$ and final $w = 0.4$), and $c_1 = c_2 = 2$. The swarm size was 20. The goodness function was 1-*cve*. *cve* is a 10-fold cross-validation error estimation procedure. Error in each fold was estimated by the percentage of miss-classified test samples using a nearest centroid method in Euclidean space. A centroid is defined as the mean of a given set of samples of the same class. Thus, after estimating all centroids for corresponding training classes in each gene, the nearest centroid for a predicting sample is the centroid whose Euclidean distance is minimal, as follows:

$$class = \min_k(\sqrt{\sum(x_i - c_{ki})^2}) \quad (4)$$

where x_i is the value of the i gene and centroid c_{ki} is the mean for gene i in class k. We have used, mainly, a nearest centroid classifier for its simplicity and high speed. However, we also made comparisons with more powerful classifiers like SVM.

All runs were performed in a Dell PowerEdge SC1435 with two dual AMD opteron processors and 8Gb of memory based on CentOS Linux Distribution (http://www.centos.org/). No more than one run per core processor was performed at the same time. Scripts were written in Java. We used official Sun Java(TM) SE Runtime Environment (build 1.6.0-10-b33) and the official virtual machine Java HotSpot (TM) 64-Bit Server VM (build 11.0-b15, mixed mode) for all runs.

For the support vector machines-recursive feature elimination, we used the R implementation in the package e1071 (Chang and Lin, 2001). For the support vector machines-forward selection, we added genes one by one following the order given by the p-value from an f-test. This forward-selection strategy is similar to that in PAM (Tibshirani et al., 2002) and the Prophet tool in GEPAS (Montaner et al., 2006).

Dataset	*All Acc*	*PSO Algorithm*	*Best Model Size*	*Best Model Acc*	*Accuracy Mean*	*Accuracy SD*	*Features Mean*	*Features SD*	*Time (hr)*
Breast-Cancer	0.667	uuPSO	13	0.923	**0.842**	0.026	**13**	2	**0.74**
		sbPSO	1470	0.756	0.686	0.009	1463	26.1	113.67
		XuPSO	7	0.872	0.827	0.016	‡20	17.6	5.14
		Wang	1386	0.782	0.758	0.015	1447	25.9	89.11
Leukemia-Yeoh	0.983	uuPSO	14	1	0.981	0.016	**14**	1.3	**0.61**
		sbPSO	1143	1	**1**	0	1210	23.8	*515.88
		XuPSO	35	1	0.999	0.002	170	77.3	5.8
		Wang	1154	1	0.997	0.002	1210	25.3	*403.76
Colon	0.871	uuPSO	12	0.984	**0.949**	0.013	**12**	2.2	**1.03**
		sbPSO	957	0.887	0.884	0.007	996	10.3	61.55
		XuPSO	5	0.952	0.937	0.006	65	33.2	3.74
		Wang	946	0.887	0.879	0.008	1000	22.4	56.07
Ovarian	0.846	uuPSO	10	1	**0.999**	0.003	**13**	2.2	**6.34**
		sbPSO	7591	0.877	0.874	0.001	7594	71.2	*2293.44
		XuPSO	6	1	0.997	0.005	40	33.2	42.17
		Wang	7424	0.881	0.88	0.002	7540	72.7	*1424.68
Leukemia-Golub	0.806	uuPSO	14	0.944	**0.879**	0.023	**14**	1.6	**1.54**
		sbPSO	3515	0.875	0.859	0.007	3550	47.9	*407.72
		XuPSO	100	0.875	0.844	0.012	184	146.9	12.43
		Wang	3529	0.903	‡0.874	0.015	3555	44.1	195.05

Table 2. Comparison of PSO algorithms: the accuracy (Acc) and number of feature (size) of the best model found among 100 runs is shown in best-model columns. accuracy is the number of correctly predicted samples divided by the total. The mean and standard deviation (SD) of the accuracy and number of features were estimated from the resulted models (100 in most runs). Compared to uuPSO, all model accuracies and number of features were significant using a Wilcoxon rank sum test at $p < 0.0005$ except those marked with ‡ where $p > 0.05$. time was estimated for the 100 runs. A star (*) marks times estimated from partial results where at least 20 runs have finished. This estimated time should not be largely affected since run-time standard deviation is low. For example, for the ovarian dataset the standard deviation per run was 0.138 and 0.696 hours for sbPSO and Wang PSO respectively. The accuracy using all features is shown in column "All Acc" for comparison. Xu PSO was ran at $f = 0.1, 0.3, 0.5, 0.7$, and 0.9. The best result is shown. In four datasets $f = 0.5$ was the best in terms of accuracy and number of features except for the leukemia Golub dataset where $f = 0.7$ was better. Best results are shown in bold.

4. Results

4.1 Comparison with other PSO methods

We first compared our algorithm with the sbPSO. For the uuPSO runs, we used an overall controlling proxy parameter, size =10, then b = size, u = size, e = 1, n = 0.5*size, and m = 1.5*size. The results summarized in Table 2 are encouraging. Our algorithm increased remarkably the classification accuracy in all datasets, decreased the selected features from thousands to a handful, and decreased the computation time from days to about an hour. Best model accuracy improved from around 7.3% in Leukemia-Golub to 18.1% in BC. Moreover, remarkable differences are observed in model size and computation time where our algorithm gets better results by around two orders of magnitude. Overall, these results clearly show that our algorithm is able to obtain better predictive models from functional genomics data with thousands of features in a fraction of time.

Dataset		#	*uuPSO*			*Tabu Search IBPSO*		
				Genes Selected			*Genes Selected*	
Type	**Classes**	**Genes**	**Fitness**	**#**	**%**	**Fitness**	**#**	**%**
9_Tumors	11	5726	**100.00**	149	2.6	81.63	2941	51
11_Tumors	26	12533	**100.00**	535	4.27	97.35	3206	26
14_Tumors	9	15009	**100.00**	634	4.22	74.76	8539	57
Brain_Tumor1	5	5920	**100.00**	14	0.24	95.89	2913	49
Brain_Tumor2	4	10367	**100.00**	161	1.55	92.65	5086	49
Leukemia1	3	5327	95.83	5	0.09	**100.00**	2577	48
Leukemia2	3	11225	94.44	5	0.04	**100.00**	5609	50
Lung_Cancer	5	12600	**100.00**	14	0.11	99.52	6958	55
SRBCT	4	2308	95.18	5	0.22	**100.00**	1084	47
Prostate_Cancer	2	10509	93.14	4	0.04	**95.45**	5320	51
DLBCL	2	5469	94.81	3	0.05	**100.00**	2671	49
Average			**97.58**		**1.22**	**94.30**		**17**

Table 3. Comparison between uuPSO and tabu search ibPSO: the fitness and number of feature (#) of the best model found among 100 runs is for the uuPSO algorithm while the results from tabu search ibPSO were extracted from (chuang et al., 2009). (%) shows the percentage of genes selected from the total (# genes).

The Xu PSO implementation (Xu et al., 2007) also tries to decrease the number of selected features by using a different strategy. There, the number of selected features is affected by biasing the binary activation decision using a parameter *f* (see section 2.3). For comparison, we ran the Xu algorithm (XA) for several values of *f*. We also compared the Wang algorithm (WA) that introduced the concept of updating a subset of features by an unusual implementation of a unique particle velocity whereas uuPSO use a candidate list of features. For the uuPSO runs, we used size = 5 or 10, then b = size, u = size, e = 1, n = 0.5*size, and m = 1.5*size. Results are shown in Table 2. This table shows that our implementation performed better than WA and XA in accuracy, number of selected features, and computation time. The WA algorithm is not able to decrease the number of active features presumably due to the initialization procedure. In XA, the maximum accuracy found at f = 0.5 may compete, but goodness is not sustained probably due to abrupt changes in the number of selected features. Contrary, uuPSO goodness is stable in terms of number of features along the run (lower SD). In addition, uuPSO is far quicker. Also, in order to find competitive models, we would have to perform several XA runs changing the *f* parameter.

We previously published (Martinez et al., 2010) that we obtained models with better classifications and fewer selected features than IBPSO (Chuang et al., 2008) which is another implementation of PSO. In these works, the algorithms were tested using 11 different datasets with distinct characteristics. The same authors of IBPSO presented an optimized algorithm based on tabu search and support vector machines (Chuang et al., 2009), tested with the same datasets and obtained better results than their previous version. In Table 3, we show the results running the same models found in (Martinez et al., 2010) with support vector machines and one-versus-all mode. In average (and in 6 of 11 datasets), we got higher classification accuracies than the Tabu-Search IBPSO algorithm, reinforcing the idea that is possible to choose models with few variables without sacrificing prediction power.

In summary, our algorithm is superior to four different PSO implementations in accuracy, number of features and time, supporting our objective of obtaining models with fewer genes.

4.2 Biological interpretation of features in models

In order to summarize the 100 models generated from the BC dataset, we selected the top 10 most frequent genes as a representative model (see Figure 1). The gene MMP14, a metalloprotease, has been recently related in breast cancer progression in the transition from preinvasive to invasive growth (Ma et al., 2009).This agrees with the expression of MMP14 in the BC dataset where higher values are observed in metastatic tumors. SLC27A2, a cholesterol homeostasis mediator, has been implicated in pancreatic neoplasm (Hansel et al., 2004). FMO1 is a monooxygenase involved in the NADPH-dependent oxidative metabolism of many drugs such as tamoxifen (Katchamart and Williams, 2001), which is used as breast cancer treatment in postmenopausal treatments. The expression levels of LAMB3 have been found to be increased in malignant tumors and correlated with the depth of invasion (Kita et al., 2009). However, in the BC dataset, LAMB3 seems to be less expressed in metastatic tumors. ORM1 is increased in the plasma of cancer patients (Budai et al., 2009). This concurs in the BC dataset where the expression of ORM1 appears to be increased in metastatic tumors. These results suggest that our algorithm is detecting genes related to BC physiology.

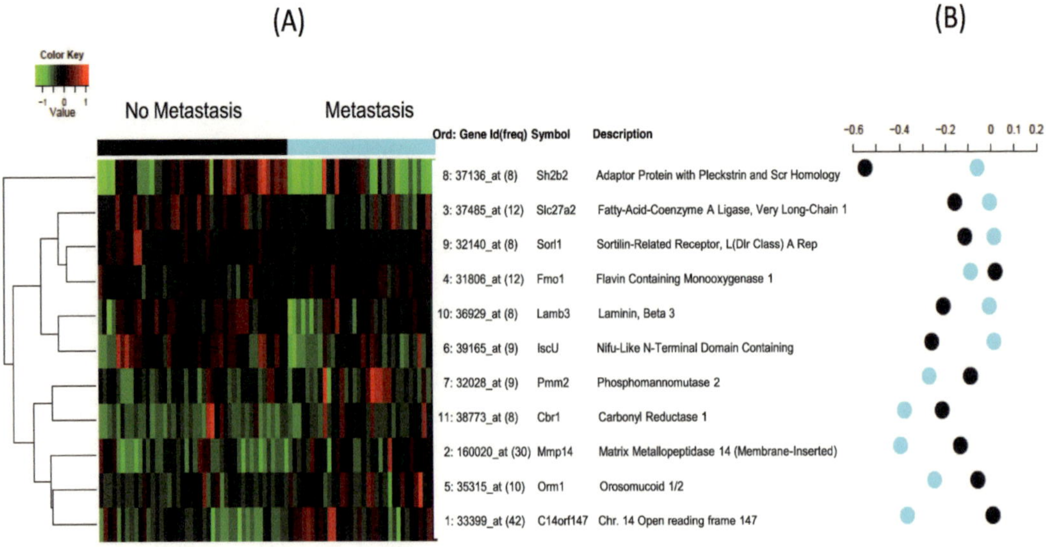

Fig. 1. Representative genes selected by our algorithm from 100 runs for the BC dataset. (A) A heatmap representation of the most frequent genes. Darker (red) or lighter (green) colors represent higher or lower expression respectively. Ord represents the order of genes given by frequency in 100 models (shown in parenthesis). (B) Class centroid for each gene. Negative values represent under-expression relative to a common reference.

4.3 Analysis of the adaptations of the *uuPSO* algorithm

Previous paragraphs have shown that our algorithm is capable of generating better and more compact models in a fraction of the time used by other methods. The next few paragraphs provides further details of the uuPSO algorithm to show the main effects of proposed adaptations. For illustrative purposes, we used only Breast Cancer and Leukemia-Yeoh datasets.

4.3.1 Overall size tests

The inspiration for our proposal is driven by the idea of decreasing the number of active features. Therefore, we compared the overall behavior attempting to control this number from 5 to 400. For this, we set size={5,10,20,100,400} as a proxy and the parameters of our adaptations were kept proportional to *size*: *b=size*, *u=size*, *e*=0.2**size*, *n=size-(size*/2), *m=size*+(*size*/2). Results are shown in Figure 2. In the BC dataset (Figure 2 A-B), overall accuracy seems more similar in late epochs than in early epochs. During the first 250 epochs, the best run achieved 84% of average accuracy using *size*=25 while the worst reached 79% using *size*=5. However, at the end of the run (epoch=1000), the former remained in 84% while the last increased to 83%. That is, it was more difficult to find 25 features than only 5. The average number of active features for the best particle slightly increased during the first 50 epochs then decreased slowly. Nevertheless, this number was very close to the initial value of size and was not limited by the limits imposed by *n* and *m*. For the LY dataset, overall accuracy was very similar (Figure 2 C-D). The number of active features also tended to increase from the initial value of *size*. The smallest average accuracy was 95% for *size*=5 but tending for model sizes around 8, which was limited by the *m* parameter used. This suggests that the decrease in accuracy is due to the low number of features used. This is sensible because the number of classes for LY dataset is 5, so, the use of 8 features is a compromise between high accuracy at low number of features. Overall, these results show that our implementation is able to control the number of active features and support our proposal that a high number of features for accurate classification of functional genomics data is not necessary.

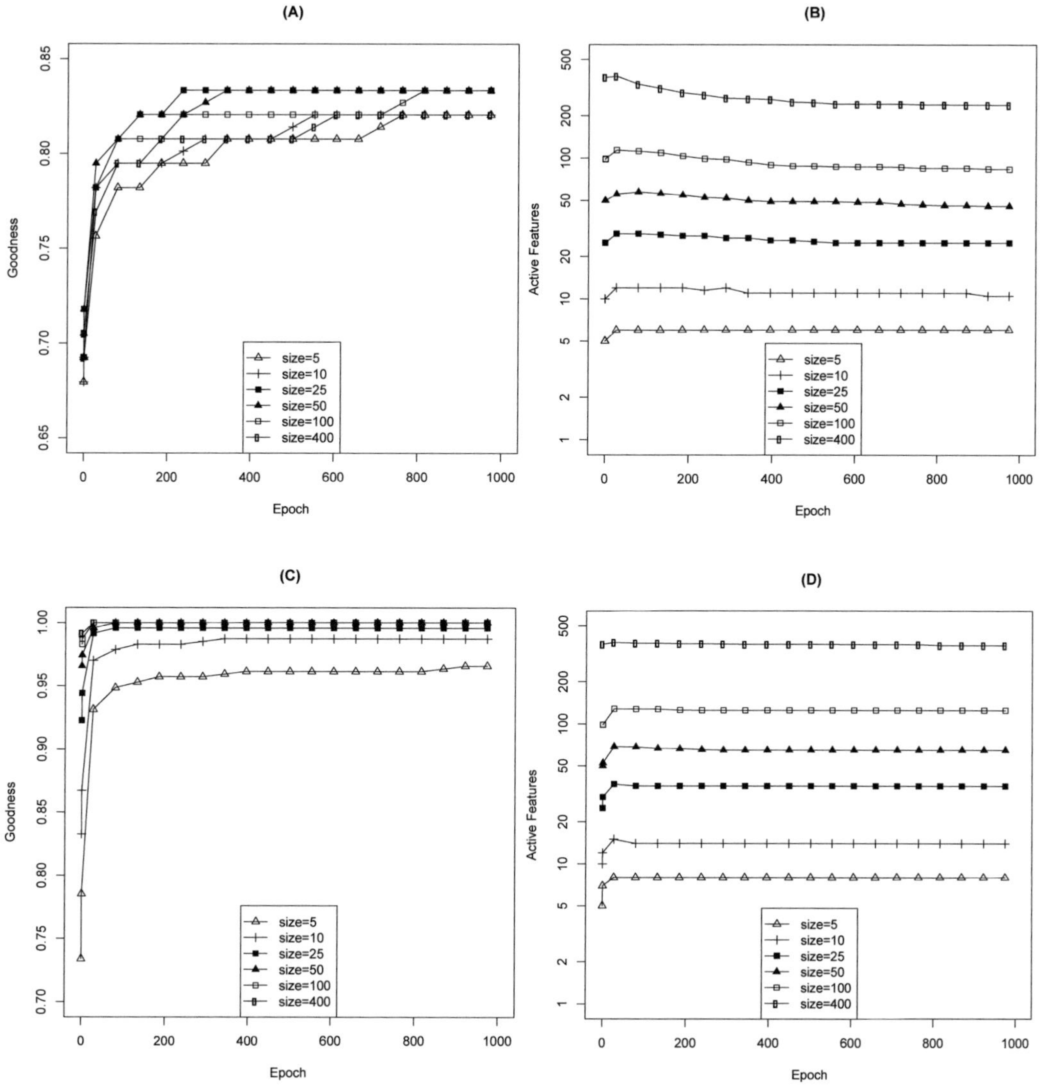

Fig. 2. Size tests for the BC (A-B) and LY (C-D) datasets. (A-C) Accuracy evolution. (B-D) Dynamics of the number of active features. Every point represents the median of the best particle in 100 runs.

4.3.2 Initialization

The runs presented above, which changed all parameters coordinately, show the overall behavior for different settings. However, the effects of each adaptation are not well appreciated. Therefore, we tested each adaptation separately. To challenge the initialization adaptation, we varied b from 5 to 400 setting b={5,10,25,50,100,400} while other parameters were kept fixed (u=10, e=1, n=2, m=600). Results are shown in Figure 3. For the BC dataset (Figure 3 A-B), accuracy was clearly smaller for b=400 within the first 50 epochs. On the other hand, for the LY dataset the accuracy was higher for larger values of b (Figure 3 C-D). For both BC and LY datasets, the final number of active features decreased when b decreased. Such decrease would be beneficial for our purposes since potential biomarker

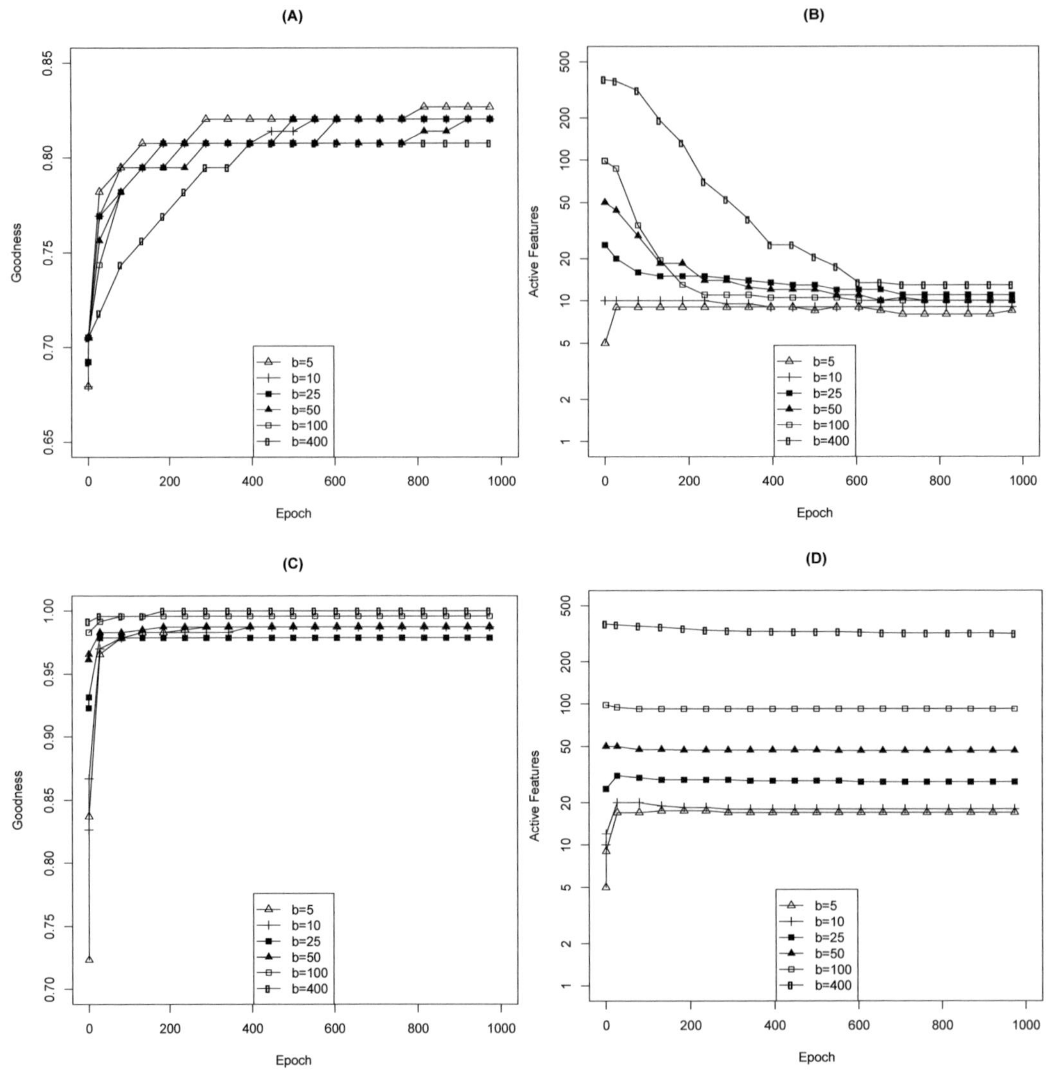

Fig. 3. Initialization tests for the BC (A-B) and LY (C-D) datasets. (A-C) Accuracy evolution. (B-D) Dynamics of the number of active features. Points as in Figure 2.

models would become more compact. Nevertheless, when initialization was smaller than update (b =5) for the BC dataset, the number of active features increases. This increase was also observed in LY for b <= 20. For the BC dataset a trend for around 10 active features is clearly observed even for b =400. In this case, it took 600 epochs to decrease the number of active features from 400 to less than 20 and to reach the same level of accuracy than in the other runs. The decrease in the number of features and the poor accuracy for runs with high b suggest that the number of active features is excessive. This may happen when the classifier is overloaded with noisy features. On the other hand, for the LY dataset, the number of active features does not decrease systematically such as that in the BC dataset. Presumably due to high accuracies in LY that are already close to 1 (the maximum possible value); thus no major evolutive pressure is present. Overall, runs tend to adjust the number of active features depending on the starting point and the accuracy pressure.

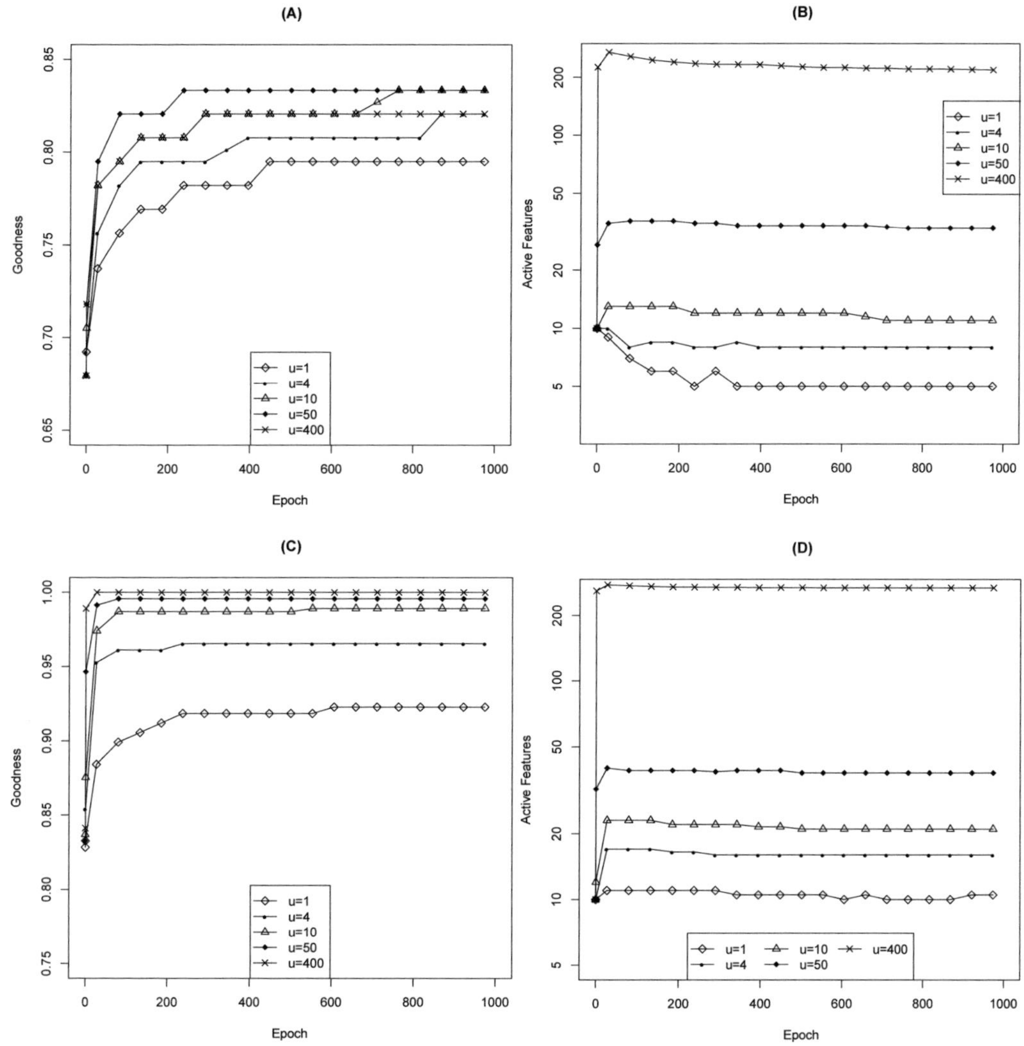

Fig. 4. Update tests for the BC (A-B) and LY (C-D) datasets. (A-C) Accuracy evolution. (B-D) Dynamics of the number of active features. Points as in Figure 2.

4.3.3 Updates

In the initialization test there was a tendency for sizes around 10 for the BC dataset, which is similar to the number of updates in those runs. This may suggest that number of active features is somehow related to updates. For this reason and to analyze the overall effect of the number of updates, we next tested the number of updates from 1 to 10 (u=1,4,10,50,400) holding all other parameters fixed (b=10, e=1, n=5, m=500). Results shown in Figure 4 propose that in general, the overall goodness increased when increasing the number of updates for low values of u in the BC and LY datasets. However for u =400, a decrement in fitness was observed in the BC dataset. This is consistent with our idea that updating a large number of dimensions is not beneficial. For the number of active features, a similar but undesirable behavior was observed in early epochs, increasing the number of updates was accompanied by an increase in the number of active features. Nevertheless, in the BC dataset, the number of active features decreased for u =1,4. Under these configurations, every particle must select 1 or 4 features respectively from at least 11 to at most 31 features composed by extreme scenarios from the set of global best, local best, its own, and random features. So, in u =1,4, deactivation was more productive than activation in the update process. This may be related to the fact that the BC is a two-classes dataset whereas LY is a five-classes one where more genes would be beneficial. Therefore, the observed results suggest that the number of updates is indirectly related to the number of active features through accuracy pressure. However, a specific number of updates may increase or decrease the number of initially active features depending on the value of the parameter and particularities of the dataset such as the number of classes.

4.3.4 Innovation

Differences between datasets were also observed when testing the number of innovations from 1 to 10 (e={1,2,4,6,8,10}; b=10, u=10, n=5, m=15). Results shown in Figure 5 for the BC and LY datasets respectively indicate that accuracies did not change drastically. However, the number of active features was sensitive to the number of innovation. For the BC dataset, the number of active features increased along with the innovation parameter. When e =10, every particle has to choose 10 updates from around 20 to 40 possible features in which 10 are new random features. Consequently, the probability of choosing new features increases, which explains the increase in active features in early epochs when the swarm is heterogeneous. For the LY dataset, the number of active features was marginally sensitive to innovation and opposite to the BC dataset. This can be explained because the LY dataset contains several features related to classes (represented by high accuracies in runs at all sizes within the first 50 epochs). In this case, new random features are not essential for the swarm because prediction is highly accurate using those already contained within the swarm. Indeed, results suggest that a large number of new random features are not beneficial and that new features are not a major driving force in the LY dataset.

In summary, there is tendency to increase the number of active features when the swarm is heterogeneous which may or may not be advantageous depending on the dataset. Innovation is a mechanism to increase heterogeneity.

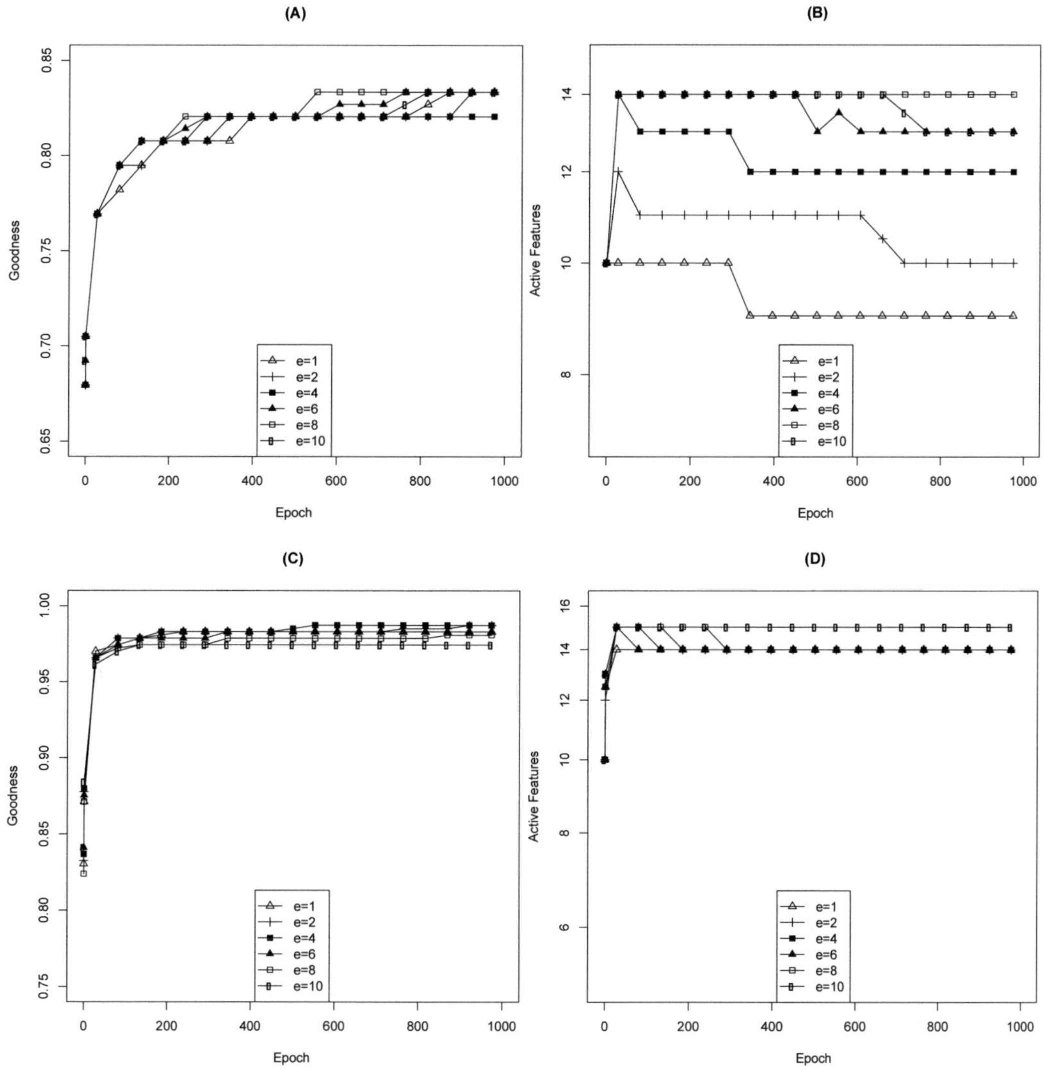

Fig. 5. Innovation tests for the BC (A-B) and LY (C-D) datasets. (A-C) Accuracy evolution. (B-D) Dynamics of the number of active features. Points as in Figure 2.

4.3.5 Constrained number of features

The last adaption was designed in order to force the number of active features to lie within a range. In this context, we would not expect major accuracy differences in changing the values of n and m. To confirm this, we conducted runs varying n =5,6,7,8,9 coordinately with m =15,14,13,12,11 respectively (using e=1, b=10, and u=10) (only ran for the BC dataset for illustrative purposes). No differences were apparent in accuracy (data not shown), but small changes were observed in the number of active features that corresponded to the limits imposed. Interestingly, a peak in the distribution of the number of active features of the final best particle was observed at the value of n in all runs as shown in Table 4. For example, for n=9 and m=11, around 60%, 30% and 10% of the best particles were generated with 9, 10, and 11 active features respectively. This tendency toward lower values indicates that the optimal number of active features needed could be lower than 9. Considering these observations, there is a tendency for the number of active features closer to 6. A consequence of this result is that the shape of this distribution may suggest an estimation of the optimal value of the number of active features.

n	m	5	6	7	8	9	10	11	12	13	14	15
10	10						**100**					
9	11					**62**	28	10				
8	12				**41**	13	18	20	8			
7	13			**24**	13	18	15	13	15	2		
6	14		15	7	16	**18**	8	17	13	5	1	
5	15	7	8	9	18	16	**20**	8	5	4	4	1

Table 4. Distribution of the number of active features, from 5 to 15, in runs at different values of n and m for the BC dataset. The highest frequency is shown in bold.

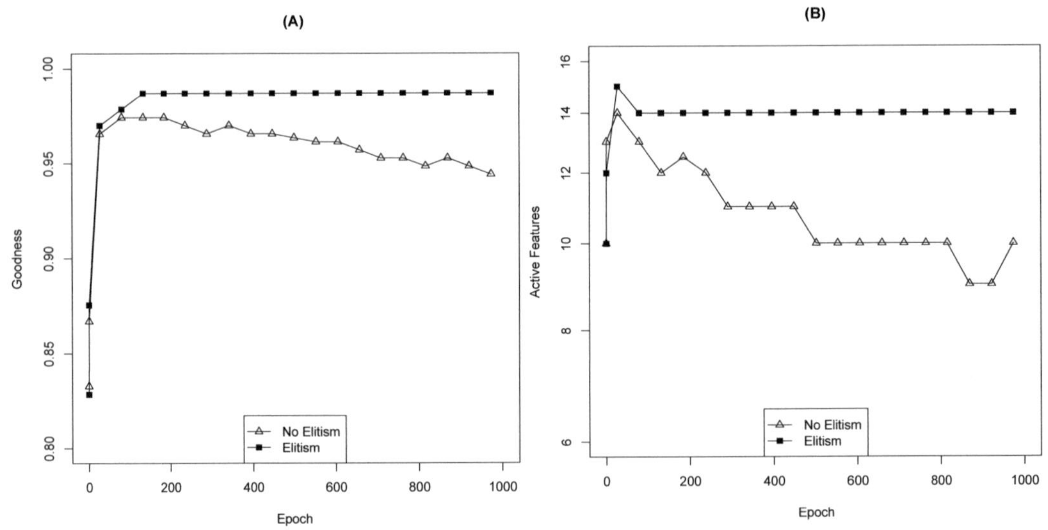

Fig. 6. Elitism tests for the LY dataset. (A) Accuracy evolution. (B) Dynamics of the number of active features. Points as in Figure 2.

4.3.6 Elitism

In the experiments described in previous paragraphs we used an elitism scheme in which the best particle is not updated. In general, it is accepted that elitism is a good practice (Eberhart et al., 2001). However, the effects of elitism are not so obvious in our implementation. Therefore we tested also the consequences of using elitism versus not using such scheme. Other parameters were set to b=10, u=10, e=1, n=5, m=15. Representative results are shown in Figure 6. As expected, the use of elitism had benefits in accuracy. On the contrary, elitism has also adverse effects by increasing the number of active features.

4.4 Simulation studies

The experiments explained in detail in 2 datasets and overall in 5 to 11 diverse datasets, clearly show that the PSO adaptations proposed here are superior to other PSO algorithms for functional genomics datasets and improved efficacy on the search of small feature subsets from large datasets. Moreover, they also exhibit better control of the number of active features than other implementations. Although our results suggest that uuPSO may be used for any other dataset, how do we know that the algorithm is actually finding good features? In this context, the biological interpretation plays a major role. However, in order to test the general applicability of our proposed algorithm, we challenged the search capabilities of uuPSO testing whether few features can be found from a large dataset mainly filled of noisy features. In such tests, simulated datasets in which data is generated by a model then injecting features carrying desired properties are commonly the choice. In this context, we generated a simulated dataset containing 2426 features for 78 samples (34 metastases, 44 non-metastases). Each feature was generated by a normal distribution with $\mu = 0$ and $\sigma = 1$. This will be referred as a "noise filled" dataset. Then we added 5 features with $\mu = 2$ and $\sigma = 1$ for metastasis sample and 5 features with $\mu = -2$ and $\sigma = 1$ for the non-metastasis samples (features 2427 to 2436). We ran uuPSO at least 1,000 times before and after adding these 10 features. Results show that *uuPSO* is able to find the 10 added features, which is represented by better accuracies, as shown in Table 5.

Simulated Dataset	*Accuracy Mean*	*SD*	***Top 10 Selected Features (frequency %)***
Noise Filled	0.80	0.02	1878(42), 2198(11), 408(9), 1280(7), 227(7), 243(7), 1799(7), 176(7), 1461(6), 2269(6)
Noise Filled + 10 predictive	0.99	0.02	2435(15), 2430(14), 2428(14), 2433(13), 2434(12), 2431(10), 2429(10), 2436(10), 2427(9), 2432(8)

Table 5. Comparison of the simulated dataset with and without 10 predictive features.

Although this result is encouraging, simulated datasets are bound to the model used, which may generate simpler datasets that could not capture the complexity of observed datasets. Therefore, to include the original functional genomics data complexity we used the BC dataset to generate a class-unrelated dataset. We generated a dataset as negative control by removing those features that are somehow related to samples class. For this, it is sensible to think that good candidates are precisely those selected using our feature selection procedure. Consequently we ran our algorithm 100,000 times ($b = 10$, $u = 10$, $e = 10$, $n = 5$, $m = 15$) resulting in the same number of feature subsets. Then, we counted the number of times each feature was selected within the 100,000 resulted models as shown in Figure 7A. The most frequent features were then removed to generate a negative dataset (see Figure 7B). To choose a cut-off value for feature removal, we estimated the expected number of times a feature would be selected by random chance in the total number of genes selected within the 100,000 runs. This was estimated by a binomial distribution (p=1/2920, tries=1,426,097 which is the total number of features in the 100,000 models generated). The expected frequency was 524 at p-value < 0.05.

We consider that this value is very conservative since we used raw p-values uncorrected for multiple tests. The number of features whose frequency surpasses this value was 494. Consequently the negative datasets carried 2,426 features. The number of 100,000 was chosen in order to be confident that the rank of top genes would not change among different runs. Indeed ranks between two runs of 10,000 and 90,000 have no major differences (see Figure 7A inset). If our algorithm cannot find related features in this negative dataset, a decrease in the final accuracy would be expected. As projected, the mean accuracy in 1000 runs for the negative dataset was 72% (labeled with BOTTOM in Figure 7B) while the same indicator in the original dataset was 82% (labeled with FULL in Figure 8B). Then, we inserted only the original top 10 features to the negative dataset (representing 0.4% of the 2,436 total features) and counted how many times the same top 10 features were found in the best models for 1000 runs. We also performed this procedure for top 20, 50, 100, 200, 300, 400 and 494 originally removed features. Results are shown in Figure 8A. We found that the high accuracy is easily restored after the first insertion (labeled TOP10 in Figure 8B). However, results show that the next 10 features were needed to fully restore the original observed accuracy distribution (labeled TOP20 in Figure 8B). We found all 10 and 20 top inserted features and more than 90% among the top 100 injected features. These results indicate that most frequent features (and presumably those more related to classes) are easily found even in highly noisy scenarios (99.6% of noisy features). Nevertheless, search efficiency was decreased to 60% when 494 top features were added. Within this, top 50 features were always found. Therefore, the search capability was uncertain only for those features ranked in the order of hundreds, presumably, because of random effects.

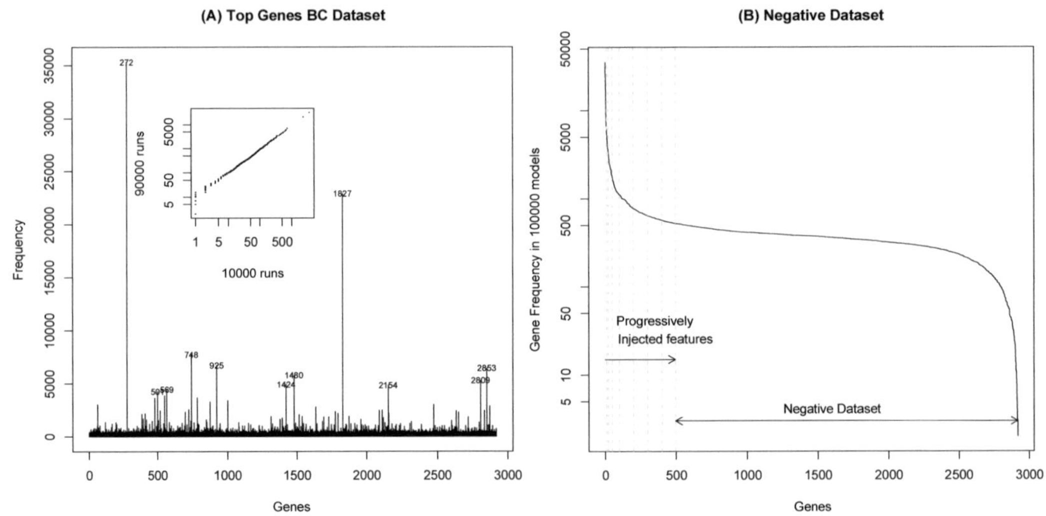

Fig. 7. (A) Top genes found in 100,000 runs for the BC dataset. Inset: Comparison of feature selection frequency for 10,000 and 90,000 runs. (B) Generation of the negative dataset and positive added features. Features were sorted by the number of times they were found in the best particle for 100,000 runs. Top 494 were removed to generate the negative dataset. Top features were then injected progressively to the negative dataset: first 10, then 20, 50, 100, 200, 300, 400 and 494 (from leftmost dashed line to rightmost dashed line).

We then asked about the amount of information that uuPSO is able to find in the original dataset. That is, the improvement attributed to the uuPSO. For this, we generated random models of equal sizes than those observed in the models generated for the negative dataset. These models would represent the amount of information (given by accuracy) found by random chance. Similarly, we generated series of 20 random models recording only the best in each series. These would represent the best models that drive the search at the beginning of the swarm optimization procedure. Results show that the baseline for the amount of information is about 54% given by random models in the negative dataset (labeled with Random in Figure 9B). The accuracy distribution from the best of the random series indicates that uuPSO starts with 66% accuracy (labeled with Best Random in Figure 8B), which is then improved to 72% during the uuPSO process (labeled with BOTTOM in Figure 8B). Overall, these results show that the average improvement by uuPSO in the BC dataset is 16% (from 66% to 82%) when good predictors are present.

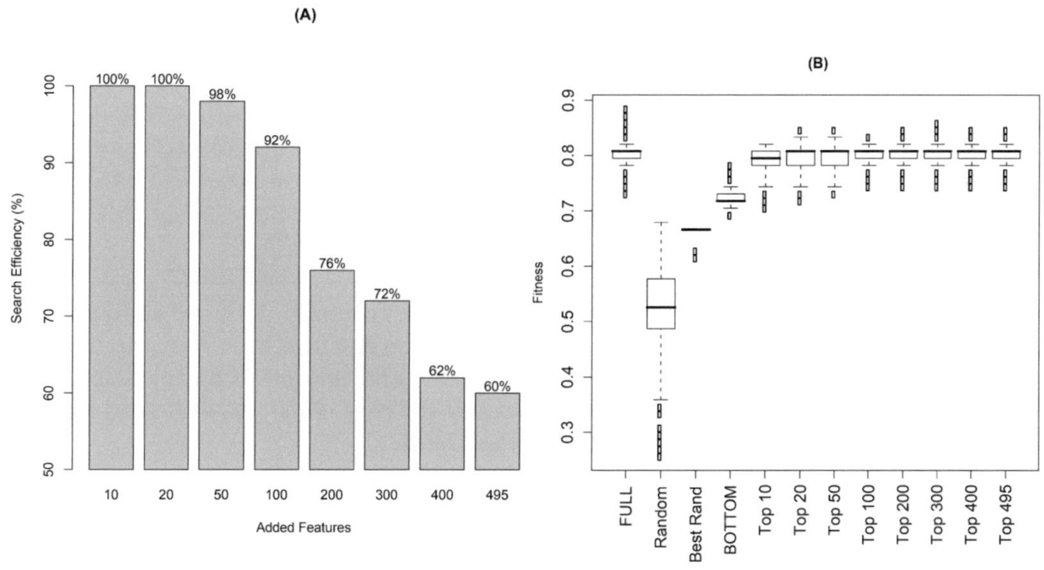

Fig. 8. (A) Search efficiency in the top added features. (B) Fitness distribution for uuPSO search capability tests.

4.5 Comparison with other feature selection methods and classifiers

In order to show that the uuPSO methodology is able to find alternative models and that is not dependent to the nearest centroid classifier (NC) used here, we also used a state-of-the-art support vector machine (SVM) classifier with a linear kernel ((Chang and Lin, 2001), java implementation). The results shown in Table 6 clearly demonstrate that uuPSO also finds good predictive models using a SVM classifier.

Although the differences are marginal relative to the NC classifier, the accuracy of SVM models was superior in all databases. Moreover, the models found using SVM were generally smaller. These differences are consistent with the perception that SVM is a powerful classifier. However, we note a huge difference in processing time, which should correspond to the complex training procedure of SVM, to the java implementation used, or to our coupling implementation of this library. In the Ovarian dataset, uuPSO using SVM found models with 100% accuracy in early epochs explaining the small difference in processing time for this dataset.

Database	*Classifier*	*Best-model*		*Accuracy*		*Features*		*Time*
		Size	*Acc*	*Mean*	*SD*	*Mean*	*SD*	*(hr)*
Breast Cancer	NC	13	0.923	0.842	0.03	13	2	0.7
	SVM	12	0.974	**0.904**	0.03	13	1	*862.0
Leukemia-Yeoh	NC	14	1	0.981	0.02	14	1	0.6
	SVM	11	1	**0.996**	0.01	14	2	*954.3
Colon	NC	12	0.984	0.949	0.01	12	2	1
	SVM	8	1	**0.987**	0.02	13	2	*585.7
Ovarian	NC	10	1	0.999	0	13	2	6.3
	SVM	10	1	**1**	0	15	2	6.9
Leukemia-Golub	NC	14	0.944	0.879	0.02	14	2	1.5
	SVM	15	0.958	**0.927**	0.02	12	2	*5722.7

Table 6. Comparison of uuPSO algorithm using the nearest centroid (NC) and support vector machine (SVM) classifiers. The goodness (Accuracy) and number of features from the best model found among 100 runs is shown. Goodnesses and features mean and standard deviation (SD) were estimated along 1000 epochs and 100 runs. Time was estimated for 100 runs. A star (*) marks times estimated from partial results.

To show the utility of uuPSO as a competitive feature selection alternative, we compared uuPSO with a state-of-the-art backward elimination strategy such as SVM-Recursive Feature Elimination (Guyon et al., 2002) and a Forward-Selection strategy (Tibshirani et al., 2002; Montaner et al., 2006). The former (SVM-RFE) considers all features and remove the worst feature in each cycle whereas the last (SVM-FS) considers the best feature and includes the next ranked feature in each cycle (based in univariate ranking such as t-test or f-test). The results of the comparison summarized in Table 7 suggest that models generated by uuPSO are competitive. However, there are some differences in the comparison of SVM-RFE and SVM-FS with uuPSO. SVM-RFE and SVM-FS procedures "see" all data to create a rank of the importance of the features related to the problem irrespective of the 10-fold-CV used to estimate the error in the feature selection step. A consequence is that the estimated error is more optimistic than the estimation of others cross-validation strategies. In our experiments using uuPSO, the SVM classifier never is aware of all data. In each of the 10 cycles of the 10-fold-CV, the SVM classifier sees only the training set and makes prediction of the test set. To observe a possible effect of this issue, we made a simple experiment in SVM-RFE changing the estimation of the rank using all data by an average rank generated by SVM-RFE from each of the 10 folds used in the cross-validation. The results, shown in Table 7 column SVM-RFE-CV, demonstrate that uuPSO is sometimes better generating smaller models.

Database	*uuPSO NC*		*uuPSO SVM*		*SVM RFE*		*SVM FS*		*SVM RFE-CV*	
	Acc	*Size*	*Acc*	*Size*	*Acc*	*Size*	*Acc*	*Size*	*Acc*	*Size*
Breast Cancer	0.92	13	0.97	12	1	13	0.83	9	1	50
Leukemia-Yeoh	1	14	1	11	1	8	1	51	1	11
Colon	0.98	12	1	8	1	9	0.89	4	1	27
Ovarian	1	10	1	10	1	3	1	34	1	21
Leukemia-Golub	0.94	14	0.96	15	1	12	0.86	9	1	13

Table 7. Comparison of uuPSO algorithm using the nearest centroid (NC) and support vector machine (SVM) classifiers versus support vector machine recursive feature elimination algorithm (SVM-RFE) and support vector machine forward selection algorithm (SVM-FS).

A more important difference of uuPSO compared to SVM-RFE and SVM-FS is the potential to generate several versions of good classifiers using a different set of features. In SVM-RFE and SVM-FS strategies, the pre-computed rank is fixed in the feature selection procedure. Therefore, alternative models are almost identical. Contrary, given the random nature of PSO, uuPSO is able to generate unrelated models with the same or similar predictive power (see Table 8 for the features selected in the top two models). For genomics data, this is useful in research and clinical scenarios to investigate the biological mechanism of the genes involved and to select models based on biological knowledge, already installed infrastructure, commercial availability, or patent protected issues. Indeed, as seen in Table 8,

Dataset	*Method*	*Accuracy*	*Selected Features*
Breast Cancer	uuPSO NC	0.923	78,116,329,672,745,760,835,925,2023,2064,2721,2847, 2871
		0.923	222,272,286,856,965,1204,1396,1480,1509,1610,2145, 2172,2422,2910
	uuPSO SVM	0.974	303,393,542,1286,1291,1370,2047,2172,2176,2721,2873, 2919
		0.974	18,78,832,1254,1515,1644,1965,2092,2185,2187,2367, 2462
	SVM RFE	1	2873,272,1002,706,268,2137,521,705,879,1695,1845, 1387,979
		1	2873,272,1002,706,268,2137,521,705,879,1695,1845, 1387,979,1793

Dataset	*Method*	*Accuracy*	*Selected Features*
Leukemia Yeoh	uuPSO NC	1	695,698,781,913,950,1069,1094,1275,1432,1609,1665,1702,1913,2155
		0.996	496,754,928,942,1175,1188,1281,1287,1519,1589,2287
	uuPSO SVM	1	51,523,934,995,1029,1153,1370,1441,1590,1969,2333
		1	15,151,422,429,708,968,1193,1220,1313,1340,1699,2007
	SVM RFE	1	708,2231,399,1139,1193,1588,781,1420
		1	708,2231,399,1139,1193,1588,781,1420,2118
Leukemia Golub	uuPSO NC	0.944	36,206,321,1830,2238,2685,3020,3239,3411,3621,4717,4915,6451,6643
		0.917	259,514,518,1291,2125,2396,2403,2912,3367,3934,4735,6352,6553
	uuPSO SVM	0.958	66,529,2610,2621,2644,3316,4377,4558,5147,5348,5751,5897,6050,6541,6577
		0.944	20,811,1332,1882,1887,2293,2860,2890,4319,6024,6761
	SVM RFE	1	997,1868,306,951,6876,6024,2520,6345,3559,5492,1650,1805
		1	997,1868,306,951,6876,6024,2520,6345,3559,5492,1650,1805,3036
Colon	uuPSO NC	0.984	182,234,549,566,613,738,788,880,1060,1210,1493,1549
		0.968	137,508,739,924,1110,1597,1698
	uuPSO SVM	1	163,380,496,764,787,1065,1324,1796
		1	19,399,440,450,611,689,1146,1679,1843,1960
	SVM RFE	1	1924,1482,1649,1843,1668,788,1935,1597,1221,124,1895,1976,1671
		1	1924,1482,1649,1843,1668,788,1935,1597,1221,124,1895,1976,1671,1094,1325
Ovarian	uuPSO NC	1	2192,2236,3258,5036,7552,8062,13207,13612,13871,15058
		1	747,2238,2633,3174,3224,3370,3561,5226,10968,12915
	uuPSO SVM	1	2235,2493,4098,4642,5808,6494,7235,12560,14006,14086
		1	1039,1682,2169,2235,2834,3703,8285,8556,11785,14707,15053
	SVM RFE	1	2239,2240,1681
		1	2239,2240,1681,2527

Table 8. Feature content of the best two models selected by three methods.

models generated by uuPSO using SVM are not similar to those generated by SVM-RFE. This suggests that uuPSO is able to explore other possibilities that cannot be explored with SVM-RFE. Therefore, uuPSO can also be used in conjunction to other methods for feature selection. In addition, uuPSO may use any classifier that can generate competitive models with different gene content. All this indicates that uuPSO is a valuable tool for the computational biology community.

5. Discussion

We have proposed and studied some the uuPSO algorithm for feature selection that successfully select small feature subsets from large-scale datasets. The selection of few highly predictive features is important in diagnosis for biological and clinical fields where an experiment has to be done for each feature. Thus, a reduced number of features would be simpler, cheaper, and easier to understand and interpret. Other fields would also prefer small models than large ones to avoid overwhelming and perhaps overfitting. We have shown in several datasets containing thousands of features than our algorithm is superior in terms of accuracy, lower number of selected features, and processing time compared to others PSO algorithms. We have also shown that designed models are meaningful biologically. In addition, uuPSO can be seen as a generalization of PSO where sbPSO is a special case (for k = total number of features, $b = k / 2$; $u = k$; $e = 0$; $n = 1$; $m = k$).

Our novel combination of subset initialization, subset update, and number of features, namely under-updated PSO, was critical in the successful selection of small feature subsets. We found that the number of updates is very close to the total active number of features. Therefore, we believe that the update-all process is the main reason why sbPSO fails for large datasets. Presumably, because a high number of features introduce such high levels of noise, that classification is confused resulting in poor prediction..

Our constrained updates adaption is somehow similar to that proposed by (Wang et al., 2007) in which the strategy was to update a subset of dimensions. However, in our approach, the choice of the specific subset to update is different and is based on dissimilar rationale. Wang used a unique velocity related to the number of bits allowed to change and does not consider the effect of the local best particle. In addition, Wang et al. initializes all features as in the usual PSO activating the half of the features by random chance. This may explain the poor performance of the Wang et al. procedure for datasets with thousands of features. Our vision to update a subset of particles is completely different. Here, contrary to Wang et al., we envisioned the number and the selection of updates as a constrained imitation in which not all features can be imitated at the same time. In this framework, our results indicate that the goodness increase when increasing the number of updates, until a certain limit. So, there are an optimal number of variables to update. In addition, the initialization plays an important role. Although uuPSO may recover from a high number of initial active features, a mild initialization may be more useful. We have shown that the proposed adaptations are successful and relevant in the context of small feature subset selection. Also our PSO implementation seems to be better than others.

One problem in our implementation is that it is necessary to start with a guess of the optimal number of features. However, which is the optimal number of features? So far we attempted to select small feature subsets of size k. Ideally, we would like that k lies between 5 and 15. Based in the results shown here, this goal is achievable. However this is far from being general and could correspond to dataset dependency. Thus, to analyze a dataset for the first time, we would suggest to use a conservative base number such as 5, 10 or 20 depending on the resulted goodness and the number of classes.

From the computational size, the superb performance in processing time may allow us to run systematic selections for several datasets and perhaps design a web service open to the scientific community. We will work in this direction shortly. Our algorithm should run faster and proportionally to the total number of features than the plain sbPSO. This is relevant since the future of microarray data analysis points out to the implementation of meta-analysis, where the number of samples are increased, thus more processing will be needed.

From the experiments performed with simulated datasets, our results clearly show that our algorithm is capable of finding the most differentially expressed genes. Table 5 supports our claim since the top 10 selected features after adding the predictive variables were precisely the variables with the best predictive power (features 2427 to 2436) and also with almost perfect classification accuracy. The search capability tests suggest that uuPSO is powerful to find important features even in the presence of 99.6% of noisy features. We showed that top 50 features are easily discovered among 1000 runs and that the search capability began to decrease for more than the top 100 genes. However, for our purpose of obtaining models composed from a few number of genes, we think that the search capability is good enough without losing information.

For illustrative purposes, we used 10-fold-cross-validation procedure considering all available data. However, it is recommended to use a blind subset to test models after the feature selection process. For the LY dataset, if the data is split in 66% for training and 33% for blind test, the accuracy of the representative model is 100% when evaluated in the blind set. This is equal to the accuracy obtained using all data. If the same procedure is performed in the BC dataset, the accuracy of the representative model is 66%. This discrepancy can be attributed to differences in the number of samples and the clinical definitions of classes. The BC dataset contains only 78 samples whereas the LY dataset contains 233. In addition, the classes in LY dataset were based on chromosomal rearrangements (Yeoh et al., 2002) whereas in the BC dataset were based on a progression end-point indicator which is biologically more complex. For example, the no metastasis class was determined by the fact that no metastases were present during the following 5 years. However, it is unknown whether some of these samples would develop metastases in the following years. Therefore, the particular molecular state of samples in the no metastasis class can be more heterogeneous than the classes in the LY dataset. Despite these concerns, the most frequent genes are conserved in both training schemes and the genes found shown in Figure 1 seem to be related to BC. For biomarker design purposes, we recommend to use large enough datasets that are representative of the biological phenomena and that can be used for proper train-test schemes.

We tested two classifiers (nearest centroid and SVM) to guide the search of features with successful results. This suggest that the use of uuPSO can be extended to other applications such as regression, time to event (survival analysis), or other custom associations between features and outcomes by using a suitable goodness function. We used the classification accuracy to make selection pressure for smaller models. However, the goodness function can also be used to explicitly select fewer features (Alba et al., 2007). For example, using goodness = accuracy * w_1 + size * w_2. Setting w_2 to negative values would tend to select particles having smaller models. However, a problem arises when more accurate models are replaced by worse ones that are smaller. Nevertheless, incipient results suggest that improvements are only marginal and may depend on others factors such as number of epochs (data not shown).

Another advantage from our method is that it can provide models with distinct variables but with the same level of accuracy. This can be useful for biologists or medical doctors, because if they have more options of possible genes to study with techniques like PCR, they can select the genes according to other criteria like molecular function, pathways, etc.

6. Conclusions

We proposed an adapted sbPSO algorithm, named uuPSO, for feature selection that allow the selection of small feature subsets from large-scale datasets. All these adaptations have a significant impact in searching small and accurate multivariate feature subsets. Results showed that good subsets were composed of around 5-20 features. These subsets performed well in classification tasks previously shown to be difficult. The proposed algorithm was successful in selecting small feature subsets from five large functional genomics datasets. Biology and simulation results confirm that our algorithm is able to find features related to sample classes. We also showed that the algorithm is able to find important features even in the presence of 99.6% of noisy features. Comparisons with other methods show that uuPSO is able to find competitive models that could not be found with SVM-RFE or SVM-FS. Therefore, uuPSO can be used in addition to these or other feature selection methods. We also tested uuPSO coupled with two classifiers (SVM and nearest centroid) and show that both can find competitive models with different selected features but same accuracy. Consequently, uuPSO could be a framework and a valuable tool in computational biology for biomarker design.

7. Acknowledgements

We would like to thank Arturo Berrones for his helpful comments, advices and criticism, which had help to improve this work. We also appreciate the manuscript corrections kindly suggested by David Mathieson, Amalia Cuellar, Gabriela Ruiz, Jose Tamez, Lucio Florez, and Sergio Martinez. This research was supported by Catedras de Investigacion grant CAT172 from ITESM Campus Monterrey and by the CONACyT grant 083929.

8. References

Alba, E., García-Nieto, J., Jourdan, L., and Talbi, E. (2007). Gene selection in cancer classification using pso/svm and ga/svm hybrid algorithms. *In IEEE Congress on Evolutionary Computation*, 284-290.

Alon, U., Barkai, N., Notterman, D. A., Gish, K., Ybarra, S., Mack, D., and Levine, A. J. (1999). Broad patterns of gene expression revealed by clustering analysis of tumor and normal colon tissues probed by oligonucleotide arrays. *Proceedings of the National Academy of Sciences of the United States of America* 96, 6745-6750.

Bello, R., Gomez, Y., Nowe, A., and Garcia, M. (2007). Two-step particle swarm optimization to solve the feature selection problem. In *ISDA '07: Proceedings of the Seventh International Conference on Intelligent Systems Design and Applications*, 691-696. IEEE Computer Society, Washington, DC, USA.

Bolstad, B. M., Irizarry, R. A., Astrand, M., and Speed, T. P. (2003). A comparison of normalization methods for high density oligonucleotide array data based on variance and bias. *Bioinformatics* 19, 185-193.

Budai, L., Ozohanics, O., Ludnyi, K., Drahos, L., Kremmer, T., Krenyacz, J., and Vkey, K. (2009). Investigation of genetic variants of ?-1 acid glycoprotein by ultra-performance liquid chromatography mass spectrometry. *Analytical and Bioanalytical Chemistry* 393, 991-998.

Carzaniga, T., Sarti, D., Trevino, V., Buckley, C., Salmon, M., Wild, D., Deh, G., and Falciani, F. (2007). Microarrays Technology through Applications. In: *The analysis of Cellular Transcriptional Response at the Genome Level: Two Case Studies with Relevance in Bacterial Pathogenesis*, 125-154. Taylor & Francis Group.

Chang, C. and Lin, C. (2001). LIBSVM: a library for support vector machines. Software available at http://www.csie.ntu.edu.tw/cjlin/libsvm.

Chuang, L., Chang, H., Tu, C., and Yang, C. (2008). Improved binary PSO for feature selection using gene expression data. *Computational Biology and Chemistry* 32, 29-38.

Chuang, L.-Y., Yang, Cheng-Huei, & Yang, Cheng-Hong. (2009). Tabu search and binary particle swarm optimization for feature selection using microarray data. *Journal of computational biology*, 16(12), 1689-1703.

Eberhart, R., Shi, Y., and Kennedy, J. (2001). *Swarm Intelligence*. The Morgan Kaufmann Series in Artificial Intelligence. Morgan Kaufmann, San Francisco, CA, USA.

Golub, T. R., Slonim, D. K., Tamayo, P., Huard, C., Gaasenbeek, M., Mesirov, J. P., Coller, H., Loh, M. L., Downing, J. R., Caligiuri, M. A., Bloomfield, C. D., and Lander, E. S. (1999). Molecular classification of cancer: Class discovery and class prediction by gene expression monitoring. *Science* 286, 531-537.

Guyon, I. and Elisseeff, A. (2003). An introduction to variable and feature selection. *Journal of Machine Learning Research* 3, 1157-1182.

Guyon, I., Weston, J., Barnhill, S., and Vapnik, V. (2002). Gene selection for cancer classification using support vector machines. *Machine Learning* 46, 389-422.

Hansel, D., Rahman, A., House, M., Ashfaq, R., Berg, K., Yeo, C., and Maitra, A. (2004). Met proto-oncogene and insulin-like growth factor binding protein 3 overexpression correlates with metastatic ability in well-differentiated pancreatic endocrine neoplasms. *Clinical Cancer Research* 10, 6152-6158.

Hieter, P. and Boguski, M. (1997). Functional genomics: It's all how you read it. *Science* 278, 601-602.

Katchamart, S. and Williams, D. E. (2001). Indole-3-carbinol modulation of hepatic monooxygenases cyp1a1, cyp1a2 and fmo1 in guinea pig, mouse and rabbit. *Comparative Biochemistry and Physiology Part C: Toxicology & Pharmacology* 129, 377-384.

Kita, Y., Mimori, K., Tanaka, F., Matsumoto, T., Haraguchi, N., Ishikawa, K., Matsuzaki, S., Fukuyoshi, Y., Inoue, H., Natsugoe, S., Aikou, T., and Mori, M. (2009). Clinical significance of lamb3 and col7a1 mRNA in esophageal squamous cell carcinoma. *European Journal of Surgical Oncology* (EJSO) 35, 52-58.

Ma, X., Dahiya, S., Richardson, E., Erlander, M., and Sgroi, D. (2009). Gene expression profiling of the tumor microenvironment during breast cancer progression. *Breast Cancer Research* 11, R7.

Martinez, E., Alvarez, M. M., and Trevino, V. (2010). Compact cancer biomarkers discovery using a swarm intelligence feature selection algorithm. *Computational Biology and Chemistry* 34, 244-250.

Montaner, D., Trraga, J., J.Huerta-Cepas, Burguet, J., Vaquerizas, J., Conde, L., Minguez, P., Vera, J., Mukherjee, S., Valls, J., Pujana, M., Alloza, E., Herrero, J., Al-Shahrour, F., and Dopazo, J. (2006). Next station in microarray data analysis: Gepas. *Nucleic Acids Research* 34, W486_W491. URL http://dx.doi.org/10.1093/nar/gkl197.

Neumann, J., Schnrr, C., and Steidl, G. (2005). Combined svm-based feature selection and classification. *Machine Learning* 61, 129-150.

Petricoin, E., Ardekani, A., Hitt, B., Levine, P., Fusaro, V., Steinberg, S., Mills, G., Simone, C., Fishman, D., Kohn, E., and Liotta, L. (2002). Use of proteomic patterns in serum to identify ovarian cancer. *Lancet* 359, 572-577. URL http://dx.doi.org/10.1016/S0140-6736(02)07746-2.

Saeys, Y., Inza, I., and Larrañaga, P. (2007). A review of feature selection techniques in bioinformatics. *Bioinformatics* 23, 2507-2517.

Sauer, S., Lange, B., Gobom, J., Nyarsik, L., Seitz, H., and Lehrach, H. (2005). Miniaturization in functional genomics and proteomics. *Nature Reviews Genetics* 6, 465-476.

Shen, K., Ong, C., Li, X., and Wilder-Smith, E. (2008). Feature selection via sensitivity analysis of svm probabilistic outputs. *Machine Learning* 70, 1-20.

Takahashi Monteiro, S. and Yukio, K. (2007). Applying particle swarm intelligence for feature selection of spectral imagery. In *ISDA '07: Proceedings of the Seventh International Conference on Intelligent Systems Design and Applications*, 933-938. IEEE Computer Society, Washington, DC, USA.

Tibshirani, R., Hastie, T., Narasimhan, B., and G.Chu (2002). Diagnosis of multiple cancer types by shrunken centroids of gene expression. *Proceedings of the National Academy of Science* USA 99, 6567-6572.

Trevino, V. and Falciani, F. (2006). Galgo: an r package for multivariate variable selection using genetic algorithms. *Bioinformatics* 22, 1154-1156.

van 't Veer, L., Dai, H., van de Vijver, M., He, Y., Hart, A., Mao, M., Peterse, H., van der Kooy, K., Marton, M., Witteveen, A., Schreiber, G., Kerkhoven, R., Roberts, C., Linsley, P., Bernards, R., and Friend, S. (2002). Gene expression profiling predicts clinical outcome of breast cancer. *Nature* 415, 530-536.

Vapnik, V., 1998. Statistical Learning Theory. Wiley-Interscience.

Wang, X., Yang, J., Teng, X., Xia, W., and Jensen, R. (2007). Feature selection based on rough sets and particle swarm optimization. *Pattern Recognition Letters* 28, 459-471.

9

Predicting Corporate Forward 2 Month Earnings

Michael F. Korns
The Shang Grand Tower U17E, Makati, Manila, Philippines

1. Introduction

The discipline of Symbolic Regression (SR) has matured significantly in the last few years. There is at least one commercial package on the market for several years (http://www.rmltech.com/). There is now at least one well documented commercial symbolic regression package available for Mathematica (www.evolved-analytics.com). There is at least one very well done open source symbolic regression package available for free down load (http://ccsl.mae.cornell.edu/eureqa).

In addition to our own ARC system [6], currently used internally for massive financial data nonlinear regressions, there are a number of other mature symbolic regression packages currently used in industry including [8] and [9]. Plus there is an interesting work in progress by McConaghy [10].

Nonlinear symbolic regression (SR) has not been widely applied to financial problems because of SR's difficulties optimizing imbedded constants. Optimizing imbedded constants is often a critical requirement in many financial applications. However, recent integrations of swarm intelligence (SI) with symbolic regression support a level of maturity and sophistication making nonlinear regression and nonlinear CART available for real world financial applications.

In this chapter we investigate the integration of two popular swarm intelligence algorithms (Bees, and Particle Swarm), and one popular evolutionary computation algorithm (Differential Evolution) with standard genetic programming symbolic regression to help optimize imbedded constants in a real world financial application: the prediction of forward 12 month earnings per share. We make the observations: that standard genetic programming does not optimize imbedded constants well; that swarm intelligence algorithms are adept at optimizing constants; and that allowing imbedded constants in SR greatly increases the size of the search space.

In the body of the chapter it is shown that the differences between the three popular constant managing algorithms is minimal for optimizing imbedded constants; yet without any swarm intelligence standard GP symbolic regression fails to optimize imbedded constants effectively.

We proceed with a general introduction to symbolic regression and the size of the search space.

Symbolic Regression is an approach to general nonlinear regression which is the subject of many scholarly articles in the Genetic Programming community. A broad generalization of general nonlinear regression is embodied as the class of *Generalized Linear Models* (GLMs) as described in [11]. A GLM is a linear combination of **I** basis functions $\mathbf{B_i}$; i = 1,2, ... I, a dependent variable **y**, and an independent data point with **M** features **x** = <x_1, x_2, x_3, ...x_m>: such that

1 $$y = \gamma(x) = c_0 + \sum_{i=1}^{I} c_i B_i(x) + err$$

As a broad generalization, GLMs can represent any possible nonlinear formula. However the format of the GLM makes it amenable to existing linear regression theory and tools since the GLM model is linear on each of the basis functions $\mathbf{B_i}$.

For a given vector of dependent variables, Y, and a vector of independent data points, X, symbolic regression will search for a set of basis functions and coefficients which minimize *err*. In [12] the basis functions selected by symbolic regression will be formulas as in the following examples:

2 $B_1 = x_3$
3 $B_2 = x_1+x_4$
4 B_3 = sqrt(x_2)/tan(x_5/4.56)
5 B_4 = tanh(cos(x_2*.2)*cube(x_5+abs(x_1)))

If we are minimizing the least squared error, ***LSE***, once a suitable set of basis functions {**B**} have been selected, we can discover the proper set of coefficients {**C**} deterministically using standard univariate or multivariate regression. The value of the GLM model is that one can use standard regression techniques and theory. Viewing the problem in this fashion, we gain an important insight. Symbolic regression does not add anything to the standard techniques of regression. The value added by symbolic regression lies in its abilities as a search technique: how quickly and how accurately can SR find an optimal set of basis functions {**B**}.

The immense size of the search space provides ample need for improved search techniques In standard Koza-style tree-based Genetic Programming [12] the genome and the individual are the same Lisp s-expression which is usually illustrated as a tree. Of course the tree-view of an s-expression is a visual aid, since a Lisp s-expression is normally a list which is a special Lisp data structure. Without altering or restricting standard tree-based GP in any way, we can view the individuals not as trees but instead as s-expressions such as this depth 2 binary tree s-exp: (/ (+ x_2 3.45) (* x_0 x_2)), or this depth 2 irregular tree s-exp: (/ (+ x_2 3.45) 2.0).

In standard GP, applied to symbolic regression, the non-terminal nodes are all operators (implemented as Lisp function calls), and the terminal nodes are always either real number constants or features. The maximum depth of a GP individual is limited by the available computational resources; but, it is standard practice to limit the maximum depth of a GP individual to some manageable limit at the start of a symbolic regression run.

Given any selected maximum depth k, it is an easy process to construct a maximal binary tree s-expression U_k, which can be produced by the GP system without violating the selected maximum depth limit. As long as we are reminded that each f represents a function node while each t represents a terminal node, the construction algorithm is simple and recursive as follows.

U_0: t
U_1: (f t t)
U_2: (f (f t t) (f t t))
U_3: (f (f (f t t) (f t t)) (f (f t t) (f t t)))
U_k: (f U_{k-1} U_{k-1})

Any basis function produced by the standard GP system will be represented by at least one element of U_k. In fact, U_k is isomorphic to the set of all possible basis functions generated by the standard GP system.

Given this formalism of the search space, it is easy to compute the size of the search space, and it is easy to see that the search space is huge even for rather simple basis functions. For our use in this chapter the function set will be the following functions: **F** = {**+ - * / abs sqrt square cube cos sin tan tanh log exp max min ℵ**} (where ℵ(a,b) = ℵ(a) = a). The terminal set is the features $\mathbf{x_0}$ thru $\mathbf{x_m}$ and the real constant **c**, which we shall consider to be 2^{64} in size. Where |**F**| = 17, **M**=20, and **k**=0 , the search space is S_0 = **M**+2^{64} = 20+2^{64} = 1.84x10^{19}. Where **k**=1, the search space is S_1 = |**F**|*S_0*S_0 = 5.78x10^{39}. Where **k**=2, the search space grows to S_2 = |**F**|*S_1*S_1 = 5.68x10^{80}. For **k**=3, the search space grows to S_3 = |**F**|*S_2*S_2 = 5.5x10^{162}. Finally if we allow three basis functions **B**=3 for financial applications, then the final size of the search space is S_3*S_3*S_3 = 5.5x10^{486}.

Clearly even for three simple basis functions, with only 20 features and very limited depth, the size of the search space is already very large; and, the presence of real constants accounts for a significant portion of that size. For instance, without real constants, S_0 = 20, S_3 = 1.054x10^{19}, and with **B**=3 the final size of the search space is 1.054x10^{57}. It is our contention that since real constants account for such a significant portion of the search space, symbolic regression would benefit from special constant evolutionary operations. Since standard GP does not offer such operations, we investigate the enhancement of symbolic regression with swarm intelligence algorithms specifically designed to evolve real constants.

As we apply our enhanced symbolic regression to an important real world investment finance application, the prediction of forward 12 month earnings per share, we discover a number of accuracy, believability, and regulatory issues which must be addressed. Solutions for those issues are provided and we proceed to apply an enhanced symbolic regression algorithm to the problem of estimating forward corporate earnings per share.

This chapter begins with a discussion of Symbolic Regression theory in Section (2) and with important theoretical issues in Section (3). Methodology is discussed in Section (4), then Sections (5) through (10) discuss the algorithms for Standard GP Symbolic Regression and the enhancements for merging swarm intelligence with standard GP symbolic regression. In Section (11) we compare the performance of standard GP symbolic regression with enhanced symbolic regression on a set of illustrative sample test problems. Sections (12) thru (15) give a background in investing and discuss the essential requirements for applying symbolic regression to predicting forward 12 month earnings in a real world financial setting. Finally, Sections (17) thru (19) compare the performance of enhanced symbolic regression with the swarm algorithm being Differential Evolution, the bees Algorithm, or Particle Swarm.

2. Symbolic regression theory

In standard Koza-style symbolic regression [12], a Lisp s-expression is manipulated via the evolutionary techniques of mutation and crossover to produce a new s-expression which can be tested, as a basis function candidate in a GLM. Basis function candidates that produce better fitting GLMs are promoted.

Mutation inserts a random s-expression in a random location in the starting s-expression. For example, mutating s-expression (4) we obtain s-expression (4.1) wherein the sub expression "tan" has been randomly replaced with the sub expression "**cube**". Similarly, mutating s-expression (5) we obtain s-expression (5.1) wherein the sub expression "cos(x_2*.2)" has been randomly replaced with the sub expression "**abs(x_{2+} x_5)**".

4 B_3 = sqrt(x_2)/tan(x_5/4.56)
4.1 B_5 = cos(x_2)/***cube***(x_5/4.56)
5 B_4 = tanh(cos(x_2*.2)*cube(x_5+abs(x_1)))
5.1 B_6 = tanh(**abs(x_{2+} x_5)***cube(x_5+abs(x_1)))

Crossover combines portions of a *mother* s-expression and a *father* s-expression to produce a *child* s-expression. Crossover inserts a randomly selected sub expression from the *father* into a randomly selected location in the *mother*. For example, crossing s-expression (5) with s-expression (4) we obtain *child* s-expression (5.2) wherein the sub expression "cos(x_2*.2)" has been randomly replaced with the sub expression "**tan(x_5/4.56)**". Similarly, again crossing s-expression (5) with s-expression (4) we obtain another *child* s-expression (5.3) wherein the sub expression "x_5+abs(x_1)" has been randomly replaced with the sub expression "**sqrt(x_2)**".

4 B_3 = sqrt(x_2)/tan(x_5/4.56)
5 B_4 = tanh(cos(x_2*.2)*cube(x_5+abs(x_1)))
5.2 B_7 = tanh(**tan(x_5/4.56)***cube(x_5+abs(x_1)))
5.3 B_8 = tanh(cos(x_2*.2)*cube(**sqrt(x_2)**))

These mutation and crossover operations are the main tools of standard GP, which functions as described in Algorithm 2, randomly creating a population of candidate basis functions, mutating and crossing over those basis functions repeatedly while consistently promoting the most fit basis functions. The winners being the collection of basis functions which receive the most favorable least square error in a GLM with standard regression techniques.

3. Theoretical issue

A theoretical issue with standard GP symbolic regression is the poor optimization of embedded constants under the mutation and crossover operators. Notice that in basis functions (4) and (5) there are real constants embedded inside the formulas. These embedded constants, **4.56** and **.2**, are quite important. That is to say that basis function (4) behaves quite differently than basis function (4.2) while basis function (5) behaves quite differently than basis function (5.4).

4 B_3 = sqrt(x_2)/tan(x_5/**4.56**)
4.2 B_9 = sqrt(x_2)/tan(x_5)
5 B_4 = tanh(cos(x_2***.2**)*cube(x_5+abs(x_1)))
5.4 B_{10} = tanh(cos(x_2)*cube(x_5+abs(x_1)))

The behavior can be quite startling. For instance, if we generate a set of random independent variables for <x_1, x_2, x_3, ...x_m> and we set the dependent variable, y = sqrt(x_2)/tan(x_5/**4.56**), then a regression on y = sqrt(x_2)/tan(x_5) returns a very bad LSE. In fact the bad regression fit continues until one regresses on y = sqrt(x_2)/tan(x_5/**4.5**). It is only until one regresses on y = sqrt(x_2)/tan(x_5/**4.55**) that we get a reasonable LSE with an R-Square of .56. Regressing on y = sqrt(x_2)/tan(x_5/**4.555**) achieves a better LSE with an R-Square of .74. Of course regressing on y = sqrt(x_2)/tan(x_5/**4.56**) returns a perfect LSE with an R-Square of 1.0.

Clearly, in many cases of embedded constants, there is a very small neighborhood, around the correct embedded constant, within which an acceptable LSE can be achieved.

In standard Koza-style symbolic regression [12], the mutation and crossover operators are quite cumbersome in optimizing constants. As standard GP offers no constant manipulation operators per se, the mutation and crossover operators must work doubly hard to optimize constants. For instance, the only way to optimize the embedded constant in s-expression (5) would be to have a series of mutations or crossovers which resulted in an s-expression with multiple iterative additions and subtractions as follows [12].

4 B_3 = sqrt(x_2)/tan(x_5/4.56)
4.2 B_3 = sqrt(x_2)/tan(x_5/(1.0+3.2))
4.3 B_3 = sqrt(x_2)/tan(x_5/((1.0+3.2)+.3))
4.4 B_3 = sqrt(x_2)/tan(x_5/(((1.0+3.2)+.3)+.07))
4.4 B_3 = sqrt(x_2)/tan(x_5/((((1.0+3.2)+.3)+.07)-.01))

Characteristically, the repeated mutation and crossover operations which finally realize an optimized embedded constant also greatly *bloat* the resulting basis function with byzantine operator sequences [18]. On the other hand swarm intelligence techniques are quite good at optimizing vectors of real numbers. So the challenge is how to collect the embedded constants found in a GP s-expression into a vector so they can be easily optimized by swarm intelligence techniques.

Recent advances in symbolic regression technology including Abstract Expression Grammars (*AEGs*) [3], [4], [5], [6], and [13] can be used to control bloat, specify complex search constraints, and expose the embedded constants in a basis function so they are available for manipulation by various swarm intelligence techniques suitable for the manipulation of real numeric values. This presents an opportunity to combine standard genetic programming techniques together with swarm intelligence techniques into a seamless, unified algorithm for pursuing symbolic regression.

The focus of this chapter will be an investigation of swarm intelligence techniques, used in connection with AEGs, which can improve the speed and accuracy of symbolic regression search, especially in cases where embedded numeric constants are an issue hindering performance.

4. Methodology

Our methodology is influenced by the practical issues in applying symbolic regression to a real world investment finance problem. First there is the issue that current standard GP symbolic regression cannot solve selected simple test problems required for the successful application of SR to predicting forward corporate earnings per share. This includes the methodological challenge of enhancing standard GP with swarm intelligence and modifying the necessary encodings to accommodate both GP and swarm intelligence algorithms. Second there is the issue of adapting symbolic regression to run in a real world financial application with massive amounts of data. Third there is the issue of modifying symbolic regression, as practiced in academia, to conform to the very difficult U.S. Securities Exchange Commission regulatory environment.

Sections (5) thru (10) discuss the methodological challenge of enhancing standard GP symbolic regression so that it can be effective when applied to the real world problem of predicting forward 12 month corporate earnings per share. In Section (11), the behavior of GP symbolic regression with and without the enhancement of swarm intelligence is compared on a few sample test problems.

For the sample test problems, we will use only statistical best practices out-of-sample testing methodology. A matrix of independent variables will be filled with random numbers. Then the model will be applied to produce the dependent variable. These steps will create the training data. A symbolic regression will be run on the training data to produce a champion *estimator*. Next a matrix of independent variables will be filled with random numbers. Then the model will be applied to produce the dependent variable. These steps will create the testing data. The *estimator* will be regressed against the testing data producing the final LSE and R-Square scores for comparison.

Sections (17) thru (19) compare the behavior of GP symbolic regression with and without swarm intelligence on a real world problem namely the forward estimation of corporate earnings on a database of stocks from 1990 thru 2009.

For the forward estimation of corporate earnings, this paper uses an historical database of approximately 1200 to 1500 stocks with daily price and volume data, weekly analyst estimates, and quarterly financial data from Jan 1986 to the present. The data has been assembled from reports published at the time, so the database is highly representative of what information was realistically available at the point when trading decisions were actually made.

From all of this historical data, twenty years (*1990 thru 2009*) have been used to support the results shown in this research. This two decade period includes a historically significant bull market decade followed by an equally historically significant bear market decade.

Multiple vendor sources have been used in assembling the data so that single vendor bias can be eliminated. The construction of this point in time database has focused on collecting weekly consolidated data tables, collected every Friday from Jan 3, 1986 to the present, representing detailed point in time input to this study and cover approximately 1200 to 1500 stocks on a weekly basis. Each stock record contains daily price and volume data, weekly analyst estimates and rankings, plus quarterly financial data as reported. The primary focus is on gross and net revenues.

The efficacy of several different swarm intelligence techniques are examined by running a full experimental protocol for each technique. Standard genetic programming, *without swarm intelligence techniques*, will be the base line for this study. We are interested in determining if the addition of swarm intelligence techniques improves symbolic regression performance – and if so, which swarm techniques perform best.

Our historical database contains 1040 weeks of data between January 1990 and December 2009. In a full training and testing protocol there is a separate symbolic regression run for each of these 1040 weeks. Each SR run consists of predicting the *ftmEPS* for each of the 1200 to 1500 stocks available in that week. A sliding training/testing window will be constructed to follow a strict statistical out-of-sample testing protocol.

For each of the 1040 weeks, the training examples will be extracted from records in the historical trailing five years behind the selected record BUT *not including any data from the selected week or ahead in time.* The training dependent variable will be extracted from the historical data record exactly 52 weeks forward in time from the selected record BUT *not including any data from the selected week or ahead in time.* Thus, as a practical observation, the training will not include any records in the first 52 weeks prior to the selected record - *because that would require a training dependent variable which was not available at the time.*

For each of the 1040 weeks, the testing samples will be extracted from records in the historical trailing five years behind the selected record *including all data from the selected week BUT not ahead in time.* The testing dependent variable will be extracted from the historical data record exactly 52 weeks forward in time from the selected record.

Each experimental protocol will produce 1040 symbolic regression runs over an average of 275,000 records for each training run and between 1200 and 1500 records for each testing run. Three hours will be allocated for training. Of course 1040 X 2 (*training and testing*) separate R-Square statistics will be produced for each experimental protocol. We will examine the R-Square statistics for evidence favoring the addition of swarm intelligence over the base line and for evidence favoring one swarm intelligence technique over another.

Finally we will need to adapt our methodology to conform to the rigorous United States Securities and Exchange Commission oversight and regulations on investment managers. The SEC mandates that every investment firm have a compliance officer. For any automated forward earnings prediction algorithm, *which would be used as the basis for later stock recommendations to external clients or internal portfolio managers,* the computer software code used in each prediction, the historical data used in each prediction, and each historical prediction itself, must be filed with the compliance officer in such form and manner so as to allow a surprise SEC compliance audit to reproduce each individual forward prediction exactly as it was at the original time of publication to external clients or internal portfolio managers.

Of course this means that we must provide a copy of all code, all data, and each forward prediction for each stock in each of the 1040 weeks, to our compliance officer. Once management accepts our symbolic regression system, we will also have to provide a copy of all forward predictions on an ongoing basis to the compliance officer.

Furthermore there is an additional challenge in meeting these SEC compliance details. The normal manner of operating GP, SI, and symbolic regression systems in academia will not be acceptable in a real world compliance environment. Normally, in academia, we recognize that symbolic regression is a heuristic search process and so we perform multiple SR runs, each starting with a different random number seed. We then report based on a statistical analysis of results across multiple runs. This approach produces *different results* each time the SR system is run. In a real world compliance environment such practice would subject us to serious monetary fines and also to jail time.

The SEC compliance requirements are far from arbitrary. Once management accepts such an SR system, the weekly automated predictions will influence the flow of millions and even billions of dollars into one stock or another and the historical back testing results will be used to sell prospective external clients and internal portfolio managers on using the system's predictions going forward.

First the authorities want to make sure that as time goes forward, *in the event that the predictions begin to perform poorly,* we will not simply rerun the original predictions again and again, with a different random number seed, until we obtain better historical performance and then substitute the new better performing historical performance results in our sales material.

Second the authorities want to make sure that, *in the event our firm should own many shares of the subsequently poorly performing stock of "ABC" Corp,* that we do not simply rerun the current week's predictions again and again, with a different random number seed, until we obtain a higher ranking for "ABC" stock thus improperly influencing our external clients and internal portfolio managers to drive the price of "ABC" stock higher.

In order to meet SEC compliance regulations we have altered our symbolic regression system, used in this chapter across all experiments, to use a pseudo random number generator with a pre-specified starting seed. Multiple runs always produce *exactly the same results.*

5. GP and swarm in symbolic regression

In standard Koza-style tree-based Genetic Programming [12] the genome and the individual are the same Lisp s-expression which is usually illustrated as a tree. Of course the tree-view of an s-expression is only a visual aid, since a Lisp s-expression is normally a list which is a special Lisp data structure. Without altering or restricting standard tree-based GP in any way, we can view the individuals not as trees but instead as s-expressions.

6 depth 0 binary tree s-exp: 3.45
7 depth 1 binary tree s-exp: (+ x2 3.45)
8 depth 2 binary tree s-exp: (/ (+ x2 3.45) (* x0 x2))
9 depth 2 irregular tree s-exp: (/ (+ x2 3.45) 2.0)

Up until this point we have not altered or restricted standard GP in any way; but, now we are about to make a slight alteration so that the standard GP s-expression can be made swarm friendly. Let us use the following s-expression.

10 (* (/ (- x0 3.45) (+ x0 x2)) (/ (- x5 1.31) (* x0 2.1)))

In this individual (10), the real constants are embedded within the s-expression and are inconvenient for swarm algorithms. So we are going to add an annotation to the individual (10). We are going to add enumerated constant nodes, and we are going to add a constant chromosome vector creating a new individual (11). The individual (11) will now have three components: an abstract s-expression (11), the original s-expression (11.1), and a constant chromosome (11.2) as follows.

11 (* (/ (- x0 **c[0]**) (+ x0 x2)) (/ (- x5 **c[1]**) (* x0 **c[2]**)))
11.1 s-exp: (* (/ (- x0 3.45) (+ x0 x2)) (/ (- x5 1.31) (* x0 2.1)))
11.2 c: <3.45 1.31 2.1>

Individual (11) evaluates to the exact same value as (10). Each real number constant in (10) has been replaced with an indexed vector reference of the type **c[*i*]**, where **c** is a vector of real numbers containing the same real numbers originally found in (10). While this process adds some annotation overhead to (10), it does expose all of the real number constants in a vector which is swarm intelligence friendly.

At this point let us take a brief pause. Examine the original s-expression (10) also (11.1) and compare it to the new annotated abstract version (11). Walk through the evaluation process for each version. Satisfy yourself that the concrete s-expression (11.1) and the abstract annotated (11) both evaluate to exactly the same interim and final values.

We have made no restrictive or destructive changes in the original individual (10). Slightly altered to handle the new constant vector references and the new chromosome annotations, any standard GP system will behave as it did before. Prove it to yourself this way. Take the annotated individual (11), and replace each indirect reference with the proper value from the constant vector. This converts the abstract annotated (11) back into the concrete s-expression (11.1). Let your standard GP system operate on (11.1) any way it wishes to produce a new individual (11^.1). Now convert (11^.1) back into an abstract annotated version with the same process we used to annotate (10).

Furthermore, if we have a compiled a machine register optimized version, γ(x), of (10), we do not even have to perform expensive recompilation in order to change a value in the constant chromosome. We need only alter the values in the constant chromosome and re-evaluate the already compiled and optimized γ(x).

Armed with these newly annotated individuals, let's take a fresh look at how we might improve the standard process of genetic programming during a symbolic regression run. Consider the following survivor population in a standard GP island.

12.1 (* (/ (- x0 3.45) (+ x0 x2)) (/ (- x5 1.31) (* x0 2.1)))
12.2 (cos (/ (- x4 2.3) (min x0 x2)))
12.3 (* (/ (- x0 5.15) (+ x0 x2)) (/ (- x5 -2.21) (* x0 9.32)))
12.4 (sin (/ (- x4 2.3) (min x0 x2)))
12.5 (sin (/ (- x4 2.3) (avg x0 x2)))
12.6 (* (/ (- x0 3.23) (+ x0 x2)) (/ (- x5 -6.31) (* x0 7.12)))
12.7 (* (/ (- x0 2.13) (+ x0 x2)) (/ (- x5 3.01) (* x0 2.12)))

First of all, the GP mutation and crossover operators do not have any special knowledge of real numbers. They have a difficult time isolating and optimizing numeric constants. But the situation gets worse.

As generation after generation of training has passed, the surviving individuals in the island population have become specialized in common and predictable ways. Individuals (12.2), (12.4), and (12.5) are all close mutations of each other. Evolution has found a form that is pretty good and is trying to search for a more optimal version. GP is fairly good at exploring the search space around these individuals.

However, (12.1), (12.3), (12.6), and (12.7) are all identical forms with the exception of the values of their embedded numeric constants. As time passes, the survivor population will become increasingly dominated by variants of (12.1) and in time its progeny may crowd out all other survivors. GP has a difficult time exploring the search space around (12.1) largely because the form is already optimized – it is the constant values which need additional optimization.

In swarm friendly AEG enhanced symbolic regression system, the individuals (12.1), (12.3), (12.6), and (12.7) are all viewed as constant homeomorphs and they are stored in the survivor pool as one individual with another annotation: a swarm constant pool as follows.

13.1 (* (/ (- x0 **c[0]**) (+ x0 x2)) (/ (- x5 **c[1]**) (* x0 **c[2]**)))
  13.1.1 (* (/ (- x0 3.45) (+ x0 x2)) (/ (- x5 1.31) (* x0 2.1)))
  13.1.2 c: <3.45 1.31 2.1>
  13.1.3 Swarm Constant Pool
  13.1.3[0] <3.45 1.31 2.1>
  13.1.3[1] <5.15 -2.21 9.32>
  13.1.3[2] <3.23 -6.31 7.12>
  13.1.3[3] <2.13 3.01 2.12>
13.2 (cos (/ (- x4 2.3) (min x0 x2))) {*annotations omitted*}
13.3 (sin (/ (- x4 2.3) (min x0 x2))) {*annotations omitted*}
13.4 (sin (/ (- x4 2.3) (avg x0 x2))) {*annotations omitted*}

The AEG enhanced SR system has combined the individuals (12.1), (12.3), (12.6), and (12.7) into a single constant homeomorphic canonical version (13.1) with all of the constants stored in a swarm constant pool inside the individual. Now the GP island population does not become dominated inappropriately. Plus, we are free to apply swarm intelligence algorithms to the constants inside (13.1) without otherwise hindering the GP algorithms in any way.

The remainder of this chapter is devoted to comparing the effects of several hybrid algorithms on symbolic regression accuracy in predicting forward twelve month corporate earnings. The chosen algorithms are Standard Koza-style GP, GP with Particle Swarm, GP with Differential Evolution, and GP with the Bees algorithm.

6. AEG conversion algorithm

The Abstract Expression Grammar constant conversion algorithm is a straight forward search and replace type algorithm in which a standard Koza-style s-expression is converted into an annotated AEG individual as shown in Algorithm (1).

Algorithm 1: AEG Conversion

```
Input: in // Koza-style s-expression
Output: out // AEG annotated individual
Parameters: k, r, n, N
```

Summary: *AEG Conversion removes all of the constants from an input s-expression and places them in a vector where swarm intelligence algorithms can easily optimize them. The output is a constant vector and the original s-expression modified to refer indirectly into the constant vector instead of referencing the constants directly.*

```
set out = <aexp,sexp,c,pool> // empty AEG individual
set out.aexp = in
set out.sexp = in
set out.c = <..empty vector of reals..>
set out.pool = <..empty vector of vectors..>
set N = length of out.aexp
for n from 0 until N do
 if out.aexp[n] is a real number constant then
   set r = out.aexp[n]
   set k = length of out.c
   set out.c[k] = r
   set out.aexp[n] = "c[k]" // replace r with c indexed reference
 end if
set out.pool[0] = out.c
return out
```

7. GP algorithm

Symbolic Regression with standard GP [8], [9], [10], and [12] evolves the GLM's basis functions as Lisp s-expressions. Evolution is achieved via the population operators of mutation, and crossover. We use a simple elitist GP algorithm which is outlined in Algorithm (2). The inputs are a vector of N training points, X, a vector of N dependent variables, Y, and the number of generations to train, G. Each point in X is a member of $R^M = <x_1,x_2,\ldots,x_m>$. The fitness ***score*** is the root mean squared error divided by the standard deviation of Y, ***NLSE***.

Algorithm 2: Standard GP

```
Input: X // N vector of independent M-featured training points
Input: Y // N vector of dependent variables
Input: G // Number of generations to train
Output: champ // Champion s-expression individual
Parameters: K, P
```

Summary: *Standard GP searches for a champion s-expression by randomly growing and scoring a large number of candidate s-expressions, then iteratively creating and scoring new candidate s-expressions via mutation and crossover. After each iteration, the population of candidate s-expressions is truncated to those with the best score. After the final iteration, the champion is the s-expression with the best score.*

```
function: mutateSExp(me)
```

Summary: *mutateSExp randomly alters an input s-expression by replacing a randomly selected sub expression with a new randomly grown sub expression.*

```
me = copy(me)
set L = number of nodes in me // me is a list of Lisp Pairs
set s = generate random s-expression
set n = random integer between 0 and L
set me[n] = s // Replaces nth node with s
```

```
 return me
end fun
function: crossoverSExp(mom,dad)
```

Summary: *crossoverSExp randomly alters a* ***mom*** *input s-expression by replacing a randomly selected sub expression in* ***mom*** *with a randomly selected sub expression from* ***dad****.*

```
 dad = copy(dad)
 mom = copy(mom)
 set Ld = number of nodes in dad // dad is a list of Pairs
 set Lm = number of nodes in mom // mom is a list of Pairs
 set n = random integer between 0 and Lm
 set m = random integer between 0 and Ld
 set mom[n] = dad[m]  // Replaces nth node with mth node
 return mom
end fun
main logic
for k from 0 until K do // Initialize population
 set w = generate random s-expression
 set population.last = score(w)
end for k
sort population by fitness score
truncate population to P most fit individuals
set champ = population.first
for g from 0 until G do // Main evolution loop
 for p from 0 until P do // Main evolution loop
  set w = mutateSExp(population[p])
  set population.last = score(w)
  set dad = population[p]
  set i = random integer between p and P
  set mom = population[i]
  set w = crossoverSExp(dad,mom)
  set population.last = score(w)
 end for p
 sort population by fitness score
 truncate population to P most fit individuals
 set champ = population.first
 end for g
return champ
```

Adding Abstract Expression Grammars to standard GP Symbolic Regression [3], [4], [5], and [6] evolves the GLM's basis functions as AEG individuals. Our simple modified elitist GP Algorithm (3) is outlined below. The inputs are a vector of N training points, X, a vector of N dependent variables, Y, and the number of generations to train, G. Each point in X is a member of $R^M = <x_1,x_2,\ldots,x_m>$. The fitness ***score*** is the root mean squared error divided by the standard deviation of Y, ***NLSE***.

Algorithm 3: AEG GP with Swarm

```
Input: X // N vector of independent M-featured training points
Input: Y // N vector of dependent variables
Input: G // Number of generations to train
Output: champ // Champion AEG individual
Parameters: K, P, S
```

Summary: *AEG GP with swarm searches for a champion s-expression as in standard GP (see Algorithm 2). However, before inserting s-expression candidates into the survivor population they are converted into AEGs and then merged with any similar AEGs (s-expressions with matching constant positions), then iteratively creating and scoring new candidate s-expressions via mutation, crossover, and swarm. After each iteration, the population of candidate AEG s-expressions is truncated to those with the best score. After the final iteration, the champion is the AEG s-expression with the best score.*

```
function: swarm(X,Y,aeg) // aeg = <aexp,sexp,c,pool>
  ...see Algorithm 5, 6, or 7...
  return aeg
end fun
function: convertToAEG(sexp)
  ...see Algorithm 1...
  return aeg
function: convertToSExp(aeg) // aeg = <aexp,sexp,c,pool>
  ...see Algorithm 4...
  return sexp
function: insertInPop(aeg) // aeg = <aexp,sexp,c,pool>
```

Summary: *insertInPop accepts an input AEG s-expression then searches the population of AEG candidate s-expressions for a constant homeomorphic AEG s-expression (an AEG with matching form and constant locations ... although the value of the constants may be different). If a constant homeomorphic AEG is found, the input AEG is merged with the existing canonical version already in the population; otherwise, the input AEG is inserted in the population in order of its score.*

```
 I = length of population
 for i from 0 until I do // Search population
  set w = population[i]
  if (w.aexp = aeg.aexp) then
   set w.pool = append(w.pool,aeg.pool)
   sort w.pool by fitness score
   truncate w.pool to S most fit constant vectors
   set w.c = w.pool.first
   set w.sexp = convertToSExp(w)
   return population
  end if
 end for i
 set population.last = aeg
 return population
function: mutateSExp(me) // me = <aexp,sexp,c,pool>
```

Summary: *mutateSExp randomly alters an input s-expression by replacing a randomly selected sub expression with a new randomly grown sub expression.*

```
 me = copy(me.sexp)
 set L = number of nodes in me // me is a list of Lisp Pairs
 set s = generate random s-expression
 set n = random integer between 0 and L
 set me[n] = s  // Replaces nth node with s
 set me = convertToAEG(me)
 return me
end fun
function: crossoverSExp(dad,mom)
```

Summary: *crossoverSExp randomly alters a **mom** input s-expression by replacing a randomly selected sub expression in **mom** with a randomly selected sub expression from **dad**.*

```
 dad = copy(dad.sexp)
 mom = copy(mom.sexp)
 set L_d = number of nodes in dad // dad is a list of Pairs
 set L_m = number of nodes in mom // mom is a list of Pairs
 set n = random integer between 0 and L_d
 set m = random integer between 0 and L_m
 set dad[n] = mom[m]  // Replaces nth node with mth node
 set dad = convertToAEG(dad)
 return dad
end fun
main logic
for k from 0 until K do // Initialize population
 set w = generate random s-expression
 w = score(convertToAEG(w))
 set population = insertInPop(w)
end for k
sort population by fitness score
truncate population to P most fit individuals
set champ = population.first
for g from 0 until G do // Main evolution loop
 for p from 0 until P do // Main evolution loop
   set w = swarm(population[p])
   set w = mutateSExp(population[p])
   set population = insertInPop(score(w))
   set dad = population[p]
   set i = random integer between p and P
  set mom = population[i]
   set w = crossoverSExp(dad,mom)
   set population = insertInPop(score(w))
 end for p
 sort population by fitness score
 truncate population to P most fit individuals
 set champ = population.first
 end for g
return champ
```

Conversion from an AEG individual back to a standard s-expression is accomplished as outlined in Algorithm (4).

Algorithm 4: AEG To S-Expression Conversion

Input: in // AEG annotated individual *<aexp,sexp,c,pool>*
Output: out // Koza-style s-expression
Parameters: k, r, n, N

Summary: *AEG To S-Expression Conversion accepts an AEG annotated individual and returns a Koza-style s-expression with all of the indirect constant references replaced with the direct constant values taken from the AEG constant vector.*

set out = copy(in.aexp)
set N = length of out.aexp
for n from 0 until N **do**
  if out[n] is a constant reference "c[k]" **then**
    set r = in.aexp.c[k]
    set out[n] = r // replace constant reference with constant
  end if
return out

8. AEG differential evolution

Abstract Expression Grammar GP can be used with differential evolution [7] which evolves the GLM's basis functions as AEG individuals. The DE algorithm encodes each individual as a constant vector. Each AEG <aexp,sexp,c,pool> stores the population of DE individuals in its constant **pool** and the current most fit champion as its constant vector **c**. In Algorithm (3) swarm evolution is seamlessly merged with standard GP and our AEG differential evolution algorithm is outlined In Algorithm (5).

The Differential Evolution algorithm is a straightforward attempt to keep a sorted list of the best constant vectors seen so far. Pairs of these constant vectors are selected at random along with the best constant vector seen so far. The algorithm then averages the differences between these constant vectors, in several obvious ways, to move closer to a global optimum.

Algorithm 5: AEG Differential Evolution

Input: X // N vector of independent M-featured training points
Input: Y // N vector of dependent variables
Input: in // AEG annotated individual *<aexp,sexp,c,pool>*
Output: in AEG annotated individual *<aexp,sexp,c,pool>*
Parameters: S

Summary: *AEG Differential Evolution optimizes a pool of vectors by selecting the best scoring vector along with a randomly selected pair of constant vectors, then the distances between these vectors are averaged in various ways to produce a new candidate vector to be scored. After scoring, the population of vectors is truncated to those with the best scores.*

function: randomNudge(c) // constant vector = $<c_0,c_2,\ldots,c_j>$

Summary: *randomNudge accepts an input constant vector then produces a new constant vector by adding or subtracting small random increments from each constant in the input vector.*

```
var (defaultSkew .90) (defaultRange .20)
c = copy(c)
I = length of c
for i from 0 until I do
  set r = random number from 0 to defaultRange
  set r = defaultSkew + r
  set c[i] = r*c[i]
end for i
end fun
function: search(a,b,c)
```

Summary: *search accepts* ***a*****,** ***b*****,** *and* **c** *constant vectors in an input vector pool* ***in*****.** *A new output constant vector* ***w*** *is created by randomly averaging the distances between the three vectors. The new vector* ***w*** *is used to score the AEG whose constant pool is being optimized. After scoring, the* **in** *pool is truncate to the constant vectors with the best scores. The score of the AEG is set to the score of the best constant vector in its pool.*

```
var (F .50)
w = copy(a)
I = length of a
for i from 0 until I do
  set r = random number from 0 to 1.0
  set r = F + r
  set w[i] = a[i] + (r*(b[i]-c[i]))
end for i
set in.pool.last = w
set in.c = w
score(in)
sort in.pool by fitness score
truncate in.pool to S most fit constant vectors
set in.c = in.pool.first
set in.sexp = convertToSExp(in)
return in
end fun
main logic
set I length of in.pool
if (I=0) then return in end if
set best = in.pool[0]
set j1 = random integer from 0 until I
set j2 = random integer from j1 until I
set b1 = in.pool[j1]
if (j1=0) then set b1 = randomNudge(best)
set b2 = in.pool[j2]
if (j2= j1) then set b2 = randomNudge(b2)
set r = random number from 0 until 1.0
```

```
// Modest momentum
if (r<.50) then search(best,best,b1)
// Aggressive momentum
else if (r<.80) then search(best,best,b2)
// Modest Mediation
else if (r<.85) then search(b1,best,b1)
// Aggressive mediation
else if (r<.90) then search(b2,best,b2)
// Wandering up
else if (r<.95) then search(b2,b1,b2)
// Wandering down
else set in.pool = search(b1,b2,b1)
return in
```

9. AEG Bees algorithm

Abstract Expression Grammar GP can be used with Bees algorithm [14] and [15] which evolves the GLM's basis functions as AEG individuals. Each AEG <aexp,sexp,c,pool> stores the population of Bees individuals in its constant **pool** and the current most fit champion as its constant vector **c**. In Algorithm (3) swarm evolution is seamlessly merged with standard GP and our AEG bees algorithm is outlined in Algorithm (6) below.

Our Bees algorithm has been modified to fit within the larger framework of an evolving GP environment. Therefore, the evolutionary loop is in the GP algorithm and has been removed from the Bees algorithm. Instead the Bees algorithm is repeatedly called from the main GP loop during evolution. Furthermore, we must execute the Bees algorithm on all AEG individuals with a non-empty constant pool; therefore, care must be taken such that any one AEG individual does not monopolize the search process.

The Bees algorithm gets its inspiration from the cooperative behavior of bees foraging for food. There is the concept of a visited food site (which in our case is one of the constant vectors in the constant pool) and a bee which searches these food sites and assigns them a fitness value (in our case a bee is the AEG individual wrapped around and evaluating the constant vector). Since we have only one bee (the AEG individual), when multiple bees are required, we will have our single AEG individual search multiple times.

In the original Bees algorithm, there are S food sites selected for search (in our case the AEG's constant pool). Of the S selected sites, the E fittest sites are "*elite*" sites and the remaining (S-E) sites are "non-elite" sites. In the original Bees algorithm there are B bees. Since we have only one bee (the AEG individual), we will have our AEG individual search B times. Of the total B bees available, BEP bees are recruited to search the neighborhood around each elite food site, and BSP bees are recruited to search the neighborhood around each non-elite food site. The remaining BRP bees search at random anywhere they please. This all assumes that B = BEP+BSP+BRP.

In the original Bees algorithm, *for each elite food* site there are BEP neighborhood searches performed, *for each non-elite food* site there are BSP neighborhood searches performed, and there are BRP random searches performed in each iteration of the main evolutionary loop.

Thus the total number of searches devoted to all elite food sites can be expressed as (E*BEP), while the total number of searches devoted to all non-elite food sites can be expressed as ((S-E)*BSP), and the total number of random searches can be expressed by the fraction BRP. From these counts of total searches performed, we can derive the probability that an elite site will be searched, that a non-elite site will be searched, and that a random search will be performed. These computed percentages will be the parameters of our modified Bees algorithm: BEp, BSp, and BRp.

Algorithm 6: AEG Bees Algorithm

Input: X // N vector of independent M-featured training points
Input: Y // N vector of dependent variables
Input: in // AEG annotated individual *<aexp,sexp,c,pool>*
Output: in AEG annotated individual *<aexp,sexp,c,pool>*
Parameters: BEp, BSp, BRp, E, S

Summary: *AEG Bees Algorithm optimizes a pool of vectors by incrementally selecting each vector from the pool of constant vectors, then either producing a new candidate vector in a random neighborhood around the selected vector or producing a new random vector. The new vector is scored. After scoring, the population of vectors is truncated to those with the best scores.*

function: neighborSearch(c) // constant vector = $\langle c_0, c_2, \ldots, c_j \rangle$

Summary: *neighborSearch accepts an input constant vector then produces a new constant vector by adding or subtracting small random increments from each constant in the input vector. The new vector is scored and inserted into the constant pool.*

```
w = copy(c)
d = copy(c)
I = length of c
J = length of in.Pool
// compute local neighborhood radius vector
for j from 1 until J do
  for i from 0 until I do
   set d[i] += (abs(in.Pool[j-1][i]-in.Pool[j][i])/(J-1))
  end for i
 end for j
 // Search the local neighborhood
for i from 0 until I do
 set r = random number from 0 to (2*d[i])
 set r = r - d[i]
 set w[i] = w[i]+r;
end for i
 set in.pool.last = w
 set in.c = w
 score(in)
 sort in.pool by fitness score
 truncate in.pool to S most fit constant vectors
 set in.c = in.pool.first
 set in.sexp = convertToSExp(in)
```

```
end fun
function: randomSearch()
```

Summary: *randomSearch produces a new constant vector by randomly setting a value to each constant in the new vector. The new vector is scored and inserted into the constant pool.*

```
 w = random constant vector
 set in.pool.last = w
 set in.c = w
 score(in)
 sort in.pool by fitness score
 truncate in.pool to S most fit constant vectors
 set in.c = in.pool.first
 set in.sexp = convertToSExp(in)
 return in
end fun
main logic
vars (I_e starts at 0) (I_f starts at E)
set I length of in.pool
if (I=0) then return in end if
set ce = if (I_e<E) then in.pool[I_e] else in.pool.first end if
set I_e = I_e + 1
if (I_e>=E) then set I_e = 0 end if
set cf = if (I_f<I) then in.pool[I_f] else in.pool.first end if
set I_f = I_f + 1
if (I_f>=I) then set I_f = E end if
set choice = random integer between 0 and 1.0
if (choice<BEp) then neighborSearch(ce) end if
if (choice<BSp) then neighborSearch(cf) end if
if (choice<BRp) then randomSearch() end if
return in
```

10. AEG particle swarm

Abstract Expression Grammar GP can be used with particle swarm [2] which evolves the GLM's basis functions as AEG individuals. In Algorithm (3) swarm evolution is seamlessly merged with standard GP and our AEG particle swarm algorithm is outlined in Algorithm (7) below.

Our Particle Swarm (PSO) algorithm has also been modified to fit within the larger framework of an evolving GP environment. Therefore, the evolutionary loop is in the GP algorithm and has been removed from the PSO algorithm. Instead the PSO algorithm is repeatedly called from the main GP loop during evolution. Furthermore, we must execute the PSO algorithm on all AEG individuals with a non-empty constant pool; therefore, care must be taken such that any one AEG individual does not monopolize the search process.

The PSO algorithm gets its inspiration from the clustering behavior of birds or insects as they fly in formation. There is the concept of an individual swarm member called a particle, the current position of each particle, the best position ever visited by each particle, a velocity for each particle, and the best position every visited by any particle (the global best). In our case, each particle will be one of the constant vectors in our AEG individual's constant pool. A fitness value will be assigned to each constant by wrapping the AEG individual around the constant vector and scoring.

Each AEG <aexp,sexp,c,pool> stores the population of PSO individuals in its constant **pool** and the current most fit champion as its constant vector **c**. However, implementing the PSO algorithm requires adding a few new items to our AEG individual. Let ***aeg*** be an AEG individual in our system. The best position ever visited by any particle will be designated as ***aeg*.best** (global best). The best position ever visited by each particle, i, will be designated as ***aeg*.pool[i]→best** (local best). The velocity of each particle, i, will be designated as ***aeg*.pool[i]→v**. The score of a constant vector, ***c***, will be designated as **fitness(*c*)**. And, of course, each particle, i, is nothing more than one of the constant vectors in the AEG individual's constant pool ***aeg*.pool[i]**.

Algorithm 7: AEG Particle Swarm

```
Input: X // N vector of independent M-featured training points
Input: Y // N vector of dependent variables
Input: in // AEG annotated individual <aexp,sexp,c,pool>
Output: in AEG annotated individual <aexp,sexp,c,pool>
Parameters: W_L, W_G, W_V, S
```

Summary: *AEG Particle Swarm optimizes a pool of vectors by randomly selecting a pair of constant vectors from the pool of constant vectors. A new vector is produced when the pair of vectors, together with the global best vector, are randomly nudged closer together based upon their previous approaching velocities. The new vector is scored. After scoring, the population of vectors is truncated to those with the best scores.*

```
main logic
vars (I_c starts at 0)
set J = length of in.pool
if (J<=0) then return in end if
i = I_c
c = copy(in.pool[i])
v = copy(in.pool[i]→v)
if (v = null) then
 set v = random velocity vector
 set in.pool[i]→v = v
end if
lbest = in.pool[i]→best
if (lbest = null) then
 set lbest = c
 set in.pool[i]→best = lbest
end if
gbest = in.best
if (gbest = null) then
 set gbest = c
 set in.best = gbest
```

```
end if
// Compute the velocity weight parameters
maxg = maximum generations in the main GP search
g = current generation count in the main GP search
W_L = .25 + ((maxg - g)/maxg) // local weight
W_G = .75 + ((maxg - g)/maxg) // global weight
W_V = .50 + ((maxg - g)/maxg) // velocity weight
I = length of c
set r1 = random number from 0 to 1.0
set r2 = random number from 0 to 1.0
// Update the particle's velocity & position
for i from 0 until I do
  set lnudge = (W_L*r1*(lbest[i]-c[i]))
  set gnudge = (W_G*r2*(gbest[i]-c[i]))
  set v[i] = (W_V*v[i])+lnudge+gnudge
  set c[i] = c[i]+v[i]
end for i
// Score the new particle position
set in.c = c
score(in)
// Update the best particle positions
if (fitness(c)>fitness(lbest)) then lbest = c end if
if (fitness(c)>fitness(gbest)) then gbest = c end if
in.best = gbest
set in.pool.last = c
set in.pool.last→best = lbest
set in.pool.last→v = v
// Enforce elitist constant pool
sort in.pool by fitness score
truncate in.pool to S most fit constant vectors
set in.c = in.pool.first
set in.sexp = convertToSExp(in)
// Enforce iterative search of constant pool
set I_c = I_c + 1
if (I_c>=S) then set I_c = 0 end if
return in
```

11. Sample test problems

Several sample test problems have been collected upon which we can compare the performance of standard GP symbolic regression and hybrid AEG symbolic regression. Each of these test problems contains an embedded real constant which greatly affects the behavior of the formula during regression. If our theory is correct, these test problems should receive better results with AEG symbolic regression than with standard GP symbolic regression. The test problems are as follows.

14.1 y = -2.3 + (0.13*sin(**4.1***x2))

14.2 y = 3.0 + (2.13*log(**1.3**+x4))
14.3 y = 2.0 - (2.1*cos(**9.8**/x0))

Two symbolic regressions are performed for each test problem: standard GP symbolic regression, and AEG symbolic regression (using the Bees Algorithm 6). Clearly the AEG symbolic regressions perform much better than standard GP symbolic regression. Table 1 shows the results.

Formula	NLSE GP	RSQ GP	NLSE AEG	RSQ AEG
14.1	.47	.77	0.0	1.0
14.2	.18	.96	0.0	1.0
14.3	.36	.81	0.0	1.0

Note: *NLSE is the least squared error divided by the standard deviation of Y, and RSQ is the R-Square statistic from the regression. An NLSE of 0.0 is perfect while an RSQ of 1.0 is perfect.*

Table 1. Sample Test Problem Regressions

Clearly the AEG symbolic regression runs are discovering and optimizing the embedded constants correctly; however, the standard GP symbolic regression runs are unable to optimize the constants and get confused. It is simply too difficult for standard GP to optimize these difficult embedded constants *using only mutation and crossover*. Furthermore, the standard GP runs produce estimators which are far from the correct form. The following are the top five estimators, produced by the standard GP symbolic regression, for test problem (14.1).

14.1.1 y = 4.6+(-2.45*(sqrt(log(x0))));
14.1.2 y = -11919+(-0.86*((-13824+log(x0))));
14.1.3 y = -1891+(-0.8624*((-2197+log(x0))));
14.1.4 y = -2073+(-0.8624*((-2401+log(x0))));
14.1.5 y = -1749+(-0.8624*((-2025+log(x0))));

The results are so absolute that statistical analysis is unnecessary. Standard GP symbolic regression cannot solve these problems, while AEG symbolic regression always solves these problems exactly. Furthermore, it is clear that the standard GP run is trying to optimize constants but it has gotten stuck in a local minimum with the wrong formula and its population of champions is dominated by the attempt to optimize constants rather than trying to find a better fitting formula.

Incidentally, it made no difference when the Bees Algorithm was replaced with the Differential Evolution Algorithm or with the Particle Swarm Algorithm. The results of an AEG symbolic regression on the sample test problems was a perfect score no matter which swarm algorithm was chosen.

Furthermore, on the issue of scientific reproducibility, we have included detailed algorithms in this chapter. No matter what random seed is used, standard GP SR will not optimize sample problems 14.1, 14.2, and 14.3 in any practical time. This is because the population operators available to standard GP SR do not manage imbedded constants. Plus no matter what random seed is used, SR with any one of the three popular swarm algorithms will optimize the sample problems 14.1, 14.2, and 14.3 very quickly. These results are easily scientifically reproduced.

Now that we have tested AEG symbolic regression on several sample test problems, achieving much better performance than standard GP symbolic regression, it is time to compare AEG with standard GP symbolic regression on a real world investing problem: estimating forward 12 month earnings per share for a database of companies between 1990 and 2009. We begin with some background on investing. In addition, we will also compare the results of the three different swarm intelligence algorithms.

12. Investing strategies

Value investing [1] has produced several of the wealthiest investors in the world including Warren Buffet. Nevertheless, value investing has a host of competing strategies including momentum [16] and hedging [17].

One of the most difficult challenges in devising a securities investing strategy is the a priori identification of pending regime changes. For instance, momentum investing strategies were very profitable in the 1990's and not so profitable in the 2000's while value investing strategies were not so profitable in the 1990's but turned profitable in the 2000's. Long Short hedging strategies were profitable in the 1990's and early 2000's but collapsed dramatically in the late 2007 thru 2008 period. Knowing when to switch from Momentum to Value, Value to Hedging, and Hedging back to Value was critical for making consistent above average profits during the twenty year period from 1990 thru 2009.

The challenge becomes even more difficult when one adds the numerous technical and fundamental buy/sell triggers to currently popular active management investing strategies. Bollinger Bands, MACD, Earning Surprises, etc. all have complex and dramatic effects on the implementation of securities investing strategies, and all are vulnerable to regime changes. The question arises, "*Is there a simple securities investing strategy which is less vulnerable to regime changes than other strategies?*".

An idealized value investing hypothesis is put forward: "*Given perfect foresight, buying stocks with the best future earning yield* ***(Next12MoEPS/CurrentPrice)*** *and holding for 12 months will produce above average securities investing returns*".

Using our database *of the 1500 Valueline stocks from 1986 thru 2009*, we studied three ideal concentrated portfolios: five, twenty five, and fifty stock portfolios. Each of these idealized concentrated portfolios are sampled each month for the twenty years from 1990 thru 2009. Fixed holding periods of one month, one quarter, and one year were examined. The per annum compound return for each decade and each holding period are shown in Table 2 along with the compounded returns, including dividends, of the Standard & Poor's 500 for each decade.

The data supports the conclusion that the ideal hypothesis yields highly above average investing profits for all portfolio sizes and all holding periods across both decades. Furthermore the ideal hypothesis appears less vulnerable to regime changes than many other popular active securities investment strategies given that the 1990s decade was a raging bull environment while the 2000s decade was a terrible bear environment.

Holding period	Decade	5 stocks	25 Stocks	50 Stocks
month	1990s	76%	69%	63%
month	2000s	120%	69%	53%
quarter	1990s	58%	73%	64%
quarter	2000s	69%	74%	53%
year	1990s	48%	46%	41%
year	2000s	103%	61%	45%
SP500	1990s	18%	18%	18%
SP500	2000s	(2%)	(2%)	(2%)

Note: *Per annum compound returns for each decade.*

Table 2. Returns for idealize future earnings yield

13. Buying current earnings yield

Of course the ideal hypothesis is impossible to implement because it requires perfect foresight which is, in the absence of time travel, unobtainable. Nevertheless the ideal hypothesis represents the theoretical upper limit on the profits realizable from a strategy of buying future revenue cheaply; yet, the theoretical profits are so rich that one cannot help but ask the question, "*Are there revenue prediction models which will allow one to capture some portion of the profits from the ideal hypothesis?*".

The easiest revenue prediction model involves simply using the current year's trailing 12 month revenue as a proxy for future revenue.

The data supports the conclusion that even using this current revenue proxy model buying the top five, twenty five, and fifty stocks with the highest ***(current12MoEPS/currentPrice)*** produces above average securities investing profits, *as least for the 1500 Valueline stocks*, as shown in Table 3.

Holding period	Decade	5 stocks	25 Stocks	50 Stocks
month	1990s	29.0%	16.5%	16.6%
month	2000s	8.2%	11.4%	15.4%
quarter	1990s	41.7%	14.9%	14.9%
quarter	2000s	22.7%	13.5%	15.6%
year	1990s	36.4%	17.6%	15.6%
year	2000s	42.1%	19.7%	17.4%
SP500	1990s	18%	18%	18%
SP500	2000s	(2%)	(2%)	(2%)

Note: *Per annum compound returns for each decade.*

Table 3. Returns for current revenue prediction

Clearly using this current revenue prediction model buying the top five, twenty five, and fifty stocks with the highest ***(current12MoEPS/currentPrice)***, produces above average securities investing profits, in most cases, *especially with one year holding periods.*

Like buying stocks *with the best future earning yield* ***(Next12MoEPS/CurrentPrice)***, buying current earnings yield ***(current12MoEPS/currentPrice)*** is an ideal method. By *ideal* we mean that all information is known and exact. There is no predictive aspect, no guess work. We already know what current earnings are for any stock.

Nevertheless, buying a stock with low PE but whose future 12 month earnings will plummet bringing on bankruptcy is an obviously poor choice. So why is low PE investing so successful given that future 12 month earnings can vary significantly? Placing current earnings yield investing in this context puts a new spin on this standard *value investing* measure. In this context we are saying that current earnings yield (also known as low PE investing) works precisely to the extent that *current earnings are a reasonable predictor of future earnings*! In situations where current earnings are NOT a good predictor of future earnings, then current earnings yield investing looses it efficacy.

This agrees with our common sense understanding. For instance, given two stocks with the same high current earnings yield, where one will go bankrupt next year and the other will double its earnings next year; we would prefer the stock whose earnings will double. Implying that, in the ideal, current earnings are just a data point. We want to buy *future earnings* cheap!

Precisely because the per annum returns from this current revenue prediction model are far less than the returns achieved with perfect prescience, we must now look for more accurate methods of net revenue prediction.

14. Future revenue prediction *inputs*

One very simplistic revenue prediction input model involves simply adding last year's revenue delta to current revenue as a prediction of future revenue, as follows:

15 2010EPS = (2009EPS-2008EPS)+2009EPS
...to generalize, we have:
15.1 forwardRevenue = (revenue-pastRevenue)+revenue

Another simple revenue prediction input is the broker estimates. Each week there appears a broker consensus estimate for the next 12Mo EPS for each of the stocks in our database. This broker revenue prediction can be used as a model for future revenue.

If we combine a number of these simple future revenue prediction inputs together we can construct a set of consensus inputs for prediction of future revenue. Constructing this consensus revenue inputs requires the following components.

16 margin = (currentEPS/currentSPS)
17 brokerEPS = *broker consensus estimate*
18 forwardEPS = (currentEPS-pastEPS)+currentEPS
19 projectEPS = (4*(currentEPS-pastQtrEPS))+currentEPS
20 forwardSPS = (currentSPS-pastSPS)+currentSPS
21 projectSPS = (4*(currentSPS-pastQtrSPS))+currentSPS
22 forwardSEPS = forwardSPS*margin
23 projectSEPS = projectSPS*margin

The five bolded elements above (brokerEPS, forwardEPS, projectEPS, forwardSEPS, and projectSEPS) are the consensus inputs to all of our future revenue prediction efforts in the remainder of this chapter.

15. Future revenue: *GP-only*

Each week we can construct a GP-only symbolic regression estimate (using Algorithm 2) for next 12Mo EPS for each of the stocks in our database, using the following five inputs as dependent variables: **brokerEPS**, **forwardEPS**, **projectEPS**, **forwardSEPS**, and **projectSEPS**. Each week we train a symbolic regression model on approximately 375,000 training examples (250 weeks of backward historical data times approximately 1,500 stocks), and each week we use the newly trained symbolic regression model to predict the earnings per share of each stock in our database for the new week. This is a text book case of in-sample-training with out-of-sample-testing using a sliding forward 250 week training window.

The per annum returns using this symbolic regression revenue prediction model buying the top five, twenty five, and fifty stocks with the highest ***(regression12MoEPS/currentPrice)*** produces above average securities investing profits as shown in Table 4.

Holding period	Decade	5 stocks	25 Stocks	50 Stocks
month	1990s	33.2%	17.9%	18.2%
month	2000s	9.7%	13.2%	17.6%
quarter	1990s	43.9%	16.8%	15.1%
quarter	2000s	25.6%	15.3%	18.5%
year	1990s	39.2%	18.8%	17.8%
year	2000s	45.6%	21.2%	18.9%
SP500	1990s	18%	18%	18%
SP500	2000s	(2%)	(2%)	(2%)

Note: *Per annum compound returns for each decade.*

Table 4. Returns for GP-only

Clearly using the GP-only symbolic regression revenue prediction model buying the top five, twenty five, and fifty stocks with the highest ***(regression12MoEPS/currentPrice)*** produces above average securities investing profits, in most cases. *In fact, compared with all simple prediction methods shown so far, for reasonably diversified fifty stock portfolios, the annual hold returns are the best we have seen so far.*

Nevertheless, despite the satisfying accuracy and high returns, there are issues with the GP symbolic regression model. The main issue with the GP regression approach is a fundamental issue of believability. Every mathematical model, however highly correlated with market behavior over a period, must withstand the test of believability.

Because the standard GP process is difficult to constrain, many of the basis functions reach sizes and complexities beyond reasonable. For instance, in March of 1998 the GP regression creates an earnings model containing the term: ***tanh(forwardEPS/brokerEPS)***. This strains the credulity of any fund portfolio manager and is very difficult to explain using standard financial concepts. It clearly works statistically in that training period; but, it is not believable.

Worse still, in order to achieve its high accuracy, the GP regression process drives the coefficients on some of the basis functions to negative values. This also creates a financial model which does not make common sense, and is therefore **unbelievable**. When the champion estimator, produced by symbolic regression is ridiculous, it undermines the acceptance of the whole symbolic regression process vis a vis investing, and no fund manager will risk assets based upon the SR models.

For instance, for the month of April 2001 the GP regression method creates an earnings model with a highly weighted basis function where the coefficient for **forwardEPS** is negative. ...

24 eps = ...+(-1.293*forwardEPS2)+...

Since forwardEPS is the result of adding last year's earnings growth to this year's earnings to get an estimate for next year, a negative coefficient has the SR model telling us that companies with big earnings growth last year are bad! AND the larger last year's earnings growth the ***worse*** the model penalizes the company.

A statistician will immediately suspect over fitting in this SR champion model. Professional investors are less kind in their incredulity. Unfortunately standard GP symbolic regression produces many champions with these believability problems.

Many of the champion estimator models produced by standard GP symbolic regression simply do not pass the common sense test. Investing large amounts of risk assets based on these GP models is very problematic *because of the GP model's fundamental lack of believability.* Even in the unlikely event that management were to sign off, regulatory and compliance sign off would be impossible.

16. Basis function constraints using AEG

Abstract Expression Grammars (AEGs) can be used to constrain the basis functions searched in a symbolic regression so that the believability issues with standard GP are resolved [6] and [13]. In our case it is reasonable and believable to constrain the basis functions to either sigmoid or Classification and Regression Tree (CART) sigmoid.

Using our five future revenue predictions as inputs to a nonlinear sigmoid regression, we can construct a more believable prediction model. Our first attempt will be to stay with an almost linear regression, but where the model coefficients are forced into the sigmoid domain. The model coefficients cannot go negative and they cannot rise above 1.0. This creates a more believable regression model in which the coefficients act more like significance weights attached to each of the five input EPS predictions as follows.

25 eps = c_1***brokerEPS**+ c_2***forwardEPS**+ c_3***projectEPS**
+ c_4***forwardSEPS**+ c_5***projectSEPS**
where $0 \le c_i \le 1.0$ for $1 \le i \le 5$

In this sigmoid linear regression model each coefficient represents the significance given to one of the five input predictions. Therefore if c_1=.2 while c_2=.4, the model is saying that the higher the brokerEPS estimate and the higher the forwardEPS estimate the better; BUT, the model gives twice as much weight to forwardEPS estimates as it does to brokerEPS estimates. This is a far more intuitively believable model.

Also it is possible to construct a more sophisticated sigmoid Classification and Regression Tree (CART) model by using the sigmoid model (24) as a template for four leaf nodes of a simple classification tree as follows.

25.1 $\mu_1 = c_1$***brokerEPS**+ c_2***forwardEPS**+ c_3***projectEPS**
+ c_4***forwardSEPS**+ c_5***projectSEPS**
where $0 \le c_i \le 1.0$ for $1 \le i \le 5$
25.2 $\mu_2 = c_6$***brokerEPS**+ c_7***forwardEPS**+ c_8***projectEPS**
+ c_9***forwardSEPS**+ c_{10}***projectSEPS**
where $0 \le c_i \le 1.0$ for $6 \le i \le 10$
25.3 $\mu_3 = c_{11}$***brokerEPS**+ c_{12}***forwardEPS**+ c_{13}***projectEPS**
+ c_{14}***forwardSEPS**+ c_{15}***projectSEPS**
where $0 \le c_i \le 1.0$ for $11 \le i \le 15$
25.4 $\mu_4 = c_{16}$***brokerEPS**+ c_{17}***forwardEPS**+ c_{18}***projectEPS**
+ c_{19}***forwardSEPS**+ c_{20}***projectSEPS**
where $0 \le c_i \le 1.0$ for $16 \le i \le 20$

We can then place these sigmoid leaf nodes into a simple CART formula as follows.

25.5 eps = $(v_1<v_2)?((v_3<v_4)?\mu_1:\mu_2):(v_5<v_6)?\mu_3:\mu_4)$
where **V = {brokerEPS,forwardEPS,projectEPS, forwardSEPS,projectSEPS}**
where $v_i \varepsilon$ **V** for $1 \le i \le 4$

In this sigmoid CART nonlinear regression model each of the four leaf nodes is a sigmoid nonlinear model of the type shown in (24). Each of the decision variables, v_i, is one of the five possible inputs.

By constraining the basis functions searched to be either sigmoid or CART sigmoid, we automatically eliminate the issues associated with GP-only future revenue prediction, and we achieve future earnings models which pass the test all important test of believability.

Unfortunately, having imposed these important basis function constraints, we encounter an additional issue. GP-only symbolic regression is very poor at evolving real number constants. These constraints place a heavy emphasis on the evolution of real number constants within the basis function and its sigmoid coefficients. Therefore we must add, to our hybrid AEG algorithm, evolutionary techniques which are better able to evolve real number constants. The remainder of this chapter will compare the efficacy of three hybrid evolutionary algorithms on the task of future revenue prediction.

17. GP with particle swarm

Testing the algorithm in (6.1) and limiting our basis functions to either sigmoid or CART sigmoid as in Section 13, each week we can construct a symbolic regression estimate for next 12Mo EPS for each of the stocks in our database, using the following five inputs as dependent variables: **brokerEPS**, **forwardEPS**, **projectEPS**, **forwardSEPS**, and **projectSEPS**.

Each week we train a symbolic regression model on approximately 375,000 training examples (250 weeks of backward historical data times approximately 1,500 stocks), and each week we use the newly trained symbolic regression model to predict the earnings per share of each stock in our database for the new week.

The per annum returns using this symbolic regression revenue prediction model buying the top five, twenty five, and fifty stocks with the highest ***(regression12MoEPS/currentPrice)*** produces above average securities investing profits as shown in Table 5.

Holding period	Decade	5 stocks	25 Stocks	50 Stocks
month	1990s	21.2%	26.1%	22.2%
month	2000s	7.6%	13.9%	17.8%
quarter	1990s	12.9%	29.2%	25.1%
quarter	2000s	9.2%	14.7%	19.2%
year	1990s	37.7%	26.3%	21.3%
year	2000s	5.6%	22.5%	22.6%
SP500	1990s	18%	18%	18%
SP500	2000s	(2%)	(2%)	(2%)

Note: *Per annum compound returns for each decade.*

Table 5. Returns for GP with Particle Swarm

Clearly using the GP with particle swarm symbolic regression revenue prediction model buying the top five, twenty five, and fifty stocks with the highest ***(regression12MoEPS/currentPrice)*** produces above average securities investing profits, in most cases. *In fact, compared with GP-only prediction methods, adding particle swarm has increased accuracy significantly – while adding believability.*

18. GP with differential evolution

Testing the algorithm in (6) and limiting our basis functions to either sigmoid or CART sigmoid as in Section 13, each week we can construct a symbolic regression estimate for next 12Mo EPS for each of the stocks in our database, using the following five inputs as dependent variables: **brokerEPS**, **forwardEPS**, **projectEPS**, **forwardSEPS**, and **projectSEPS**.

Each week we train a symbolic regression model on approximately 375,000 training examples (250 weeks of backward historical data times approximately 1,500 stocks), and each week we use the newly trained symbolic regression model to predict the earnings per share of each stock in our database for the new week.

The per annum returns using this symbolic regression revenue prediction model buying the top five, twenty five, and fifty stocks with the highest ***(regression12MoEPS/currentPrice)*** produces above average securities investing profits as shown in Table 6.

Holding period	Decade	5 stocks	25 Stocks	50 Stocks
month	1990s	20.6%	26.8%	22.6%
month	2000s	7.4%	14.8%	18.6%
quarter	1990s	13.6%	29.0%	24.3%
quarter	2000s	9.6%	14.2%	18.8%
year	1990s	37.9%	27.4%	23.8%
year	2000s	5.3%	21.3%	21.5%
SP500	1990s	18%	18%	18%
SP500	2000s	(2%)	(2%)	(2%)

Note: *Per annum compound returns for each decade.*

Table 6. Returns for GP with Differential Evolution

Clearly using the GP with differential evolution symbolic regression revenue prediction model buying the top five , twenty five, and fifty stocks with the highest ***(regression12MoEPS/currentPrice)*** produces above average securities investing profits, in most cases. *However the GP with differential evolution algorithm does not yield a significant improvement over GP with particle swarm.*

19. GP with Bees algorithm

Testing the algorithm in (7) and limiting our basis functions to either sigmoid or CART sigmoid as in Section 13, each week we can construct a symbolic regression estimate for next 12Mo EPS for each of the stocks in our database, using the following five inputs as dependent variables: **brokerEPS**, **forwardEPS**, **projectEPS**, **forwardSEPS**, and **projectSEPS**.

Each week we train a symbolic regression model on approximately 375,000 training examples (250 weeks of backward historical data times approximately 1,500 stocks), and each week we use the newly trained symbolic regression model to predict the earnings per share of each stock in our database for the new week.

The per annum returns using this symbolic regression revenue prediction model buying the top five , twenty five, and fifty stocks with the highest ***(regression12MoEPS/currentPrice)*** produces above average securities investing profits as shown in Table 7.

Holding period	**Decade**	**5 stocks**	**25 Stocks**	**50 Stocks**
month	1990s	107.6%	66.7%	43.7%
month	2000s	9.8%	16.9%	19.3%
quarter	1990s	51.3%	37.9%	31.5%
quarter	2000s	10.5%	18.3%	19.4%
year	1990s	26.8%	30.0%	22.2%
year	2000s	15.4%	28.9%	24.0%
SP500	1990s	18%	18%	18%
SP500	2000s	(2%)	(2%)	(2%)

Note: *Per annum compound returns for each decade.*

Table 7. Returns for GP with Bees Algorithm

Clearly using the GP with Bees Algorithm symbolic regression revenue prediction model buying the top five, twenty five, and fifty stocks with the highest ***(regression12MoEPS/currentPrice)*** produces above average securities investing profits, in most cases. *In fact, compared with all other prediction methods* (referring to fifty stock portfolios, which have less statistical variance than smaller portfolios) *adding the Bees algorithm has increased accuracy significantly over GP-only and is a slight improvement over GP with particle swarm and GP with differential evolution.* However, the Bees slight performance improvement over DE and PSO is not statistically significant under rigorous statistical analysis.

20. Summary

Having no population operators of its own which specialize in constant optimization, it is our contention that standard GP symbolic regression can benefit greatly when enhanced with swarm intelligence algorithms specializing in constant optimization. A method of integrating standard GP with swarm intelligence, Abstract Expression Grammars is introduced.

The importance of constants in symbolic regression is studied. It is shown that the size of the search space, for even simple financial applications, is very large and that a significant portion of that size is due to the presence of constants.

Several sample test problems, with embedded constants, are presented with standard GP symbolic regression unable to solve any of the problems while AEG enhanced SR is always able to solve each of the problems exactly. It made no difference which swarm algorithm was used - DE, Bees, or PSO. It was the presence of AEG integrated swarm intelligence which made the test problems tractable.

Theoretical, methodological, and regulatory issues applying standard GP symbolic regression to an important investment finance application are discussed. Symbolic regression is enhanced, using AEG, to be applicable to the prediction of forward 12 month earnings per share. A number of bloat and believability issues applying SR to predicting forward 12 month earnings are addressed and solved with AEG.

AEG enhanced symbolic regression is used to predict forward 12 month earnings per share on approximately 1500 stocks from 1990 to 2009. Three distinct swarm intelligence algorithms are compared: DE, Bees, and PSO. All three swarm algorithms perform well, providing earnings predictions in a format easily acceptable by portfolio managers and regulatory compliance officers.

Incidentally, comparing t-statistics, f-statistics, variance, information ratio and p-values shows it made no difference when the Bees Algorithm was replaced with the Differential Evolution Algorithm or with the Particle Swarm Algorithm. The results of an AEG symbolic regression on predicting future 12Mo eps was statistically similar for all swarm algorithms compared. It was the integration with any of the three swarm algorithms which made symbolic regression effective for forward earning prediction.

Enhancing standard GP with Abstract Expression Grammar hybrid algorithms solves a number of regression accuracy, believability, and regulatory issues when using symbolic regression in financial applications. Based upon our experiments in this chapter, standard GP symbolic regression has serious issues when applied to financial applications; while, swarm enhanced SR shows real promise in the financial domain.

Furthermore using AEG to add swarm intelligence algorithms to SR significantly enhanced accuracy in future 12 month revenue prediction and produced above average securities investing profits in the historical period 1990 to 2009. Significantly this superior performance was undeterred by the bearish market environment of the 200 decade.

Directions for future research include investigating whether or not there are other swarm algorithms which would show real statistical significantly improved results over DE, Bees, and PSO? Is AEG the optimal GP SI integration approach to symbolic regression, or is there another integration approach which is superior?

21. References

[1] Graham, Benjamin, and David Dodd. 2008. Securities Analysis. New York, New York, USA. McGraw-Hill.

[2] Kennedy, J.; Eberhart, R. 1995. Particle Swarm Optimization. *Proceedings of IEEE International Conference on Neural Networks*. IV. pp. 1942–1948.

[3] Korns, Michael F. 2007. Large-Scale, Time-Constrained Symbolic Regression-Classification. In Riolo, Rick, L, Soule, Terrance, and Wortzel, Bill, editors, Genetic Programming Theory and Practice V, New York, New York, USA. Springer, pp. 299–314.

[4] Korns, Michael F., and Nunez, Loryfel, 2008. Profiling Symbolic Regression-Classification. In Riolo, Rick, L, Soule, Terrance, and Wortzel, Bill, editors, Genetic Programming Theory and Practice VI, New York, New York, USA. Springer, pp. 215–228.

[5] Korns, Michael F., 2009. Symbolic Regression of Conditional Target Expressions. In Riolo, Rick, L, Soule, Terrance, and Wortzel, Bill, editors, Genetic Programming Theory and Practice VII, New York, New York, USA. Springer, pp. 211–228.

[6] Korns, Michael F., 2010. Abstract Expression Grammar Symbolic Regression. In Riolo, Rick, L, Soule, Terrance, and Wortzel, Bill, editors, Genetic Programming Theory and Practice VIII, New York, New York, USA. Springer, pp. 109–128.

[7] Price, Kenneth, Storn, Rainer, Lampinen, Jouni 2009. Differential Evolution: A Practical Approach to Global Optimization. New York, New York, USA. Springer.

[8] Guido Smits, Ekaterina Vladislavleva, and Mark Kotanchek 2010, Scalable Symbolic Regression by Continuous Evolution with Very Small Populations, in Riolo, Rick, L, Soule, Terrance, and Wortzel, Bill, editors, *Genetic Programming Theory and Practice VIII*, New York, New York, USA. Springer, pp. 147–160.

[9] Flor Castillo, Arthur Kordon, and Carlos Villa 2010, Genetic Programming Transforms in Linear Regression Situations, in Riolo, Rick, L, Soule, Terrance, and Wortzel, Bill, editors, *Genetic Programming Theory and Practice VIII*, New York, New York, USA. Springer, pp. 175–194.

[10] Trent McConaghy, Pieter Palmers, Gao Peng, Michiel Steyaert, Goerges Gielen 2009, Variation-Aware Analog Structural Synthesis: A Computational Intelligence Approach. New York, New York, USA. Springer.

[11] J.A., Nelder, and R. W. Wedderburn, 1972, *Journal of the Royal Statistical Society, Series A, General*, 135:370-384.

[12] John R Koza 1992, Genetic Programming: On the Programming of Computers by Means of Natural Selection. Cambridge Massachusetts, The MIT Press.

[13] Korns, Michael F., 2011. Accuracy in Symbolic Regression. In Riolo, Rick, L, Soule, Terrance, and Wortzel, Bill, editors, Genetic Programming Theory and Practice IX, New York, New York, USA. Springer (*to be published in winter 2011*).

[14] Pham, D., Ghanbarzadeh, A., Koc, E., Otri, S., Rahim, S., and Zaidi, M. 2005. "The Bees Algorithm". Technical Report Cardiff University.

[15] Parpinelli, R. S., and Lopes, H. S., 2011. New inspirations in swarm intelligence: a survey. *Int Journal of Bio-inspired Computation*. Vol 3. Number 1.

[16] Bernstein, J., 2001. Momentum Stock Selection: Using The Momentum Method for Maximum Profits. New York, New York, McGraw Hill

[17] Nicholas, J., 2000. Market-Neutral Investing: Long/Short Hedge Fund Strategies. New York, New York, Bloomberg Press.

[18] Poli, Riccardo, McPhee, Nicholas, Vanneshi, Leonardo, 2009. Analysis of the Effects of Elitism on Bloat in Linear and Tree-based Genetic Programming. In Riolo, Rick, L, Soule, Terrance, and Wortzel, Bill, editors, Genetic Programming Theory and Practice VI, New York, New York, USA. Springer, pp. 91–110.